THE GREAT RESET

The Globalist Plan vs. Heaven's Victory

By Ted Flynn

Maxkol Communications

Cover of Light House: Shutterstock
Published and printed in the USA
© MaxKol, 2022
ISBN Number: 978-0-9634307-7-9
Design Layout: Paul McNamara
Cover Design by: Faith and Family Publications

Publisher:

For bulk or case orders contact: tflynn333@icloud.com

Distributor:
Signs and Wonders of Our Time
P.O Box 345
Herndon, Virginia 20170
E-mail: signsorders@gmail.com
Phone: (703) 707-0799
Website: Sign.org

This book of the law shall not depart out of your mouth,
but you shall meditate on it day and night,
that you may be careful to do according to all that is written in it;
for then you shall make yourself prosperous,
and then you shall have good success.

JOSHUA 1:8

Men of Israel, hear these words Jesus of Nazareth,
a man attested to you by God with mighty works and wonders
and signs which God did through Him in your midst,
as you yourselves know.

ACTS 2:22

Have no anxiety about anything, but in everything by prayer
and supplication with thanksgiving let your request be made to God.
And the peace of God, which passes all understanding,
will keep your hearts and your minds in Christ Jesus.
Finally, brethren, whatever is true, whatever is honorable,
whatever is just, whatever is pure, whatever is lovely,
whatever is gracious, if there is any excellence,
if there is anything worthy of praise, think about these things.

PHIL. 4: 6-8

Table of Contents

Acknowledgements

As anyone who has worked on a project, they soon realize that it becomes a joint effort with others to accomplish it. Someone is doing something else that enables that person to devote the time and effort for the given task. This has also been the case here as well. My wife Maureen and I would spend countless hours speaking about the direction of the culture and the Church, after talking to thousands of people a year as an extension of Signs of the Times Apostolate, which is now in its 33rd year publishing a magazine. The Sign.org website, run by Colleen Flynn, has a world-wide audience and is where we hear from people the most. What we hear loud and clear from subscribers and friends, is that people are experiencing a great deal of stress. We would spend time talking about many sensitive and volatile subjects, and where people of faith are headed. Always asking what is the best response for people navigating these shoals to make sense of the profound changes in our midst was a primary focus of the chapters herein.

Conversations among friends took place and we are encouraged that Heaven has a plan out of this malaise, and we should not be reduced to feeling helpless. Many people were a part of that thought process. Colleen Flynn provided valuable insight into the types of articles people would be interested in hearing about, and was never shy expressing an opinion on content. Maureen Flynn took the first shot at editing for clarity and relevancy, and what topics would be most beneficial for people to be encouraged rather than depressed about our cultural decline.

However, a special and sincere thanks to Team Welter. The heavy lifting fell to Kimberley Welter to polish, refine, and bring clarity to serious subject matter. The hours she spent polishing, her family surely sacrificed in other areas, so she could get the job done. It is never a singular effort by anyone when there are family responsibilities. Kimberley hits the trifecta for a friend and editor: she knows the material and is bright, she is conscientious and fastidious about details of the Divine, and she is a faithful disciple of the Lord and His Mother's agenda. Potent traits to have as an advocate for any job.

Also, the same can be said for Meredith and Danny Flynn. Meredith would be the one doing the layout for the Friday e-mail blast when the material was complete that saw a global audience.

Chriss Rainy was of help pushing the project over the finish line, doing a great job of being like a precision machinist fine-tuning in all respects.

Also, as important, is the St. Joseph Prayer Group. This is where discussions would take place around the table on the subjects addressed in the book year after year. There is always a fresh and Godly perspective with an educated opinion on the unique times in which we live—and solutions for peace of soul. There is always a delicate balance of being hopeful, yet a realist, with the daily onslaught of negative news. For all, a warm thank you, as no man is an island.

Introduction

The chapters enclosed are from articles that were written over a four-year period. The longer ones were only in *Signs and Wonders for Our Times* magazine, and others were posted on our website Sign.org. They deal with the vast secular and religious issues of our day, and what our response should be to the crisis we see in our cultural decline.

Many were written during the Covid 19 pandemic when there wasn't a person or family not affected to a greater or lesser degree by the disunity we witnessed over serious issues. Lines of demarcation over Covid were drawn, and there was division. The Covid 19 disruption is a dress rehearsal for far more draconian measures coming our way. At some point it will be "show me your papers" as in World War II. Next time it will be a digital version of that in some form, and if there isn't compliance with the state, your accounts for things you do every day for a living may be deactivated and frozen.

There are several general themes of the articles. One, the world is in the midst of a transformative process that has happened before at certain points in history, but none as significant as we see now. America is seeing the changing of the guard so to speak, and this is the normal ebb and flood of civilization itself. One ruling empire is deposed and another rises. Empires are not usually conquered from without, but commit suicide from moral rot within. We are watching this in real time for the American Empire. American ideals came to the forefront after World War II and Bretton Woods, and she is fast losing global supremacy — militarily, morally and economically. It is going to be rough for many families unless they realize the Blessed Mother has said, *"I have a great plan for the salvation of mankind, and I come to tell you God exists."* If we study and are in prayer, we will see it.

Two, the Lord's prescription for peace of soul is provided in Scripture for trying times. We can lead joyful and productive lives in the midst of turmoil. It must be our blueprint going forward, or we will perish emotionally. Nothing is clearer than what Yahweh told His people through the prophet Jeremiah on how to live while in captivity. It was not just a formula for then, but today as well. It is timeless advice. It is how the Lord instructed His people through the ages to preserve their traditions and faith in times of duress. Believers will need to know and practice these principles in the coming days. In spite of the negative news there is GREAT HOPE in the future which is addressed in many of the chapters. Heaven's perspective of our times abounds in uplifting and inspirational encouragement from Scripture, historical Church teaching, and the messages of Our Lady as modern-day epistles.

A third theme discussed throughout, is how many believers allowed the depravity to escalate before they spoke up. As Jesus prayed in the Garden of Gethsemane while His apostles slept before His passion, so too many believers slept thinking all was going to stay the same. The lies and deception have been so great by communists, some believers never saw what was coming, because they didn't believe what was happening in our culture. Many have simply failed to believe that anyone could have such an evil agenda to destroy our way of life and depopulate the earth. Many were unaware that there was an evil agenda coordinated and planned by The Deep State and Freemasonry to restructure the world in their image absent of a Divine Being.

Many believers and people of good-will have been asleep for several generations, and do not fully understand that evil never sleeps. Evil has a goal to kill, destroy, and steal (John 10:10). There has been an agenda that many in the left labeled *"conspiracy theory."* Calling it that was a simple and effective ploy that allowed the left/progressives to deflect from the truth. By dismissing the individual as a fool, they can manipulate the narrative. A person only has to be in another's company for a very brief time before they both see where the other stands with their world view. Heaven is exposing evil like wheat being separated from the chaff. The agenda of Satan's army on earth is in the open for all to see if one chooses to see it. The lack of speaking up when error and immorality were being promoted and taught primarily in schools has caught up with us. We didn't just arrive here overnight. It has been a gradual decline year after year with passive people ignoring the cultural demise looking to go along to get along. Their silence has been consent. The end goal of the globalists is to silence all dissent, and with the cooperation of big tech we are far down that road.

We are witnessing such madness it is hard to put it into words that are descriptive enough of the events taking place in our world. Many who call themselves democrats, socialists, or progressives are not that: they have become outright pagan. Their actions are no different from Moloch offering up child sacrifice to pagan gods in ancient days. When a party that is ruling the Presidency, the House, and the Senate, passes legislation allowing the mutilation of a child by promoting transgenderism and refuses to pass legislation requiring life-giving measures to infants born alive after a failed abortion, that is not progressive, it is pagan. The narrative needs to be stated for exactly what it is.

To think that a person can be fired for calling a man *"confused"* while masquerading as a woman shows how far off course we are morally as a nation. It is the sane person who is punished. It is a scripted mass psychosis funded by government and multinational business that is intentionally indoctrinating youth to the kindergarten levels of school. If anyone cannot see by now there is a virulent ruthless agenda by an organized global cabal (Deep State) to overthrow the country's core beliefs through radical ideologies, they are not seeing straight — or worse in denial of it. We are presently watching a brilliantly executed overthrow of western Christian values by trained Marxists. We are living chapter one of the book of Romans where St. Paul addressed a pagan people about their personal traits and conduct. St. Paul gives many descriptions of their behavior that look like modern day America. This is another indicator of how morally depraved and reprobate America has become. People cannot see the truth because they have **darkened intellects,** and their actions are an attempt to justify their vile beliefs and habits. Nothing is more heinous and evil than the intentional corruption of the young. At this point, the blessings of God have been removed from our country due to grievous sin. As a nation we are no longer under His *"hedge of protection"* (Job 1:10).

The left and an evil cabal of people, that is now called the **Deep State,** along with the **Deep Church** of all denominations, with heavy infiltration by secret societies, have been relentlessly chipping away at our way of life for decades. They perpetuate their ideology through like-minded people promoting colleagues into positions of authority from within all types of organizations, so they may subordinate and deflect dissent from their real

Marxist atheistic agenda. In this respect evil is organized, and Heaven has a lot to say on the organizations promoting this plan. It is an ideology of godless people where its fruits are chaos in the streets. It is the rotten fruit of Satan's declaration, *"I will not serve"* (non serviam). It is the mentality of a person who wishes to resist the grace of God. It is the battle of the ages, Satan v. God, good v. evil, and this is the mother of all evil. Through millennia it plays out in the streets always in the same way. To achieve the globalist goal, God in every form must first be removed from the public square. Christian education and thought has always been in their sights and removing it from education first, as it is the single biggest goal to implement their agenda.

The term the **Great Reset** is about restructuring the world in a new image of the global elites to totally control the affairs of people, and ultimately give us all a social credit score and put us all in a digital cage. The United Nations, the World Economic Forum, secret societies, the world's largest banks, funds larger than the GDP of most nations on earth, governments, tech giants, multi and transnational corporations are working in unison, and could pull the switch any day to create a dystopian nightmare for citizenry of the world that is barely believable. If a nation bucks the *community of nations* by stepping out of bounds with independent practices, they will be cut off from trade, bank funds, sanctioned, vilified, and excommunicated and treated as an outcast. Iraq, Libya, Syria, Iran, Russia, Afghanistan, Yemen, Somalia, and other countries have experienced it. Not that they all have had honorable intentions, but it does show if any nation sings off key from the global consensus, there are consequences. The globalists have a simple but powerful formula. If a country will not be under globalist-approved central bank control, it will be invaded and dissolved as a country. Being in unity with *the community of nations* is the preeminent and primary rule for sovereign survival today. The push for climate change and green energy is a large part of the globalist plan to institute carbon credits and force digital technology surveillance on all people of the world.

Technology and government are in lockstep on the methodology and the programs to implement the **Great Reset.** The plan was hatched decades ago. To turn a phrase, there is a new sheriff in town. They are going to rule on their terms. If you disagree, they will cancel you, and thus crush you into obscurity, poverty, and oblivion. There will be one winner and one loser in this fight. There are people in control now that believe the United States Constitution, the Bill of Rights, and Christianity are obsolete and have no place in the modern world. They believe these institutions are a sinking ship because they are outdated and have been a colossal failure, and their goal is to destroy them by any means. The collapse has not been from a staccato randomness, but coordinated and planned. The invasion on the southern border should show that clearly. People speak of the democrats not having a plan to prevent millions of migrants illegally crossing into the U.S. From the beginning, the democratic plan was an open border and they lied for decades to a gullible public. Western Civilization is intentionally being deconstructed in real time. It is on such a scale, few can even believe it is possible, never mind happening.

There is also a concerted effort to redefine marriage and family with their heinous godless agenda as well. Moral relativism over the years has allowed the venomous cancerous destruction of families at the legislative level. Sister Lucy of Fatima told Cardinal Carlo Caffara that Satan's final attack would be on marriage and the family. In addition, we have a group of people brainwashed to call every action racist, thus their manic push for Critical Race Theory (CRT) to indoctrinate youth to become better global citizens and servants of the state. It is the old Malthusian doctrine that there are too many people in the world. At the very root of this thinking is the concept of sustainable development; thus the need to depopulate by limiting growth. What better way than a virus to lockdown the world and instill fear among the people and take away basic human rights. The idea goes back a long way, but in the year 1972 Dennis and Donella Meadows (Club of Rome) published a book called *Limits to Growth*. Its premise was continued population growth requires exponential quantities of resources in a world with a finite supply and is not sustainable. Their book gained enormous traction in academia and beyond, and in many ways launched the environmental movement that has in time been hijacked and mutated into much more radical and godless programs.

As we progress into the near future, at some point there will be no neutrality among people. Man is being winnowed. This is a battle for all the marbles and how we will move into future generations. You will either be **in or out** depending on your response to government dictates. Tough decisions will need to be made by families. Jesus said, *"My kingdom is not of this world"* (John 18:36). We are exiles living in a strange land. Our Lady has said to her followers, *"Right when it appears Satan is the victor, his victory will be snatched away in a trice."* Trice means quickly or in an instant. Our Lady has also said about her followers, *"You are apostles of the last times."* Navigating in these times for a believer can be difficult, so sticking to the fundamentals of the faith for peace of soul will become paramount to maintain the mental stability and equilibrium to function. Yes, there is great hope, and we need to stand on the promises and not wobble. Jesus was not *"a reed shaken by the wind,"* and neither should we be.

Heaven has a plan. One could easily be demoralized if they are just seeing the negative news and ignoring Heaven's plan. Our Lady is exposing and dismantling these groups, and she names her target specifically. Heaven will defend their people and we have to trust what Our Lady is telling us. To usher in the Triumph of the Immaculate Heart, we will see the old pass away, and this is the process that we are watching now. It is painful to watch and endure, but people must be purified as dross is removed from gold so it becomes pure. It is uplifting and encouraging to know her plan. Our Lady has told us, *"All has Been Reveled to You"* and we have been given *"the full and entire truth."* People following what Heaven has been telling us, and specifically what The Blessed Mother has said repeatedly should not be surprised by the events we see around us, even though they are so incredulous. Before we see the Triumph of the Immaculate Heart, our era must pass. This process to walk Calvary will be painful, but the Church must pass through it. We are then promised to see **the New Era, the New Times, the New Jerusalem, and the Second Pentecost.**

Nothing is more comforting than what has been prophesied at Garabandal, Spain. Promises await us for a reversion of millions of people to the ways of God. Our Lady came and gave over 2,000 messages to four young visionaries in the mountains of northern Spain from 1961-1965. These prophesied events will shake the world like nothing before in history. Many have expected the events before this time, but current events seem to be pointing that they may now be closer. Heaven is seldom early, but never late. Satan knows his time is short, thus we see the unrestrained torrent of evil. However, right when all appears lost, it will be The Woman Clothed with the Sun (Revelation 12:1-6) who crushes the head of the serpent. It will be the culmination and fruition of Genesis 3:15, *"I will put enmity between you and the woman, and between your seed and her seed; he shall bruise your head, and you shall bruise his heel."*

Nothing will be more of a bounteous display of grace than the **Warning and the Great Miracle** that has been prophesied to come with the genesis of events that originate from that small mountain village in Garabandal, Spain. It will change life as we know it. There will be no more than one year between the two events. It will be **HEAVEN'S ULTIMATE ACT OF MERCY** for a wayward people. It will be so spectacular it will change life as we know it.

The Blessed Mother has said what is coming will be the greatest miracle since the creation of the world. We don't know **exactly** what that is, but we do have some clues. It will be so significant, we will measure time with the event much in the same way we measure time now Before Christ (BC) and After Christ (AD). The Warning will show every person on earth the state of their soul as God will see it at judgment. All will know they are in a Divine Presence of unexplainable love. It has several names: the warning, a judgment in miniature, a life review, a correction of conscience, and an illumination of conscience. Heaven will meet the evil in the world on Heaven's terms because, *"Where sin abounds, grace abounds all the more"* (Romans 5:20).

A great day soon awaits us. We must embrace the future with faith and hope that Heaven knows our circumstances and hears our cries. *"Now the God of hope fill you with all joy and peace in believing, that you may abound in hope, through the power of the Holy Spirit"* (Romans 15:13). We must endure the fight until the end with vigilance, temperance, fortitude, hope and the faith like those before us. Scripture informs us, **In the End We Win**.

TED FLYNN
May 1, 2022
The Feast of Saint Joseph the Worker,
Patron of the Universal Church & Families

The Great Reset —
The Globalist's Plan vs. Heaven's Victory

In fact, at the very moment when Satan will be enthroned as the lord of the world and will think himself now the sure victor, I myself will snatch the prey from his hands. In a trice he will find himself empty-handed, and in the end the victory will be exclusively my Son's and mine. This will be the triumph of my Immaculate Heart in the world.

Message #29g, the Blessed Mother to the
Marian Movement of Priests, December 19, 1973

No matter the publication or venue, the phrase **The Great Reset** is popping up all over the place. It should be taken seriously because the goal of the Great Reset is to:

- end national sovereignty,
- end personal liberty,
- end freedom of religion,
- implement a digital currency,
- end borders,
- eliminate private property,
- implement more vaccines which actually alter our RNA,
- push a global tax for climate change administered as a new giant slush fund by government,
- allow mass migration to the West,
- and make everyone a slave to the state — and much more.

The plan had been around for years, but for the 2020 U.S. Presidential pre- and post-election time frame, it was in full force for the control of America's future. It is now everywhere — front and center. The globalists are the people behind the curtain who have planned this for years.

The globalists are going for broke, for all the marbles so to speak, and they are now in the open for all to see. It was on the cover of Time magazine with a graphic of workers on scaffolding manufacturing a new globe. It is an established fact the globe has looked the same for many years, but some want a radical makeover in their image.

The utopia of Plato in its modern form is exerting itself with very powerful and wealthy people promoting a globalist agenda. It is now extremely well organized, and uber funded. The goal line is in sight, and the godless globalists are pushing their plan through with the delicacy of a pile driver. Satan will be the master for this global reset.

For years those who followed the meetings, the agendas, and the writings of groups like the Council on Foreign Relations (CFR), the Bilderbergers, the Trilateral Commission, Skull and Bones, The World Economic Forum (WEF), and other like-minded entities, were considered fringe by many people. The United Nations is establishment controlled, and has been captured heart, mind, and soul by the Deep State, and the Deep Church. People who wrote or spoke on the organized goals of a globalist agenda were considered not only conspiracy theorists, but were mocked in public for their views.

At cocktail parties and gatherings with people who may address the subject, many people would politely move away if the subject came up, they may gently reach for a shrimp cocktail or a bourbon & ginger, and gently slink away in the opposite direction to avoid being associated with it. The thinking may be on several levels. Number one would be, *"I don't want to be associated with this thinking."* Secondly, it would be considered too far out and may hurt a reputation socially or professionally. So, they duck the discourse entirely. Their silence being consent is what allows the globalists to achieve their goals.

The question must be asked, who are the globalist conspirators? The word conspiracy in Latin means to *"breathe together."* On page 404/405 of David Rockefeller's (1915-2017) autobiography *Memoirs,* he was clear in thanking the Washington Post, the New York Times, and elite groups like the Economist (British) for keeping their meetings quiet and not publishing what was said when they met. People are now finding out, primarily because of the internet, it has been the global elite who have had a nefarious globalist agenda — for decades and generations.

They meet in stealth at the finest resorts in the world for several days a year, depending on the organization, with the most powerful people in the world running the largest corporations, think tanks and government agencies. This is the norm for the anointed attendee roll-call. To a young executive hoping to be a power broker, it is a strong inducement for a career to blossom, to be a part of that network. Fidelity to the cause guarantees mammon and influence after tasting the sweetness of the nectar. The organizations ask for member silence, and it was easily obtained with the wealth that was a by-product of this earthly kingdom.

David Rockefeller was central in most of the organizational charts to build a new world in their image. A ruling, a working, and military class right from the Utopian Dream of Plato. His grandfather at the height of his power had approximately one percent of the total GDP of the United States of America. His wealth in today's dollars would be an estimated $400 billion. The Rockefeller timing was impeccable. Right when kerosene was being eliminated from American homes because of the new invention of Edison's electricity, Henry Ford was rolling off cars from an assembly line for under $1,000, which families could well afford. The new fuel from oil was called gasoline, and John D controlled a lion's share of refineries and distribution.

To put that in perspective, that is $400 billion in today's dollars. Jeff Bezos of Amazon is worth as of this writing about $200 billion — and growing by hundreds of thousands of dollars per minute. The Rockefeller family had plans for a new way of thinking and were not wall flowers about spending money to achieve their goals. The harm they have inflicted on humanity is incalculable, albeit in their minds, they may have perceived it as laudatory.

Many have written on the goals of the global elite in the last number of years. The internet has enabled people to get educated on a subject as fast as they want, and as thoroughly as they want, on just about anything. That has been a game changer for those without power and influence. But the swamp masters will not go down without a fight because they think long term, and never quit. Politics to them is just a minor obstacle to work around no matter who holds office. Controlling currency controls public policy, and their primary agenda is to control political finance for their chosen public policies.

The global elite feel the end is in sight and their goal is within grasp. They are now in the open and forthright about their agenda. They have taken control of financial institutions, the mainstream press, NGOs, the judiciary, government agencies and personnel mainly at the SES (Senior Executive Service) level in the United States Government. They also have a very large percentage of the institutional church of all denominations under their control. It took time, but they captured the hearts of some religious leaders through state sponsored financial largesse giving state money to fund their pet charities.

Bretton Woods, New Hampshire

The last time the world had a global reset was Bretton Woods, in the White Mountains of New Hampshire, during and immediately after World War II. The allies were aware a country the size of Germany was incapable of defeating the Western world, and plans were underway to make the U.S. dollar the new reserve currency of the world supplanting Great Britain's sterling. A transfer of power was taking place, and a country the size of England no longer sailed the seas plundering from nations who didn't wear shoes to send commodities back home for the manor born and enable the gentry to enjoy the Sunday morning *"fox and hound hunts."* At Bretton Woods, plans were drawn up for a global reset. Now, more than 75 years past those meetings, new plans are being drawn up for an operational organizational chart of new players and new agendas. The *"illumined souls"* have new plans for humanity — and it is godless.

Out of Bretton Woods came the International Bank for Reconstruction and Development (IBRD), more commonly known as the five branches of the World Bank. The International Monetary Fund (IMF) sets global monetary policy, and the International Finance Corporation (IFC) is the investment banking arm for World Bank transactions. After that came the Multilateral Investment Guarantee Agency (MIGA), which is the insurance arm of the IBRD. The rules of the World Bank are if a country defaults, they can't come back to the well for further money. Dams and hydroelectric plants will no longer be possible, thus there is a strong incentive to comply with World Bank directives. With that investment came liberal social policies for compliance. This was the Global Reset after World War II.

The plan now is a new digital currency which will track every transaction, and people carrying a state sponsored digital passport. It is not a conspiracy theory. World leaders are openly addressing it to the point that Christine Lagarde, former head of the IMF, and now President of the European Central Bank (ECB), said she can see it being introduced in 2-4 years. The globalists feel their time is now with Covid 19 lockdowns allowing the opportunity that they masterminded.

The Reset allowed by World War II would have never taken place if not for the upheaval of war in the Pacific and Atlantic where an estimated 60 million people died in both theaters. As the Masonic saying goes, *"Out of chaos comes order."* And World Wars I and II were Masonic wars. Just as World War III is being planned by Masonic forces. From the Tavistock Institute and Chatham House in England came two World Wars planned in paneled conference rooms. Their plan for World War III is Christian v. Muslim. It is not a conspiracy to say so, it is an established bona fide plan playing out in real time, exactly like previous wars to an unsuspecting public.

For those who may think this is the hobgoblin of a conspiracy theorist, reflect on exactly what is being planned using Covid 19 as the instrument for global control, and a vaccine administered by them. If one does not comply with a vaccine, then one will be out from The New World Order they have planned. One must remember what we are watching today has been in the works for decades and longer. Those who subscribe to these plans we see today are being incrementally executed right under our noses. If you spoke about them years ago, you were looked at as a certifiable lunatic. The fact is people who spoke about them years ago were correct. ***This is the modern day battle for control of the hearts, minds, and souls of mankind.*** To not pay attention now to **The Great Reset,** and its agenda of global control of the masses, will make one a slave to the state. Joe Biden was chosen as their puppet, and Kamala Harris as the venomous pit bull.

The new agenda is to destroy humanity, make it a slave to state directives, destroy freedoms we have known up until now, institute a hard-core communist ideology, end private property, have people become a digital number for commerce, and eradicate religion in its totality. To have people like Joe Biden and Kamala Harris have a following, shows just how many lost and uninformed souls are out there. At its core it is communism, not socialism. Nor is it solely Marxist. They want God removed in every sector of the human condition. That is communism.

Heaven Has a Reset Plan

Where Satan abounds, grace abounds all the more. The Blessed Mother has been battling the cohort of evil with the host of heaven for millennia. Now we are in the time of the Mother. She is prophetess of the New Times, and her role as the Woman Clothed with the Sun (Revelation 12:1) is now. The time before her appearance is a time of great turmoil of all kinds in the world (Rev. 11:19). We are in those times now. As Queen Esther interceded to save her people before the king, so too the Blessed Mother will intervene in the affairs of mankind as she has done at countless apparition sites globally. She has not come for tea and crumpets, but for battle, with Saint Michael at her side. She has the cohort of Heaven behind her which is why she has been appearing at Medjugorje since June 25, 1981, and all over the world. Heaven knows with its infinite wisdom why mankind needs her messages like never before. She doesn't make a move without the endorsement and will of the Father. Those who are detractors of her messages need to deeply ponder why this grace is rejected.

President Donald Trump signed the Executive Order on foreign interference in U.S. elections on September 12, 2018, **The Feast of In the Name of Mary.** On that same feast day, 27 years earlier, September 12, 1991, in a message to the Marian Movement of Priests, the Blessed Mother said, *"It will again be **in the name of Mary**, that I will bring to completion my work **with the defeat of Masonry**, of every diabolical force, of materialism, and of practical atheism, so that all humanity will be able to attain its encounter with the Lord and be thus purified and completely renewed, with the Triumph of the Immaculate Heart in the world"* (MMP #456e).

What we are looking at with the confluence of events at the supernatural and preternatural level, is **Heaven's own version of a Global Reset Plan.** As the Blessed Mother said at Medjugorje, *"I have a great plan for the salvation* *of mankind...."* **The Triumph of the Immaculate Heart is the ultimate Global Reset**. Exactly how and when is not known, but come it will.

What does the Lord require of you? To act justly, and to love kindness, and to walk humbly with your God (Micah 6:8).

The Great Reset — Satan Plans; Heaven Wins

JESUS I TRUST IN YOU

Medjugorje — The Great Spiritual Reset: The Ultimate Clash of Darkness Versus Light

Dear children, I want you to comprehend that God has chosen each one of you, in order to use you in His great plan for the salvation of mankind. You are not able to comprehend how great your role is in God's design. Therefore, dear children, pray so that in prayer you may be able to comprehend what God's plan is in your regard. I am with you in order that you may be able to bring it about in all its fullness.

Our Lady of Medjugorje, January 25, 1987

Medjugorje is the second longest Marian apparition in the history of Christianity, and by far the most unique for many reasons. The longest apparitions were in Laus, France, and lasted a total of fifty-four years (1664-1718) to a young girl by the name of Benoite Rencurel in Saint Etienne-Le-Laus. Our Lady's apparitions in Medjugorje began on June 24, 1981, the Feast of St. John the Baptist, ushering in New Times as first the Baptist did when he announced in the time of Jesus that the Kingdom of God was coming to the world. The next day, June 25th, Our Lady appeared again, and to this day is giving messages like never before in history. At

Medjugorje, the major spokesperson is not Jesus, but His Mother. She is the daughter of the Father, the Mother of the Son, and the Spouse of the Holy Spirit. Our Lady does not move without the permissive will of the Most Holy Trinity. Our Lady came to Medjugorje with a specific mission for the salvation of all mankind.

Medjugorje has confounded secular observers and others alike for many reasons. Many theologians, and believers in general, bring an unreasoned, preconceived bias of the supernatural as an ingredient in the spiritual journey. Yet the entire anthology of the Roman Catholic Church and people we call saints demonstrates that the miraculous and mystical were often commonplace. Saints are people of great conviction and holiness and courage, and often suffering under extremely adverse circumstances. For many, suffering was a central part of their lives, whether in silence or in public. It is primarily for these reasons they were raised up as examples for people to emulate. In the early years the village of Medjugorje had similar circumstances of difficulty and the mystical was present from Day One. The supernatural became commonplace and conversions were profound and extraordinary. Yet many still do not believe, and many more still doubt for intellectual reasons often rooted in pride. The issue is that we are witnessing a modern-day gift to the world in tumultuous times and rational logic and reason alone will not bring anyone to the realization of this mystical and supernatural gift to all humanity. It reminds me of what Bernadette Soubirous said of Lourdes, *"To those who do not believe, no explanation is possible. To those who do believe, no explanation is necessary."*

There have been apparitions like Lourdes (1858), and Fatima (1917), where millions over the centuries have journeyed, but none have seen the general excitement and interest of Medjugorje for many reasons. First, as the phenomena occurred at the tail-end of the twentieth century, the widespread air travel, internet, and thousands of conferences world-wide in the 1980's and 90's principally centered around Medjugorje, allowed easy dissemination of information globally through the new millennium of the year 2000. At this time there have been a myriad of all forms of social media bringing attention to the village, and most importantly the messages. Second, as already mentioned, is its longevity. Third are the messages themselves.

Why: A Great Plan for the Salvation of Mankind

Any student of journalism will ask the basic questions of Who, What, When, Where, and Why. For Medjugorje, we know What it is, Where it is, Who is involved, and even How it evolved to a modern day phenomena like no other. What must be explored more incisively is Why? **Why of all places** in the world, did Our Lady come to a remote obscure hamlet in the mountains (with tremendous cost of travel and difficulty to get there, yet with so many repeat pilgrims making the trip)? **Why now at this point in history?**

The Why must be looked into deeper to understand what has and is still taking place there. The Blessed Mother said, *"I have a great plan for the salvation of mankind, and I come to tell you God exists."* She said she is *"appearing like never before in history,* and will appear in every home if necessary."

Mirjana once said, (date unknown) *"[T]he last secrets will be dramatic; moreover, the Virgin Mary also prophesied that a new and better world will be born of the secrets. Announced by the Virgin Mary as the Triumph of the Immaculate Heart, this new way of life on earth will crown her apparitions in what she foretold will be an era of peace."* **This is an extremely hopeful message that new and glorious times await us as we are in this painful time of transition.** Heaven has it own timetable and plan for a global reset to counter Satan's plan. It is the battle of darkness versus light.

Ivanka once asked Our Lady why she came to Medjugorje and she replied, *"because there are good believers here."* At another time, the children asked why have you chosen us who have nothing special, and she replied, *"I do not choose the best."* Some have made the journey dozens of times over the past several decades leading groups of people because they believe that visiting Medjugorje increases the odds for a favorable result of a conversion of a friend or loved one. Medjugorje is simply a powerful place of grace. Testimonies abound of profound conversions while there. A great deal of information is written about the lives of the six visionaries. This is normal for people to inquire and want to know about their lives, but the most important issue is why? To understand that we must ask what is the purpose of Our Lady's coming, and what is she trying to communicate to the world? What is she saying? What are her messages?

The History of Cross Mountain: A Faithful Generation

All the way back in the 1930's, Saint James Parish wanted to consecrate the parish to Jesus Christ the Redeemer of the world, to protect people from evil, and especially from hailstones that would destroy their harvests so frequently. Cross Mountain until 1934 was called Sipovac. To honor God the town people wanted to build a cross. Under the supervision of their pastor by the name of Fr. Bernardin Simojian, they decided to build a cross on the top of the mountain. Father Simojian wrote in his diary, *"lime, water, cement, iron, wooden material, and sand had to be taken up to that altitude, on the back of those people."* A small relic of the true cross was sent from Rome to be built into the cross. The cross was completed on March 15, 1934. It was on that day it was renamed from Sipovac to Cross Mountain. It was a cement cross, 520m above sea level, and 8.56m tall. The parish wrote on the cross, *"To Jesus Christ, Redeemer of mankind, as a sign of their faith, love, and hope, raised by the parish of Medjugorje, and the parish priest Father Bernardine."* And at the very end it said, *"From every evil, deliver us Lord."*

Cross Mountain testifies to the history of, and fidelity to, the faith of Medjugorje residents over decades. There are reasons why things happen in life, and this historical fact is significant to understand why the Blessed Mother said she chose this place: because of the faith of the people. Forty-seven years prior to 1981, the grandparents of the visionaries and village parishioners erected a permanent sign of their fidelity and faith in Jesus Christ. Wherever the Son is, the Mother is too. *"And His mercy is for those who fear him from generation to generation"* (Luke 1:50).

Medjugorje and Yugoslavia: War is Imminent

Medjugorje was not only remote, it was simple by any western standard in 1981. The way the parents of the visionaries, and the visionaries themselves, were raised is anathema to our way of living. Most people in Medjugorje didn't get electricity and indoor plumbing until 1969, the year Neil Armstrong walked on the moon and came home safely. Homes were largely made of cinder blocks with primitive roofs. Most modern conveniences were largely non-existent. Screens and air conditioning only became more common place as greater numbers of pilgrims and the inquisitive journeyed there. Chickens, goats, and livestock also disappeared from front lawns as the years went on. The only cash crop was growing tobacco in small quantities.

Into this simple community, she came under the title as the Queen of Peace. The six young children (visionaries) didn't understand the meaning at first because Medjugorje at the time was a village of tranquility and peace. But, as we know that would soon change with the war that came to the surrounding area. The war began in April of 1992, and ended in December 1995, and was the biggest conflict in Europe since World War II. It was at one point within several miles of Medjugorje itself.

The Balkans, including Yugoslavia, had suffered greatly under the tyrannical dictator, Josip Broz *"Marshal"* Tito. Tito broke with Stalin in 1948 but had served in the Soviet military after the Bolshevik Revolution of 1917. Tito governed Yugoslavia as a Soviet-style communist revolutionary from 1953 to his death in May of 1980, less than a year before Our Lady's first appearance. Yugoslavia was made up of Bosnia and Herzegovina, Croatia, Macedonia, Montenegro, Serbia, and Slovenia. Tito had governed the region under his tight control and his death was instrumental in the breakup of the county into smaller states. The several countries and provinces that made up the Balkans as a region were in turn made up of warring tribes of profoundly disparate ethnic, religious, and cultural identities that had fought out their differences in fratricidal wars for hundreds of years. The population was comprised of Muslims, Orthodox, and Christians depending on where you lived. It was a large cauldron boiling with rage from past grievances when the war broke out.

This is the underlying political climate in the region surrounding Medjugorje when the Blessed Mother first appeared in 1981. They suffered and knew hardship. Hatred had built up for generations much like we saw in the Rwandan genocide of 1994, where neighbors for years turned on each other and slaughtered one another overnight with an estimated 800,000 dead in approximately 100 days. Under Tito, this was the political, social, and economic order lived under by the families in Medjugorje for so long.

It was Our Lady Queen of Peace who freed the people from communism as well as the former USSR and Eastern Europe.

Message for Medjugorje: Message for the World

On June 25, 1993 Ivanka said, *"The Virgin showed me horrible things that will happen soon. She asked us to abandon [ourselves] to her Son with prayer."* The next day Ivanka said, *"The Virgin showed me horrible indescribable events. What I saw did not concern the secrets. These things are imminent and concern the world in general. It is like a new warning, because these grave events can be changed* **with fasting and prayer***. Conversion and abandonment to Jesus are more necessary than ever. Do not remain blind: you are unconscious, be converted. God desires that we persevere on this path."* Again, and again we see in the messages that focusing on prayer and her Son through a personal transformation is the key to what she is conveying to the world. It is actually just that, a simple message with profound implications for all humanity if we heed her call. Our Lady said it was the people being so devout in the village which was a reason why she chose Medjugorje. In addition, the people are from a very multi-ethnic and diverse background, and have also suffered for their faith, which would happen again when they endured the oncoming Bosnian War.

The **Why** is also addressed when she said at the very beginning, *"My dear angels,* (a term of endearment Croatian women used for their children and grandchildren) *I have come to tell you that God does exist, and mankind strayed from God and desires to create its own future without God.* **Mankind has to go back to God, has to convert, awaken and start to live the Gospel again."** At the wedding feast at Cana, Our Lady says, "Do whatever He tells you." Here again, true to her nature she points to Jesus. She is resolute that the turmoil in our midst in every genre of the world is because we left the Gospel message. She has a great plan for the salvation of mankind because heaven is watching and will exceed the evil that is now upon the world. Satan knows his time is short and he has an agenda to literally destroy God's civilization.

Our Lady's Battle Plan: Only Conversion and Faith Can Change the World

Our Lady's Battle Plan explains why there are so many messages for so long on so many subjects. As the prophetess of our age, Our Lady said, *"God wishes to establish in the world a devotion to my Immaculate Heart as the last means for salvation."* She says it is a four-point change for mankind: 1. **Go back to God** as the answer for the ills of mankind; 2. **Convert** to an ideological and lifestyle change consistent with faith and morals; 3. **Awaken** to the fact Jesus alone is the solution; 4. **Live the Gospel** and put faith into action no matter your profession or locale. This is her plan and she has said repeatedly over the years she needs our cooperation to carry out her plan. Each word is very emotive and requires the individual to change their focus on how they live.

Her Battle Plan is a simple one: live the faith. People need to pray more, fast, recite the rosary, go to Confession more frequently, go to daily Mass if possible, read the Scriptures, be a part of a community prayer group, and spend time in Adoration. This is her plan. How anyone could find this a radical Catholic message has confounded people who have believed in Medjugorje and listened to the detractors and critics of her messages over the years. Medjugorje is about the messages, and the rest is superfluous. It is a place of grace where conversions take place. Hearts are touched and there is a chain reaction of grace that touches many others. It is like a rock thrown on a still pond where the ripples stretch out wide.

On January 25, 2001 Our Lady said, *"Dear Children! Today I call you to renew prayer and fasting with even greater enthusiasm until prayer becomes a joy for you. Little children, **the one who prays is not afraid of the future and the one who fasts is not afraid of evil.** Once again, I repeat to you: **only through prayer and fasting also wars can be stopped—wars of your unbelief and fear for the future. I am with you and I am teaching you.** Little children: your peace and your hope are in God. That is why, draw closer to God and put Him in the first place in your life. Thank you for having responded to my call."*

Twenty years later on the same day, January 25, 2021 in a message to Marija, Our Lady said, *"Dear Children! I am calling you at this time to prayer, fasting and renunciation, that you may be stronger in faith. This is a time of awakening and of giving birth. As nature which gives itself, you also, little children, ponder how much you have received. Be joyful bearers of peace and love that it may be good for you on earth. Yearn for Heaven; and in Heaven there is no sorrow or hatred. That is why, little children, decide anew for conversion and let holiness begin to reign in your life. Thank you for having responded to my call."*

Heaven has a plan into the future we cannot see or even comprehend in its totality. But, and this is a big but, we have to Trust the Plan for it to come to fulfillment. During the Bosnian War there was an attempt to bomb Medjugorje and two providential things happened that protected it. One, a bomb was dropped in the area, and it never exploded. Two, a pilot tells the story that he knew he was in the area by his coordinates as he had just bombed Citluk, only three kilometers away. On his way to bomb Saint James he said he couldn't find it. He tells the story after being shot down and captured and said, *"When I was approaching I could no longer see anything: a sort of fog hid it from my eyes."* Medjugorje is protected ground by Heaven. So too, is Our Lady not offering spiritual insight for those who will listen and follow her plan? Our protected ground is reached by following her Battle Plan.

Saint John Paul II: Affection for Medjugorje

For those who have followed Medjugorje, Pope John Paul II and Benedict XVI were extremely favorable to Medjugorje and in numerous ways protected it during their pontificates. Pope Benedict established a commission that eventually confirmed the supernatural origins of the first seven apparitions.

On November 24, 1993, Pope John Paul II at the end of a dinner with the bishops of the Indian Ocean — according to what was reported by one of them, said, *"'As Hans Urs von Balthasar said, Mary is the Mother who warns her children. Many are hesitant about Medjugorje and the apparitions that have taken place there for so many years. But, the message has been given in a certain context: it corresponds to the situation in the country.*

"The message insists on peace, on relations between Catholics, Orthodox, and Muslims. These messages are the key to understanding what is happening

[authors' note: the war was going on at that time and 100,000 died and 2.2 million were displaced] *and what will happen in the world and of its future.'* Therefore, according to this thought (which however, I emphasize was reported by a third party) the war in the former Yugoslavia would be interpreted as a confirmation of the message of Medjugorje and the validity of the secrets concerning the world." *Revised Medjugorje: the 90's, The Triumph of the Heart,* Sr. Emmanuel, pg. 196.

Chaos in the World: Heaven's Intervention

We are in the midst of a clash of civilizations and she has a great plan to counter the wiles of Satan and his tactics. The word apocalypse means unveiling. We may be seeing some signs of this today as the corruption of the world is being exposed for all to see where people truly stand on things no matter the country you live. Every institution, no matter its size and stature, if it is not on the side of Heaven's agenda is being exposed or unmasked. The confluence of events in the world is showing just how big is this battle in our midst. The corruption of the world and its apostasy is being exposed for all to see precisely. This is surely a part of Our Lady's plan that is not yet visible but discernible for the next step in the process of Heaven's direct intervention. Satan is using every means available to enslave man, but she has a plan greater for mankind to prevail. Whether we want to call it the Great Reset is not known, but it will be her victory, and it will be seen only in retrospect, and we will then see its glorious genius.

Is this what Cardinal Karol Wojtyla (Pope John Paul II) was speaking about in 1976 at the Philadelphia Eucharistic Congress when He mentioned the historic confrontation humanity was about to go through? *"We are now standing in the face of the greatest historical confrontation humanity has gone through. I do not think that wide circles of the American society or wide circles of the Christian community realize this fully. We are now facing the final confrontation between the Church and the anti-Church, of the Gospel versus the anti-Gospel. This confrontation lies within the plans of divine Providence; it is a trial which the whole Church and the Polish Church in particular, must take up. It is a trial of not only our nation and the Church, but, in a sense, a test of 2,000 years of culture and Christian civilization with all of its consequences for human dignity, individual rights and the rights of nations."*

As the world becomes more of an arid wasteland due to the lack of faith, we can expect to see the chaos around us increasing in every setting. As government continues to grow, it invariably corrupts the character of the people. Power corrupts virtue in the citizenry, and sin becomes more accepted. Government and its people reach greater heights of debauchery. This is precisely where the world is now. It will take a Divine Act to turn this around. Darkened intellects are now running governments worldwide. The world is drowning in its own vomit, and doesn't even know it.

The Lord is hearing the cries of His people who have been in prayer and fasting. His remnant, God's people faithful to the Gospel, have been mobilized and are in spiritual battle. We have some strong indications that the Divine Plan for humanity is coming into play in incremental steps, pointing to a possible turn around in the direction of not just the United States as leader of the free world, but other countries as well. Heaven at this point in time is dismantling and defeating Freemasonry. The veil of lies and deceit are presently being lifted, and a joyful and glorious day is upon us. Heaven sees much broader than we can, and has different plans than our way of natural thinking. Trust Our Lady's plan. The Lord and His Blessed Mother are now drawing back the curtain on the world stage shining a spotlight exposing the enemies of truth worldwide.

We have a track record from a very reliable source — the Blessed Mother — as the prophetess of our age who has been appointed by the Trinity for this role at this moment in time to expose Freemasonry for what it is. What we are seeing again today is the same way she won other battles for her children in the past.

In the Name of Mary: Defeat of Masonry and Its Diabolical Forces

What exactly does the Blessed Mother say about her next target of evil? To the Marian Movement of Priests, she identifies her next target of conquest. In message number 456, **In the Name of Mary,** delivered just before the fall of the former USSR in 1991 from Slovakia, Our Lady says:

"In the name of your heavenly Mother, yes, in the name of Mary, the Turks were defeated, when they laid siege to the city of Vienna, and threatened to invade and destroy the whole Christian world. They were far superior in strength, in numbers and in weapons, and they felt that their victory was assured. But I was publicly invoked and called upon; my name was inscribed upon their banners and shouted out by the soldiers, and thus through my intercession, there took place the miracle of this victory which saved the Christian world from its destruction. It is for this reason that the Pope, instituted on this day, the feast of the Name of Mary.

"In the name of Mary, Marxist communism, which for decades had been exercising its rule and holding so many of my poor children in oppressive and bloody slavery, has been defeated in these countries. Not because of political movements or persons, but through my personal intervention, has your liberation finally come about.

"It will again be in the name of Mary that I will bring to completion my work with the defeat of Masonry, of every diabolical force, of materialism, and of practical atheism, so that all humanity will be able to attain its encounter with the Lord and be thus purified and completely renewed, with the triumph of my Immaculate Heart in the world.

"It is for this reason that I desire that the feast in honor of the name of Mary be restored, now that you are entering into the fiercest moments of the struggle and the most painful stage of the great tribulation." (MMP #456)

Several very important things are being said.

1. This message is about her agenda, not about Russia as Fatima was. It is not about the region of the Persian Gulf, North Korea, the Korean Peninsula, China, Eastern Europe, Iran, Iraq, Saudi Arabia, or counties in the forefront of geo-politics that dominate the news. She did not say, Islam, migration, immigration, sex trafficking, or apostasy of faith. It is specifically about Freemasonry. How interesting a subject under the radar to the average person not knowing its hidden agenda. Its tentacles run far, wide, and deeper than most can imagine — always operating

in secret. Man hacks at the branches of evil; Heaven goes to the root of evil.

2. The Christian world defeated the Islamic powers at the Battle of Lepanto (1571), and the Siege of Vienna (Turks, 1683), against great odds after invoking her name. Similarly, under enormous odds, the Soviet Empire stretching from Vladivostok in the East, to St. Petersburg in the west were defeated without bloodshed. The USSR just collapsed, and no one saw it coming. The CIA (an oxymoron) said they never saw its collapse coming.

3. When we march under her banner and shout out her name there is protection and victory. Victory is swift and decisive if we follow her directives under her mantle. It is her personal intervention that assures this victory, not the words of political rulers and pundits, because of her love for all people.

4. It is Our Lady who will bring about to completion her work with the defeat of Masonry and all that comes with it: every diabolical force, practical atheism, and materialism. These events will take place and are probably ingredients to the Triumph of the Immaculate Heart.

5. We are in the fiercest moments of the struggle. Much like birth pangs that increase in intensity before the birth of a child, the battle at the moment will increase and will be painful (and is) for many. Medjugorje's call to transform lives is the key part of this plan. She is fighting the largest multi-lateral institutions in the world as well as the leadership of the United Nations. Even the Vatican at this point is aligned with plans of U.N. global government to enslave all mankind through implementation of a godless system of government, void of any resemblance to Christian principles. People are talking about a **Great Reset**. The Illumination of Conscience and the Miracle, which may be a part of the secrets of Medjugorje ushering in the Triumph of the Immaculate Heart, would be a **Great *Spiritual* Reset** on Heaven's terms. What will happen at Medjugorje will be a complete paradigm shift in world affairs. It will make the parting of the Red Sea seem insignificant as a miracle and will be the equivalent of a polar shift for the world. It will be that significant.

We are witnessing evil versus good, virtue versus vice, God's cohort versus Satan's cohort, children of light versus children of darkness; and the fight is spiritual at the highest levels in Heaven. The reign of Satan as prince of this world is about to be broken by the heel of a woman who steps on the head of the serpent. Much like Queen Esther interceded to the King on behalf of her people with evil men around her seeking her destruction, the Blessed Mother is interceding on our behalf to the King of Kings, Our Lord Jesus Christ.

In message 457 to the Marian Movement of Priests, Our Lady says, *"**Thus, by means of you**, I am able to continue my motherly work of mercy, which I have begun in these countries, but which I must still bring to completion in every part of the world, for the triumph of my Immaculate Heart."* (MMP #457)

Any observer in the world today can readily admit that events globally are out of control in the church and state. One would be hard pressed to point where things are in order and functioning well. No country seems to be spared from the onslaught of evil in our midst.

In our own country, the battle for Our Lady of America is being blocked by strong Masonic forces because Heaven's promise is so great. Her promise is one of purity being restored to America if Bishops do as Our Lady asks, when she is enthroned at the Basilica of the National Shrine of the Immaculate Conception in Washington, D.C. With a promise so magnificent for all America and the world, some clergy in positions of great power are blocking her request.

"Thus, by means of you." Our Lady has said she needs us to participate in her redemptive plan for mankind. **"Your prayers, your fasting, your sacrifices…."** Heaven needs you to speak up and stop the deceit. It is your time.

Events in the World: Mirjana's Observation

In 2016 Mirjana Soldo, the oldest of the visionaries did a series of interviews that were published into a book called *My Heart Will Triumph*. It is her account of the events with their aftermath on her overview of the big picture thinking. The book is 369 pages that covers nearly every subject one would want to know from her perspective of what went on there generally since the beginning. One would find from reading the book how incisive it is, how reasoned, logical, and how normal she is in spite of so many things that have happened to her in the last forty years. It is obvious she is mentally balanced and has a great sense of humor and takes things in stride. On the last page of the book, she delivers a block buster where we are in time and the potential for the upcoming release of the secrets and what it could mean for the world. She says: *"Evil yearns to deprive us of eternal reward by luring us with temptations and then destroying us from within. More darkness on the planet equals more souls lost forever."*

"'As individuals, my dear children, you cannot stop the evil that wants to begin to rule in this world and destroy it,' [Our Lady] said on August 2, 2011, 'But according to God's will, all together, with my Son, you can change everything and heal the world.'

"Our Lady told me many things that I cannot yet reveal. For now, I can only hint at what our future holds, but I do see indications that the events are already in motion (authors note: this narrative was written in 2016). Things are slowly starting to develop. As Our Lady says, look at the signs of the times, and pray.

"I can compare it to a spring cleaning. If I want my home to be spotless, I know that I first have to turn everything upside down, I move the sofa, I stack the chairs on the table, I open all the cupboards — nothing remains in place. My home is thrown into chaos and disorder, it is unrecognizable for my children and the peace is gone. But then I clean under everything. I wipe away all the grime. I put every piece of furniture back in its rightful place. In the end, my home is more immaculate than ever.

"This is how I see all the confusion in the world today. This is how I see Our Lady's apparitions and God's plan. A truly clean house starts with a big mess. Will you be like most children and stand back while Mom cleans, or will you not be afraid to get your hands dirty and help her? Our Lady said in one of her messages, 'I desire that through love, our hearts may triumph together.'

"May the triumph of her heart begin with you."

The Secrets: Getting Closer

After years since the beginning of the apparitions in 1981 and the turmoil in the world so insidious and evil, logic would tell us we are getting much closer to the secrets being revealed, which would validate Medjugorje all the more, and what has gone on there all of these years. It has always been presumptuous and prideful to predict a date for supernatural events, but Our Lady did say, *"Look at the signs of the times and pray."*

Saint John Paul II called Medjugorje, *"the confessional of the world."* Cardinal Schonborn of Austria said, *"If it were not for Medjugorje, the seminaries of Europe would be empty."* With June of 2021 being the 40th anniversary since the apparitions began, many are anxiously waiting to see if we see some of the promised Ten Secrets released. Secrets are just that. There is a certain amount of information that has been divulged over the years by the visionaries and pieced together for some more clarity, but they are still secrets between Our Lady and the six visionaries. Heaven must have some amusement in doing this, because we know the interest over the decades with the Third Secret of Fatima.

Our Lady is remaining with us in Medjugorje through these times. She gave an answer to the length of time of the apparitions and messages when she said, *"Dear Children! My Son has allowed me to stay with you this long, to help you, and to protect you. Dear children, you cannot do it on your own."* The evil is so strong today, she is saying we need her help to endure the trial. As Jesus told Peter, *"Simon, Simon, behold, Satan has demanded to sift you like wheat"* (Luke 22:31). When we follow her prescription for protection in these times, there is a dome of protection over us.

There is no reason to fear. When the Blessed Mother came to Fatima she told the three children, *"Be not afraid; I shall do you no harm."* She said the same thing to the young children at Medjugorje when she first came. What Mother would harm her children? When Pope John Paul II came out on the balcony after being elected pope, he said the same thing. Jesus told his apostles, **"Be not afraid,"** to quell their fear. Heaven is not arbitrary, and a great plan is under way. It may be only when we can look back in retrospect that we then truly understand.

JESUS I TRUST IN YOU

3

The Warning and the Great Miracle— Like Nothing Before in History— Two Supernatural Events that Will Change the World—The Global Reset— Heaven Resets on Their Terms

And I will work wonders in the heavens above, and signs on the earth below; blood, fire, and a cloud of smoke.

Acts 2:19

Listen to me, you devout sons of mine, and blossom like a rosebush on a stream bank. Bloom like a sweet-smelling lily, and send your fragrance into the air like incense. Sing the Lord's praise and thank Him for all that He has done.... All that the Lord has done is very good: all that He commands is sooner or later done. No one should ask why things are as they are; these questions will be answered at the right time: whatever He commands is promptly done; there are no limits to His power to save.... He sees the whole of time, from the beginning to end, and nothing takes Him by surprise. No one should ask why things are as they are; everything in creation has its purpose.

Sirach 39:13-21

For those familiar with Signs and Wonders Magazine, and my writings, I have had a particular interest in the apparitions of the Blessed Mother at Garabandal Spain since the mid 1980's. Garabandal has a uniqueness all its own, which I have written extensively about it. My wife Maureen and I released a book in 1993 called **The Thunder of Justice.** The story and messages of Garabandal were the heart and the soul of the book. Garabandal is a fascinating story historically, prophetically, scripturally, and mystically. It lays the tiles together for a beautiful mosaic of Heaven's language to their people. Garabandal points to future events that are complimentary to other elements in the Catholic faith, as well as significant events that are in the Old Testament. If one understands that God, the Blessed Mother, and the Host of Heaven, have a plan for the salvation of all mankind in our troubled times, then Garabandal and its promises make even more sense.

My wife and I first visited Garabandal in 1994, and again in 2017 on pilgrimage to Fatima on its 100th anniversary as well as other sites. It was an eye-opening experience on the second visit, because we had learned so much more during that interval of time since our first visit. What was most noticeable in 2017 was how little had changed in the village. More accurately, we were stunned by it. The church had not been updated or expanded, and was still tiny, and only a few dozen more homes were built. For pilgrims, there were only two public bathrooms. Two! It was eerie in its simplicity and remoteness from the noise of the world, and what is expected to happen there at some point in the future. The miraculous that is prophesied to happen there will be unprecedented in all of history. The lack of amenities and facilities may be a part of the much bigger story when the Miracle does happen.

The Push for a Great Reset

At a point in time there are continual changes the way societies and civilizations govern and rule—and who the new governing powers will be. To have a new one, there will be one replaced. This is the story of civilization itself that historians like Will Durant and others wrote about. We see empires like Egypt under the Pharoahs, Persia, the Greeks, Alexander the Great, the Romans, Spain under the Armada, France under the Sun Kings, England sailing the seven seas for commodities and spices, and America after World War II and Bretton Woods, becoming the undisputed ruler of finance and industry globally in the twentieth century. However, never has the world seen an integrated and interconnected community of nations like we now see. It is a new phase of mankind. With so many government bodies vying for control, we see any nation that steps out of bounds from what a global elite deems appropriate, then that nation will be doomed to either obscurity or destruction. At the heart of it all is who controls central banking. On March 21, 2022 President Joseph Biden gave another indication we are in a seismic shift as nations in the past when he said, *"you know we are in an inflection point, I believe in the world economy. Not just the economy, the world. It occurs every three or four generations. As one of the top military generals told me the other day in a secure meeting, 60 million people died between 1900 and 1946, and since then we have established a liberal world order and that hadn't happened in a long while. Lot of people dying now, but nowhere near the chaos. And now's the time when things are shifting. There's gonna be a new world order out there, and we've gotta lead it. And we've gotta unite the rest of the world in doing it."*

A Reset Designed by God

All over the news is the Great Reset of the elites pushing their agenda of global control. However, the Warning and the Great Miracle of Garabandal will be Heaven's Reset on their own terms to offset the evil in our day. *Where sin abounds, grace abounds all the more* (Romans 5:20). Due to the interconnectivity of this community of nations, Heaven will have their own global solutions.

The breadth and width of the events of the prophetic events that are to happen at Garabandal are breathtaking and will defy natural law. At the time of this writing, there are five Cardinals and many bishops that are openly saying they see signs of the "end times" in our midst. More people of all faiths see we are in *"the end of times."* If one were to look at the world, mankind has run out of answers to govern itself. It is not a question of looking at the glass half full, it is seeing that mankind is on the precipice of destruction on a global basis. A spark from just about anywhere could ignite a world-wide maelstrom that could generate a massive tsunami of destruction. There would be uncontrollable wars were it not for the grace of Heaven to stop the carnage. The Blessed Mother told Sister Lucy of Fatima, *"Wars are a punishment for the sins of mankind."* The anxiety and commotion of our times are birthing a New Era. Any mother can tell you, it is a painful process before the birth of a child. The old is passing away, and New Times await us. Satan knows his time is short, thus the flurry of evil in our day. Garabandal will be a **Global Reset** not the **Great Reset** designed by men, and it will be on Heaven's terms like the world has never seen. It will offset the evil of our day, and it will happen in an instant and change the world as we know it. People will soon speak of **before** the Warning and Miracle and **after** the Warning and the Miracle. It will be like they designate centuries and millennia Before Christ (BC) and After Christ (AD).

THE GAMECHANGER — Heaven Intervenes — The Warning, the Illumination of Conscience, the Life Review, a Judgment in Miniature, the Correction of Conscience

People who have followed what the Blessed Mother has said in the past at Garabandal Spain, have been waiting in joyful hope for several events. There are millions who have been exposed to the literature and what has been said long ago even to recent mystics. Heaven has a tendency of never being late, but it never seems to be early. A prophecy will happen exactly as Heaven said it will happen if it is authentic, but not necessarily as we perceive it in our mind. The Lord's ways are not our ways. We have seen this at Guadalupe, Rue du Bac, Lourdes, Fatima, Akita, LaSalette, and other apparition sites. Heaven moves with a still small voice (I Kings 19:12), as Heaven is never in a hurry. God is a God of order, and He speaks to us gently and in small doses over a long period of time so we can absorb and internalize the message.

God's DNA is mercy and He will not abandon us. As Jesus was walking on the water in the Sea of Galilee in the midst of a storm, His words to his spiritually young apostles were, *"Fear not, it is I"* (Matt. 14:27). Very early in his pontificate Saint John Paul II would often say especially to the young, *"there is nothing to fear,"* and *"fear not."* It was a constant theme during his pontificate.

Anxiety comes from a lack of spiritual simplicity and the lack of a prayer life. To grasp the magnitude of events coming our way will require letting go of the superfluous things from our lives. What is amusing is the talk of people being "preppers." What was once a cottage industry has gone mainstream with big business engaged. When the largest retailers in the country like Sam's Club, Walmart, Target, and Costco are carrying all types of dried food sold in volume that they cannot keep in stock, it is time to take notice that many don't have great comfort in the present system or in government. Guns and ammunition have never been sold like they have in the last few years as people feel there will be a breakdown of society and have decided to take more control for protection. People are now paying more attention knowing that the present way we are living is not sustainable. Items are widely being sold for consumer use that are helpful if the electric grid goes down. Stress and anxiety are all around us.

People are heading to the woods in cabins looking for solace and safety as they build doomsdays refuges, and there is even a TV show about it. The thinking is that the system may break down, and it doesn't take a genius to see it. If people have the resources and means to head to the woods, that is their prerogative. However, their motives must be clear on why they are doing it. If it is not to help others, it will fail and will be a useless enterprise. There is no hiding from what is coming our way. A person may postpone disaster, but not totally avoid it. There will be no ultimate safety for what lies ahead — but spiritual. A person may mitigate disaster in the short term, but living off the grid is not a long-term solution. The digital control government has today is just too vast for anyone to run and hide for a long period of time.

What is amazing with all the physical prepping, is that there is little talk of spiritual preparation, the greatest preparation of all which will keep us safe. The Blessed Mother has been clear, the refuge is in her Immaculate Heart. Few ever speak of the necessary preparation to protect one's family that are spiritual. The clergy as a whole are afraid of the subject of apparitions for several reasons. **One**, they will be marginalized if they speak of these, thus they fear that. They fear man more than God, and some are men pleasers rather than God pleasers. **Two**, their Bishops frown upon them speaking on unapproved apparitions like Medjugorje, Garabandal, and others. **Three**, they don't know much about Our Lady's appearances.

What is the Lord doing? Is there a timetable? What are we to expect? No one knows the precise answers to these questions, but we are not far off from momentous changes nearly impossible to wrap our head around if what has been spoken about. Heaven has provided us some important data for us to know that these events may not be far off. What we are being told is just before the events, there will be chaos and war in the world. Due to the rapid disintegration of the way the world has existed in the past, new structures of totalitarian government are being ushered in due to the breakdown we see around us. What you once knew is no longer, and the safety net of government is gone, or at least disintegrating rapidly and not working as originally implemented.

This is not the end of the world, but what you knew in the past will be over. We will move forward in a new direction. What worked in the past is not working now, and plans are afoot for global government that will add new dimensions at a dizzying pace. Most people will wilt under the changes, and not be able to adapt and cope unless they have spiritual formation prior to the events. The speed of it all will cause many to lose employment, marriages will break up for a variety of reasons, with the most notable, spouses not in unison on ideology of what is really happening. There will be loss of property, general confusion, and capitalism itself will be transformed due to the added power of civil bodies all over the world. Just look at the force of totalitarian government control over the vaccine issue. Free-market economies are being altered due to interference from regulatory bodies that will dictate how business is done. The globalist goal is to put people in a digital cage to monitor all activities. Systems are now in place to execute that plan. The goal is Agenda 2030 under the United Nations, with the ideology of the World Economic Forum and other large multi and transnational bodies behind it. Every area of life will be affected, and no one will come away unscathed from the changes.

Just when it appears all is lost, Heaven will not abandon its children. Heaven has a plan. There will be two events, which will happen one after the other. The first is called **THE WARNING.** There are many other terms for it among credible mystics, but other terms most commonly used are the **"Illumination of Conscience/Life Review/Judgment in Miniature/ Correction of Conscience."** By and large some people may know of these events coming our way through friends and family, but it tends to be almost exclusively Catholics that have been receptive to it. Why? It has been the Blessed Mother as the Prophetess of our age saying it, preparing us for many years about what is to come. She has been appointed by the Most Holy Trinity for her task at this point in time, as we move to the culmination of the battle. Satan's cohort battling God's cohort for the soul of mankind. In Revelation 12 the Woman Clothed with the Sun is in battle as the Queen of Heaven and earth. By and large there is great prejudice against her from those who wish to dismiss her if she speaks. Good Catholics including some priests, reject the messages when she speaks, or will only address her messages in hushed terms for fear of being marginalized by their congregations or confreres. As long as she remains silent, many are fine with that. The faithful will often venerate her as a symbol in history, but they will shun her when someone speaks of her majesty and work in the world. Many think her activity stopped at Fatima and refuse to address the last 100 years. Soon, there will be no getting around what she has been saying, as we will know the appointed time by the events themselves. The events will dictate we look into what has been said at so many of her apparition sites.

The **Warning / The Illumination of Conscience / Life Review / Judgment in Miniature / Correction of Conscience** is an event that was described in more detail at the apparition in Garabandal, Spain than any other place. The reason is that the statements were so precise on what will happen at some future date. Similar statements have been mentioned by other mystics, and it will be an event like no other. What is prophesied to happen is that every person in the world will see their soul as God sees it at judgment, "*a judgment in miniature.*" Anyone who knows people who have experienced a life after death experience or near-death experience (NDE), know that they come back dramatically changed people. Many who have experienced such phenomena come back and tell of having seen Heaven, Hell, or Purgatory. These are impossible to explain aside from a personal encounter. Most are not open to these events being real, some are. It is a choice. But no one will escape this event of a "*judgment in miniature.*" Today, it is a relatively small population who know of it, but soon it will be the entire world. Never in recorded history has there been such an event. There will be no denying what has taken place. Throughout history, the Lord works with small numbers like He did with Gideon to show the victory was His alone. We will be stripped naked before God and we will see our life like a slow-motion movie picture. We will have no response before a Divine loving God, other than acknowledgment of truth. Sins that are more grievous will go slower, such as where we have hurt people with words or actions, and see our sins of omission and commission. In the presence of that Divine Truth, we will have no response other than acceptance. We will be in so much light and love, we will have no rebuttal other than the truth we have seen. Today God is our Savior, at death He will be our judge.

The Visionaries, The Story of Garabandal & Saint Michael the Archangel

Located in the Cantabrian Mountains of Northern Spain near the Bay of Biscay in a remote village called Garabandal, the Blessed Mother appeared to four young girls over 2,000 times from 1961-1965. It was during the time of Vatican II where significant changes were happening in the church. Some events were spoken of in detail by the Blessed Mother that have never been said so clearly and directly in the past. Why? Heaven must think that we are in need of such events to shock us back to God. At the end of the events, people will be on one side or the other, but not sitting on a fence. They will be hot or cold, for or against the things of God, but not neutral. It will be a time like no other in history.

San Sebastian de Garabandal was a tiny village of about 300 people in the Diocese of Santander, when the Blessed Mother first appeared in 1961. At the time of the apparition there wasn't a motor with moving parts in the entire village. The townspeople were simple and very devout. About a quarter mile to the north on a high ridge, nine pine trees tower over the village, marking the spot where Our Lady frequently appeared, and the spot where a Great Miracle is prophesied to happen in the future at the nine pines. The nine pines are tucked in a valley that is a natural amphitheater where millions can comfortably sit and look down on them.

The story of Garabandal began on the evening of June 18, 1961, when the Archangel Michael appeared to four young girls. The visionaries were: Conchita Gonzalez (age twelve), Jacinta Gonzalez (age twelve), Mari Cruz Gonzalez (age eleven), none of whom are closely related, and Mari-Loli Mazon (age twelve). He made eight silent appearances during the following twelve days. On July 1, St. Michael finally spoke to announce that on the following day the Blessed Virgin Mary would appear to them as Our Lady of Mount Carmel. The Blessed Mother then appeared on July 2 to the children. July 2 was the Feast of the Ark of the Covenant in the old liturgical calendar. Our Lady is the New Ark of the Covenant. The Ark of the Covenant contained the signs of God's presence among His chosen people and was a physical sign of Yahweh's covenant with His people. Was Our Lady showing us that she had come to do battle when she came to Garabandal?

The apparitions were preceded by three interior calls, which the girls described as joys, each one becoming stronger. After the third call, the girls would come running from different parts of the village and would arrive at the same time in the place designated by Our Lady. They would then fall to their knees in ecstasy.

The four seers described Our Lady as a beautiful young woman about eighteen years of age. She wore a white dress with a blue mantle and a brown scapular on her right arm. On her head she wore a crown of twelve stars as she appears in Revelation 12. Her hair was deep brown and parted in the center. Her face was oval with a fine nose. The girls said, *"No other woman looks like her or sounds like her."*

Each apparition affirmed and amplified one another, with similar themes on the importance of the Rosary, the Eucharist, the Mass, the Sacraments, and all that entails living a daily life in communion with God. Many who follow such events make a mistake that thinking what has been said at one apparition site (although that may be the case) will necessarily carry over to another. What is the focus here is that there will be events coming from Garabandal that will show the world God's faithfulness to His people. The old must pass, before the new can come. Before every Easter Sunday comes Good Friday and the Church at this point in time is walking the road of Calvary. At the time of Noah, his was the only righteous family to escape the flood. Genesis gives us a graphic account of the sin. We saw the same in Sodom and Gomorrah, when it was only Lot, his wife, and two daughters who escaped the wrath of God. What most people do not realize is that Lot's daughters were both betrothed, and neither made the journey out of the city after being warned. They were told not to look back, but Lot's wife disobeyed the Lord's command by turning around, and she turned to a pillar of salt. The sin of disobedience has consequences.

Heaven has an agenda and it is filled with grace. We can either accept it, or fight it. It is a personal choice. If a person is unsure whether Garabandal is true, wisdom would say to remain quiet to not quench the work of the Holy Spirit. If it is not true, it won't matter. But if it is true, nothing you can do or say will stop it. This would be a similar situation to the words of the Rabbi Gamaliel when he told the Jews not knowing what to do after the death of Jesus, as they fought amongst themselves at Pentecost. Addressing the Sanhedrin he said, *"What I suggest, therefore, is that you leave these men alone and let them go. If this enterprise, this movement of theirs, is of human origin it will break up of its own accord; but if it does in fact come from God you will not only be unable to destroy them, but you might find yourselves fighting against God"* (Acts 5:38-39). What is going to take place at Garabandal is of such mind-numbing scope, it is actually impossible to fully comprehend it. The events will be **God's ultimate acts of mercy** on a scale the world has never seen before. The Warning and the Great Miracle are both separate and distinct events on different days, but linked as one. One will follow the other.

When one sees in the modern era what the Blessed Mother and the Host of Heaven are looking to accomplish at authentic and time-tested apparition sites, there is more of a complete understanding of what is happening in the world. The messages of Garabandal address these issues. They show what Heaven is doing to bring us to a new Era of Peace, a New Jerusalem, a New Epoch — New Times. This will not be the end of the world as one could make a derisive comment, but a line of demarcation where world events transition to a New Time. We have seen transitions in history like after the Bolshevik Revolution, the French Revolution, the American Revolution, the American Civil War, World War I and II, etc. This will be much larger with a far bigger and wider global impact.

This narrative will present a short synopsis of what happened and what is expected to happen when Our Lady came and foretold future events for the world and the church. Due to the poverty of space, many poignant and important aspects of the story cannot be told, nor many of the controversies. *There are approximately two thousand messages given over four years* and innumerable stories could be told, but the point of this narrative is principally on the Warning, and the Great Miracle — the why of it, and its impact on the world, although several key messages are provided.

Mystical Phenomena

During the apparitions, many mystical phenomena were witnessed. The girls were able to detect and recognize priests who came to the village dressed in civilian clothes, trying to conceal their identities. Many times, during the ecstatic walks, the visionaries would offer these priests their crucifix to be kissed. During one of Conchita's ecstasies in 1962, two priests were kneeling down in reverence. They were gently encouraged by Conchita to stand up, in order to emphasize the deep respect that Our Lady has for priests. She taught the children to greet the priest before greeting an angel, because a priest is more important, since only a priest can consecrate bread and wine into the Body and Blood of Christ during the Holy Sacrifice of the Mass.

On occasions the young girls were subjected by investigators to burns, spotlights in their eyes, and pin pricks without showing any physical response to pain. Reports indicate that four adult men had difficulty lifting one twelve-year-old girl, yet the girls could lift each other easily to kiss Our Lady goodbye. The apparitions were accompanied by other phenomena that seemed to defy natural law, such as ecstatic falls and running fast forward and backward over very rocky terrain. For detractors of this phenomena they may want to read the story of Balaam's donkey speaking for being treated harshly (Numbers 22:21-39). Thus, the phrase, *"out of the mouth of an ass."* It is not every day a donkey speaks. Stories in the Bible don't always follow logical or natural law, yet one can barely read Scripture and not see the supernatural.

Many religious objects were kissed by Our Lady. The visionaries, while in ecstasy, would return the objects to their rightful owners even though their owners were unknown to them. The seers claimed that Our Lady guided them to the right person. Our Lady promised: *"Through the kiss I have bestowed on these objects, my Son will perform miracles, wonders, and prodigies before and after the Great Miracle."* The fulfillment of this promise has been realized by the many conversions and cures of terminally ill and addicted people around the world.

Another remarkable event emphasized at Garabandal was the importance of the Eucharist. An angel appeared bearing a golden chalice. In many photographs of Garbandal, a chalice is often suspended in mid-air. This was very common in the early years of the apparitions, as the Eucharist was central to the messages. The angel asked the children to think of the One whom they were going to receive. He taught them to recite the Confiteor (Latin for a penitential prayer said at the beginning of the Mass in prior years), after which he gave them Holy Communion. He also taught them to say the Anima Christi in thanksgiving.

These "Angelic Communions" were recorded on film, showing the movement of the girls lips, tongue, and throat. However, since these Hosts were only visible to the girls, many skeptics doubted that they were actually receiving Holy Communion. When questioned about where the Hosts came from, since only a priest could consecrate, the angel told them that the Hosts were taken from the tabernacle of the church. Therefore, a priest and not an angel had consecrated the Hosts.

On June 22, 1962, the angel told Conchita that God would perform a "special miracle." The people would be allowed to see the Sacred Host appear on Conchita's tongue at the moment she received Communion, in order that they might believe. Conchita's diary entry for June 30, 1962, stated: *"While I was in the pines I heard a voice which said that the Miracle would take place on the eighteenth of July."* The angel later instructed her to reveal this message fifteen days in advance. She was unable to receive Communion on the 18th, but did receive the mystical Communion at 1:40 AM on July 19th. This occurred in front of numerous witnesses and was filmed.

Priest Sees the Great Miracle, Father Luis Maria Andreu, S.J.

Highlighting the centrality of the priesthood to the messages of Garabandal, two priests' stories underscore that importance while emphasizing Our Lady's presence with supernatural phenomena.

Father Luis Maria Andreu, a thirty-eight-year-old Jesuit priest, was visiting Garabandal for the second time on August 8, 1961. Father Luis, while observing the visionaries during ecstasy, suddenly cried out, *"Milagro!"* four times. When driving home later that night with his friends, Father Luis said, *"What a wonderful present the Virgin has given me! How lucky we are to have a mother like that in Heaven! Today is the happiest day of my life!"* Shortly after, he lowered his head and died. In a later apparition, Our

Lady told the visionaries that Father Luis had seen her and had also seen the Great Miracle. He died of joy with his last words, *"This has been the happiest day of my life."* Our Lady also revealed to Conchita on September 14, 1965, that Father Luis' body will be exhumed and found to be incorrupt on the day after the Great Miracle. Note this will be even more of a miracle since his remains were transferred and found to be decomposed.

Father Ramon Andreu, S.J., the brother of the deceased Father Luis Andreu, S.J., was also a significant witness whose life was dramatically changed by the events of Garabandal. He was privileged to have witnessed more than 400 ecstasies. During his visits to the village, he kept a detailed record in his notebooks of everything he saw and heard. These notebooks represent some of the more valuable documentation. The most startling event for Father Ramon was the revelation from the visionaries that they had conversed with his dead brother, Father Luis. Father Ramon was told precise details of his brother's funeral and details of his personal life that were unknown to anyone but himself. On another occasion, Father Luis gave a message for his mother: *"Be happy and content for I am in Heaven and I see you every day."* This was a message of great joy for his mother, who entered the convent, and a remarkable revelation about our loved ones who have gone to Heaven. He and his brother, Father Luis, were especially chosen by Our Lady to bear witness to the incredible events of Garabandal.

Support for the Apparitions

The apparitions were contemporaneous with Vatican II. Although there exist some differences of opinion among bishops. Since 1961, the Church has never condemned them. However, bishops have held different levels of interest and openness to the apparitions. The early position by one bishop was one of caution and the apparitions were dismissed with the whole affair as *"child's play."* In 1961, Our Lady told the visionaries: *"A time will come when all four of you will contradict yourselves one with the other, when your families will also contradict themselves about the apparitions; you will even deny that you have seen me or Saint Michael."* On this occasion witnesses heard the four visionaries while in ecstasy say: *"How is it that one day we will say that we did not see you, since we are seeing you now?"* Our Lady told them: *"Because you are going to pass through the same confusion as the Church."*

These prophetic words did come to pass, as they later denied receiving the apparitions. Thus, the bishop and his successors had cause for serious reservations about the authenticity of the apparitions. Bishop Fernandez and his immediate successor Bishop Eugenio Beitia issued "Notas." These "Notas" advised caution and restricted priests from visiting the village without permission. They stated further that there was no evidence that any supernatural events had taken place. However, it is significant to note that Bishop Beitia, in his "Notas" of July 8, 1965, stated: *"... We would like to say, however, that we have found no grounds for an ecclesiastical condemnation either in the doctrine or in the spiritual recommendations that have been divulged in the events and addressed to the Christian faithful; furthermore, these recommendations contain exhortations to prayer, sacrifice, devotion to the Holy Eucharist and devotion to the Blessed Virgin under traditional, praiseworthy forms; there are also exhortations to a holy fear of the Lord, offended by our sins...."*

In a letter dated May 7, 2007 the Archbishop of Oviedo, Carlos Osoro Sierra, the Apostolic Administrator of the Diocese of Santander wrote to an American by the name of Edward Kelly. Kelly was an American who married a woman from Garabandal, and then lived in California. The letter was printed in the Garabandal Journal/Special Edition. Bishop Sierra wrote, *"I encourage you to continue maintaining this devotion to Our Mother.... I am open to all information and to every consideration about Garabandal."* From the same publication, there is a letter published in which Msgr. Stanislaus Dziwisz (Cardinal of Krakov Poland) once secretary to John Paul II, responded on behalf of the pope to a book by German author Albrecht Weber he received on Garabandal. *"May God reward you for everything, especially the deep love with which you are making the events connected with Garabandal more widely known. May the message of the Mother of God, find an entrance into hearts before it is too late. As an expression of joy and gratitude, the Holy Father gives you his apostolic blessing."* Accompanying this letter was a greeting by John Paul II in his own handwriting.

Abortion Referenced by Our Lady

Among the many prophecies of Garabandal was one that only came to light with the publication of Weber's book on Garabandal in 1992. Weber was in Garabandal on the day of Conchita's last apparition on November 13, 1965, and had a conversation with the visionary. The following excerpt from his book deals with some of what the visionary told him:

> "She (Conchita) spoke quite openly about the developments by which men in the near future would rebel against God. On the day after Our Lady's last appearance at Garabandal, Conchita asked the author, *"Can you imagine how someone could kill children in the womb without thereby killing the mother?"* The author spontaneously answered, *"No, what gave you that idea, Conchita." Well, the Blessed Mother spoke about this and she let me know that this will happen with the overflowing of the chalice."* [In the second message of June 18, 1965, the Virgin said, *"Before the cup was filling up. Now it is flowing over."*]
>
> *"Conchita said this trembling without being able to visualize what it really implied. She said it disturbed her very much but that she felt ridiculous because she hadn't understood at all how this could happen. The Blessed Virgin had not explained it to her, and up until that moment, nobody had been able to explain it to her at all."*

"Conchita would learn soon enough when abortion became legalized, even in her own country."

(This story on abortion above in its entirety is verbatim from the *The Garabandal Journal*, January/February, 2004, page 11).

Possible Data Points on the Timing of the Warning

Pope to Visit Moscow?

As mentioned, German author Albrecht Weber was devoted to Garabandal from the time of the apparitions to his death in 2014. He is buried at Garabandal, and in no way would ever wish to harm what happened there. He devoted his life to making the messages of Garabandal known. Weber is the sole origin of the story that the reigning pope would visit Moscow near the time of the Warning. Weber claimed Conchita told him that when meeting with her at the time of the apparitions in 1965. Pope Francis has expressed interest in visiting Moscow and said so on his way back to Rome after his five-day Greece and Cyprus trip in December 2021. Patriarch Kirill of Moscow then sent a representative soon after to the Vatican to work out details. Pope Francis visited the Russian Embassy on February 25, 2022 in Rome, at the beginning of the Russia Ukraine war, presumably making a plea for peace. It has been nearly 1,000 years since Eastern Orthodoxy split from Rome, so it would be a significant event. However, at the time of this writing, no date has been given for Pope Francis to visit Moscow. What is odd, is that this story had not surfaced until fairly recently about Weber's claim. After multiple decades of speculation when the Warning may take place, this story had not been spoken of or widely disseminated. However, events are now pointing to the fruition of the prophecies by just looking at the social upheaval in the world. If Weber is correct, we will know shortly.

Was the Synod on Synodality the Synod Prophesied at Garabandal?

Another event that is interesting to note on the possible timing of the Warning is that it would be around the time of a synod. Synods are not new in the Church, and there have been many since the apparitions ended in 1965. But a Spanish nun by the name of Mother Nieves Garcia who was the head of Conchita's boarding school in Spain knew Conchita since her school days, said she was told the Warning would be near the time of a Synod. Conchita had allegedly told Mother Nieves that "an important one" {Synod} would be held before the events took place. Pope Francis has initiated a program called *The Synod on Synodality* which is a two-year process of listening and dialogue that began with a solemn opening in Rome on October 9, 10, 2021. The reason it is an *"important one"* is that it has relevance to every diocese and parish in the world because there has never been one quite like it. The Synodal process will conclude in 2023. Pope Francis said about the synod, *"I invite the Church to reflect on the theme that is decisive for its life and mission. It is precisely this path of synodality which God expects the Church of the third millennium. This journey which follows in the wake of the Church's renewal proposed by the Second Vatican Council, is both a gift and a task: by journeying together and reflecting together on the journey that has been made, the Church will be able to learn through her experience which processes can help her to live communion, to active participation to open herself to mission."*

This is another controversy because many people feel that Pope Francis might use the Synod to make changes that will be more progressive than many like, taking the Church in a further direction conservatives feel will aid in the further destruction of orthodoxy and tradition. At the diocesan level there are meetings mandated by bishops with clergy participating in *listening sessions* with laity to discuss the direction of the Church. Conservatives are concerned that it will bring more of a liberal social justice agenda to these *"listening sessions"* throughout the world.

The Issue of the Number of Popes

After Pope John XXIII died, Conchita said that Our Lady told her, *"After this pope there will be only three left, but there would be a fourth pope who would govern the Church for a short time, then it would be the end of times."* This gets into a highly controversial matter as to the issue of when she said this. It is alleged there was pressure from Conchita's mother on releasing this portion of the message relating to the reign of a pope for just a short time to not create controversy for her daughter. Since John XXIII, we have had Paul VI, John Paul I, then John Paul II, Benedict XVI, and now Pope Francis. We do know that John Paul I governed only thirty-three days, which is an amazingly accurate prophecy in light of that fact it did happen. If the above is true, then that would mean the conclave electing Pope Francis ushered in the end times. It is a plausible scenario but still controversial. Initially Conchita indicated there would be only three popes before "the end times," **a New Era of humanity, not the end of the world.**

The Role of Communism is Still a Dominant Theme that Never Seems to go Away

A Mrs. Christine Bocabeille asked Mary Loli, *"Since you are not allowed to tell me the exact year of the Warning, perhaps you could tell me approximately when it will happen?"* Loli responded, *"It will be at a time when the world will most need it."* Then it was asked when is that? Loli said, **"When Russia will suddenly and unexpectedly overrun a great part of the free world.** *God does not want this to happen so quickly. In any case the Warning will come when you will see the Holy Mass cannot be celebrated freely anymore; then it will be that the world will most need the intervention of God."*

Mari-Loli did not know the date/day of the Warning, only the year. Conchita alone knows the day of the Miracle. Mari-Loli also said that the Blessed Mother told her prior to the Warning and the Great Miracle, *"A time would come, when it would look like the Church was finished, when priests would have difficulty saying Mass and talking about holy things. There would come a time when the Church would give the impression of being on the point of perishing. It would pass through a terrible test. Priests would supposedly have to hide in order to say Mass. It is then that the world will be in most need of God's intervention."* When she asked Our Lady how this would happen, Our Lady called it **"communism."** This has happened in many countries already. Whether or not it will be more widespread remains to be seen.

It is much easier to manipulate and control an individual that does not acknowledge the truth of Christianity, which is precisely why it must be removed by a tyrannical government. We have seen the brutality of communist regimes from the USSR and China and other brute dictators, but communism is simply a government where God cannot be publicly displayed. Through sophisticated social engineering, much of the west, and the world at large, exhibit a form of theoretical and practical atheism—or communism as it comes to everyday living. A world without God is the communist (global elite) goal.

The Blessed Mother once told Conchita, **"it would be like an invasion of Communism."** Premier Mikhail Gorbachev said the event that toppled the USSR was the nuclear disaster at Chernobyl April 26, 1986. The ramifications of Soviet incompetence spreading throughout western borders was no longer acceptable to the West, and Gorbachev was firm when he said it was this event that led to the 1992-1994 downfall. As the world watches the destruction of the Ukraine and the issues that it is causing world-wide, one would have to ask, has communism really fallen?

The girls described the times of tribulation as *"the return of Communism."* Four young mountain children in the early 1960's would not have any understanding of what Communism meant. In political philosophy Communism does not necessarily have to be violent, although it usually is. Communism is an ideological practice without God in the governance of the state. Due to theoretical and practical atheism globally, we increasingly see a world that does not want God in any genre or milieu of life. Classrooms across the world continue to be cesspools with a lack of any moral formation, with many countries outright reverting to paganism. This would constitute Communism returning on a much wider scale than what we have seen in the past.

Prelude to The Warning or The Illumination of Conscience

Our Lady's messages promised three events at Garabandal; a fourth is contingent upon the world's response. The first event will be a world-wide warning from God, known as The Warning. Conchita wrote in a letter on January 1, 1965: *"Our Lady said that a warning would be given to the entire world before the Miracle in order that the world might amend itself. It will come directly from God and be visible throughout the entire world."*

There will be two events to happen *within* one year. The operative word is **"within."** It may be less, but it will not be more than one year from the Warning to the Great Miracle. The word *within* doesn't mean it has to happen in the same calendar year.

Pope Paul VI (Papacy from 1963-1978) called the struggle of good and evil going on in the world "apocalyptic." Pope Paul quoted Luke 18:8: *"when the Son of Man returns will He find faith on earth,"* and said the *"smoke of Satan had entered the sanctuary."* The Blessed Mother also said at Fatima, **"In the end my Immaculate Heart will Triumph."** The Triumph of her Immaculate Heart is the return of Jesus in glory. It is never about the Blessed Mother; it is about Jesus. As the Blessed Mother said at Cana instructing the servants, *"Do whatever He tells you"* (John 2:5). The Holy Trinity has appointed her for this task specifically at this point in time. If one thing is gleaned from this entire narrative, it is this; *The refuge is her Immaculate Heart.* Looking for safety anywhere else will be of limited value and duration. Not taking away from the authority of Jesus in the least, she glorifies His Sacred Heart. She is a co-redeemer with us in His salvation plan for mankind, and what better vessel than His mother who came into the world without the stain of sin through the Immaculate Conception?

Garabandal as the other authentic apparition sites are all simple and direct. They speak in clear language about the basic tenets of the faith. Not philosophy or theology few can understand, but always go to the heart of what is true and good. When a life changing experience or a message is heard and absorbed, there is a transformation of the soul. Pope Paul VI, Saint John Paul II, Father Stefano Gobbi of the Marian Movement of Priests, and many other contemporaries of our time believed in what was said at Garabandal, and were all public in affirming it. Saint Pio (Padre Pio) St. Teresa (Mother) also believed in the validity of Garabandal. Both visited with Conchita and extended their blessings and prayers to her. Saint Pio on the occasion of his visit with her, took Conchita's hand and her crucifix that Our Lady had kissed and held them both. The crucifix had been passed through the hands of the child Jesus during the apparition of November 13, 1965.

However, what made Garabandal unique, is that the girls spoke about two events that would happen that have been spoken about by other mystics in the church like Saint Edmund Campion, and Blessed Anna Maria Taigi. Other more contemporary mystics like Servant of God Maria Esperanza of Betania/Caracas, Venezuela have addressed the same subjects.

The Warning is where each will see the state of his or her soul as God would judge it upon our death. It will be a line of demarcation in all of history. Satan's lie will be exposed for who he is, and he will know we know it. His grip will be loosened. There will still be sin in the world after the event, but a line will be drawn in the sand where there is no fear of Satan. The free will of man will still be present, but the neutrality of people will be gone. You will either be for the things of God, or not. As the Jews wandered in the desert after they left the four hundred years of captivity in Egypt, it was not long before they forgot what God had done for them. Shortly thereafter, they were making a golden calf in the desert. Manna, and quail were falling from the sky to feed the migratory people heading to the promised land, and they were soon offering up a pagan rite. It will be the same today. People will soon forget the graces they have been given during "*The Warning,*" and go back to old ways because they have not been properly formed in the faith. It is for this reason formation in the faith is so important. *"Faith comes by hearing, hearing by the Word,"* (Romans 10:17), and as the Psalmist said, *"I have hid the word of God in my heart that I may not sin against thee"* (Ps. 119:11).

Two Key Messages of Garabandal

Our Lady revealed the first message for the world. She told the girls to announce the message publicly on October 18, 1961. On this day, the children made known the message: *"Many sacrifices must be made, much penance must be done.* **We must pay many visits to the Blessed Sacrament… but first of all we must be very good… if we do not do this, punishment awaits us… already the cup is filling, and if we do not change, we will be punished."** That message given to the young girls was heavily centered on conversion and amendment of life. The Blessed Mother had a continual theme as to the urgency of our times and what would happen, IF man did not repent.

The message continued: *"**If you ask pardon with a sincere soul, He will pardon you. It is I your Mother, who through the intercession of Saint Michael, wish to say that you amend, that you are already in the last warnings and that I love you much and do not want your condemnation. Ask us sincerely and we will give to you. You should sacrifice more. Think of the Passion of Jesus."* Our Lady appeared wearing the Brown Scapular, an indication we should wear it, and taught the children how to pray the rosary. Her greatest emphasis was placed on the Eucharist and prayers for the priests.**

On January 1, 1965, the Blessed Virgin told Conchita that the Archangel Michael would appear to her on the following June 18th to deliver a final message in Mary's name for the entire world, because her first message was not heeded. Saint Michael appeared to Conchita while she was in ecstasy, which lasted approximately sixteen minutes. On June 18, 1965 the following message was delivered to the world: ***"As my message of October 18th [1961] has not been complied with and has not been made known to the world, I am advising you that this is the last one. Before the cup was filling up. Now it is flowing over. Many cardinals, many bishops, and many priests are on*** *the road to perdition and are taking many souls with them. Less and less importance is being given to the Eucharist.*

"You should turn the wrath of God away from yourselves by your efforts. If you ask His forgiveness with sincere hearts, He will pardon you. I, your mother, through the intercession of Saint Michael the Archangel, ask you to amend your lives. You are now receiving the last warning. I love you very much and do not want your condemnation. Pray to Us with sincerity and We will grant your requests. You should make more sacrifices. Think about the passion of Jesus."

There are several very important things contained in that message. First and foremost, beyond temporal concerns, is **the importance of the Eucharist and Adoration.** It states clearly if people do not change, there will be punishment. Also, some clergy are leading souls to perdition. But, not just priests, but bishops and cardinals. These are profound statements with broad implications for the Church, the family, and the culture. It would be wise to reflect on these two messages and what they mean for us today. At the time that message was issued, the challenges to Church teaching with the sexual scandal involving priests had not fully unfolded.

The last apparition for Conchita was on November 13, 1965 at the Pines. Conchita described this last conversation as happy, but Our Lady kindly chastised her: *"Conchita, why don't you go often to visit my Son in the Most Blessed Sacrament?"*

Often, people who speak today on such subjects like this in public will frequently be ridiculed. You will hear this is an Old Testament mentality on the wrathful God. This was said in the 1960's and it is not some Old Testament prophet shouting it from the rooftops. A decision must be made on our theology and our perception of who God is in our life, and come to a realization that not all is well in the world—and Heaven has a plan. It comes to one major issue: This is Heaven's agenda, we are to embrace and declare it. Living the Gospel is being asked of us. Often the more conservative element in the church focus excessively on doctrine and are critical of what the Blessed Mother is doing in the world. They will venerate and pay lip service to her titles in Heaven, but if she speaks, they can't run fast enough to get away, not wanting to be associated with it. They often forget that the gospel is about people, and fallen people at that. The more liberal groups will often dismiss it as an outdated theology for a modern world.

More often than not, they have their own agendas which usually focus on social justice to the exclusion of nearly everything else. A feel good 'luving" church. Luv everywhere, luv everyone, with few boundaries on behavior, making up new theology along the way as they consider the Church outdated. Both sides fail to see the essential issue is to do what the Holy Spirit is asking. In addition, often the Marian devotee focuses so much on the severe parts of the messages of the Blessed Mother, they see nothing but doom and gloom to the exclusion of everything else, and forget that the gospel means, *"The Good News."* There has been great fruit from many of apparition sites throughout the world over the centuries bringing people to a deeper faith.

In Revelation 2 and 3, the Holy Spirit speaks to the seven churches that will have different spirits and charisms throughout millennia. Each of the churches has a major strength. No church has it all together except the Church of Philadelphia (Rev. 3: 7-13) as it is the only church the Lord does not find fault, because it embraces love. Each of the others, it is said, *"and this I have against you"*… but Philadelphia. This is where we need to arrive. We need to be transformed to arrive at neither left nor right in our theology and philosophy, but through finding peace of soul by living the gospel, where we are to love unconditionally. Our service will come because of our love and obedience to Scripture, and the Magisterium of the Church. Social Justice needs to be rooted in what we hear in prayer and fidelity to the laws of God, not a godless leftist political agenda creating havoc in the streets.

The Transition of Civilization Takes Place, Two Events to Come — the First Will be the Warning

The first of two events will be a world-wide warning from God. Conchita wrote in a letter dated on January 1, 1965 where she said, *"Our Lady said that a Warning would be given to the entire world before the Miracle in order that the world might amend itself. It will come directly from God and be visible throughout the entire world."* Conchita wrote on June 2, 1965, *"The warning, like the chastisement is a fearful thing for the good as well as the wicked. It* will draw the good closer to God and warn the wicked the end of times is coming. *These are the last warnings."* Conchita explained *"that the warning is a purification to prepare us for the miracle. Each person on earth will have an interior experience of how he or she stands in the light of God's Justice. Believers and nonbelievers alike will experience the Warning."* Those living in a state of grace will have less severe impact from it we are also told by other mystics. Mari Loli Mazon who lived in Massachusetts before she died in 2009, was the only visionary to know the year of the Warning, but not the day of the Great Miracle. Mari Loli said, *"We will see it and feel it within ourselves, and it will be most clear that it comes from God."*

Jacinta Gonzalez said: *"The Warning is something that is first seen in the air, everywhere in the world and immediately is transmitted into the interior of our souls. It will last for a very little time, but it will seem a very long time because of its effect within us. It will be for the good of our souls, in order to see in ourselves our conscience ... the good that we have failed to do, and the bad that we have done. Then we will feel a great love towards our heavenly Parents and ask forgiveness for all our offenses. The Warning is for everybody because God wants our salvation. The Warning is for us to draw closer to Him and to increase our faith. Therefore, one should prepare for that day, but not await it with fear. God does not send things for the sake of fear but rather with justice and love. He does it for the good of all His children so they might enjoy eternal happiness and not be lost."*

Are We Close to the Warning?

How much closer to this year of the Warning could we be? At this point in America, leading political figures are far more communist than socialist. Closer to Stalinist is actually more accurate where many leaders wish to bring western countries. Worldwide, America has lagged other countries in implementing communist principles, but now she seems eager to catch up. Many are promoting a communist ideology demanding faith be removed from the culture in every way possible. If a politician won't say it, they will often try to legislate it into reality, while they personally benefit from the largesse a capitalist structure affords them to live. The "invasion of Communism" is gaining ground in the USA faster than at any time since the Great Depression of the 1930s. A world that submerges into moral relativism where sin does not exist, fits a cleaner definition of communism. Today we have people who do not obey the commandments of God, yet will attend church paying more attention to cultural and state norms than Biblical truth. In essence, a state run, politically acceptable faith void of God, is increasingly the situation in the U.S. Language engineering and social manipulation are key to controlling the populace, and maintaining a godless narrative. We are seeing Our Lady's prophecy on communism being fulfilled with state control of all social structures. Inch by inch this goal has been achieved over several generations. Taking the Bible and prayer out of the classroom by order of the U.S. Supreme Court in America was a significant step with this agenda.

The Warning is Worldwide

Father Joseph Pelletier, the late Marian scholar and author (1912-1986 and Professor at Assumption College), asked Conchita several questions and offered further insight about the events of Garabandal. Conchita's answer on June 19, 1965, is as follows: *"Here in writing is the Warning that the Blessed Virgin gave me when I was alone at the pines on January 1st of this year, 1965. The Warning that the Blessed Virgin will give us is like a chastisement. Its purpose is to draw the good nearer to God and to warn the others. I cannot reveal what the Warning will consist of. The Blessed Virgin did not tell me to announce it. Nothing further. God would like that through this warning, we amend our lives and that we commit less sins against Him."* To the question posed by Marian and Garabandal scholar Father Laffineur whether the Warning would cause death, Conchita said, *"If we die from it, it would not be from the Warning itself, but from the emotional shock that we would experience in seeing and feeling the Warning."*

Statements were made by Conchita in response to questions put to her:

Q. Will the Warning be a visible thing or an interior thing or both?

A. **The Warning is a thing that comes directly from God. It will be visible all over the world, in whatever place anyone might be.**

Q. Will the Warning reveal his personal sins to every person in the world and to persons of all faiths, including atheists.

A. *Yes, the Warning will be like the revelation of our sins, and it will be seen and felt equally by believers and non-believers, and people of any religion whatsoever.*

In reply to a question whether the Warning might be a comet that was approaching the Earth, Conchita said: *"I don't know what a comet is. If it is something that depends on man's will, I answer — no. If it is something that God will do, it is quite possible."* When the woman expressed fear, the latter replied: *"Oh, yes, the Warning will be very fearful, a thousand times worse than earthquakes."* To an inquiry concerning the nature of the Warning, Conchita answered: **"It will be like fire. It will not burn our flesh, but we will feel it bodily and interiorly."** She added, *"We shall comment on this later. All nations and all persons will experience it in the same way. No one will escape it. Even the nonbelievers themselves will experience the fear of God. Even if you hide in your room and close the blinds, you will not escape it. You will feel and see it just the same. Yes, it is true. The Blessed Virgin gave me the name of the phenomenon. It begins with an 'A.' but she did not tell me to reveal it to anyone."*

As the lady again expressed her fear, Conchita added: *"Oh, but after the Warning, you will love the good Lord very much."* To the question: *"What about the Miracle?"* she said, *"The Miracle will not delay in coming."* Conchita added an interesting observation: *"Although it is taking time to come, it will not be late. God's time is always the appropriate time."*

An important note should be added: when Conchita describes the Warning as being *"like fire,"* she means that in some way or ways it resembles fire but that it is not fire. According to Conchita, the Warning and fire have two things in common: *"they can be seen and felt, and they are very terrifying. The Warning will be seen and felt by all men and will cause great fear in men's hearts, a fear so great that it could conceivably cause some to die. To want a precise and detailed description of the phenomenon in human terms is to seek the impossible. Also, it is not necessary. This should be enough to prompt us* **to take measures now so as to be ready for the Warning when it comes.**"

Fatima and the Illumination of Conscience

The **Warning/Illumination of Conscience/Life Review/Judgment in Miniature** is a worldwide event where everyone in the world will see the state of their soul as God would judge them based upon the life they have lived. It brings one's thinking to the The Four Last Things: DEATH, JUDGMENT, HEAVEN, HELL. We will know that it is God communicating in absolute love, and there will be no rebuttal. There will be no exceptions to this. After speaking to numerous people over the last thirty years who have experienced a near-death experience (NDE), I have learned it often takes them years to emotionally and intellectually sort it out and put the event into words. The Warning will be more profound than a near death experience. There are parallels between Fatima and Garabandal.

Something that is seldom if ever spoken of is that Lucia, Francisco, and Jacinta at Fatima described something similar: seeing oneself in the Divine Light of Truth. On the very first apparition of May 13, 1917, Our Lady revealed Divine Mysteries in an aura of light exactly how the visionaries of Garabandal speak of it. Lucia wrote, *"we were able to see ourselves in God, Who was this Light, more clearly than we see ourselves in the best of mirrors."* All three of the children witnessed themselves as God would see them, and more importantly, what God was asking of them. This would make sense as the Lord would want to reinforce to the visionareis what He says will happen — did happen. This would also reinforce their belief they were not being deceived, and would have the strength to go forward and continue their mission in spite of obstacles. It enables one to minimize doubt going forward.

Just two months later on July 13, 1917, all three witnessed a vision of Hell. The impact that this would have on nine-year old Francisco Marto (9 is very young) is hard to imagine. Heaven decided it would be beneficial for these very young children to see Hell. Today, if one were to speak of Hell, many would consider it extreme or even cruel to a child as the faith has become so sanitized. Yet, Heaven thought otherwise in 1917. Up until his premature death of the Spanish flu on April 4, 1919, Francisco spent his remaining time praying the Rosary, consoling God for the sins of mankind. He would often make visits to the Blessed Sacrament to see *"the Hidden Jesus."* Everyone in the Marto family died from the Spanish flu with the exception of his father.

Why this fact is so seldom spoken about Fatima is puzzling. It can validate other apparitions where there are similar events. One can see consistencies if there is a cumulative knowledge of what happens when the Blessed Mother appears.

Another voice weighing in mystically concerning a worldwide event of great magnitude was Pius IX (Pope from 1846-1878) when he said, *"There will come a great sign which will fill the world with awe. But this will occur only after the triumph of a revolution during which the Church will undergo ordeals that are beyond description."*

Father Joseph Brennan, O.C.S., an early writer on Garabandal, summarized the prophetic statements made by saints, blessed and popes. He put it this way: *"They foretell a time of unprecedented and terrible confusion and suffering unlike anything that has ever been experienced in human history. It will affect every area of human life."*

The turbulence of our times is like birth pangs for an expectant mother. The difficult times are increasing like birth pangs, in intensity and severity.

Saint Paul never saw or followed Jesus as one of the original twelve apostles, yet he was the single most important person to promote the Gospel to the world traveling city to city after the Resurrection of Jesus. A thorough knowledge of Scripture enables one to follow the Lord's statutes, precepts, and commands. Having a cumulative knowledge of the Blessed Mother's instructions for mankind enables an individual to have a more acute and deeper understanding of our times. She is a gift, and the gift is only understood in humility and littleness absent of self and ego. Self-abandonment to Divine Providence is key.

In Isaiah, this is exactly what the Lord is saying. Isaiah writes, *"I come to gather nations of every language; they shall come and see my glory. **I will set a sign among them;** from them I will send fugitives to the nations…, to the distant coastlands that have never heard of my fame, or seen my glory; and they shall proclaim my glory among the nations. They shall bring all your brethren from all the nations as an offering to the Lord…."* This is clearly talking about the coming of a Messiah and the signs that He would make available to all the nations.

Isaiah continues what it would be like. *"As the new heavens and a new earth which I will make shall endure before me, says the Lord, so shall your name and your race endure. From one new moon to another, and from one Sabbath to another, all mankind shall come to worship before me, says the Lord"* (Is. 66:18-23).

This sign is one of supernatural deliverance and a situation where there is no answer unless it is by the hand of Almighty God Himself. The mission of Jesus is being described in this passage. The memorial of His sign is a testament to what He says will happen for His glory, and the benefit of his people. God speaks through signs to show His people He can be trusted, and what He says will happen. Could the Permanent Sign at Garabandal speak to the Jewish people and bring about the conversion foretold of Jews by St. Paul?

The Warning in Perspective

Our Lady herself explained the warning to Conchita. As Conchita explains it after receiving her last apparition: *"The Blessed Virgin Mary told me before that Jesus does not want to send the punishment in order to distress us but in order to help us and reproach us because we pay no attention to Him.* **And the Warning will be sent in order to purify us for the Miracle in which He will show us His great love,** and in *order that we may fulfill the message."*

Fear of God is a good thing, as Holy Scripture tells us, but the fear of God that is good is not the kind of fear that obsesses us, causes us to worry constantly, and ultimately robs us of our peace of mind and heart, and leads us away from God. The fear of God that is good, is the fear that draws virtuous souls to God and prompts sinners to amend their lives. The fear of the Lord translates to **"awesome majesty"** of God. This is precisely the purpose that Conchita ascribed to the Warning. It will cause a holy respect for God. Our concern at this moment should be to get closer to God, casting all sin from our lives and striving to love and serve Him better. If we do this, we will be ready for the Warning when it comes. To be sure, it will strike fear in our hearts. However, this fear will not kill us. It will bring us closer to God because we fear offending Him as a son fears offending his father who is always good to him.

The Great Miracle at the Nine Pines in Garabandal

- The second event Our Lady promised is a **Great Miracle** that will take place above the Pines.
- It will occur on a Thursday evening, at 8:30 PM Spanish time.
- Between the 8th and 16th of March, April, May, or June.
- Much of the literature mentions March, April, or May, but Conchita on television in Ireland once said, March, April, May, or June.
- According to Mari-Loli, the Miracle will take place **WITHIN ONE YEAR AFTER THE WARNING.**
- The **Miracle** will coincide with an important event in the Church.
- It will be on the feast day of a young martyr of the Eucharist.
- It will last about fifteen minutes.
- It will be seen in the sky. It will be possible to photograph and televise this event, but not touch it.
- All those in the village or in the surrounding mountains will see it.
- The sick who are present will **ALL** be cured.
- It will be **THE** greatest Miracle ever performed by Jesus for the world.

The word used here is the definite article **THE**. Ponder for a moment that word and what it may mean. There has been widespread speculation on exactly what the Grand Milagro may be, however, we only have cryptic messages of exactly what it may be.

- Sinners and non-believers will be converted. The incredulous will believe.
- Russia will be converted after the Miracle.
- Conchita, who knows the date of the Great Miracle, will announce it eight days in advance.

- Conchita tells us that the reigning Pope will see the Miracle from wherever he is.

Conchita said about this great supernatural event:

1. Before the Miracle there will be many reported "apparitions" throughout the world. She said this in December, 1962.
2. A Bishop of Santander will come along who will not believe at first but will receive a sign and allow priests to go to Garabandal for the Miracle.
3. Before the Miracle many will stop believing in Garabandal.

Based upon compiled data over a lifetime, I think the **Great Miracle** will be so extraordinary, with millions making the journey to Garabandal, it will be as the miracles the Hebrews saw leaving Egypt after 400 years of captivity. The Miracle will be an undeniable act of God. The parting of the Red Sea by Moses was a significant event by any standard of miracles in the Bible, but that was a local event where a finite number of people witnessed it. Not to dimmish the parting of the Red Sea by any means! The Warning will be an event every person in the world will witness, and the Permanent Sign after the Great Miracle at Garabandal can be seen by anyone who wishes to journey there to see it. The more details of the Garabandal story are read and digested, the more it is difficult to process all of the phenomena that happened from 1961-1965. But, when millions recount the same stories of miraculous warnings, their witness will validate its legitimacy to the most hardened skeptic. People will fall on their knees in repentance when the promised Miracle is seen from the natural amphitheater of the tranquil Cantabrian Mountains looking down upon the nine pines. That in itself is part of a much bigger story that is being scripted by Heaven. The sins of man are so great and solutions so elusive, it will take an event such as this to reorient man to God's design for living.

The Little Miracle — A Visible Host

The time the Eucharist miraculously was placed on Conchita's tongue by St. Michael, was called by her the "Little Miracle," and it became visible for all to see. The miracle of the visible Host for Conchita occurred at 1:40 A.M. on July 19, 1962. Hundreds of witnesses were present. The event was recorded on film by a businessman from Barcelona. This film was later submitted to the bishop of Santander. Witnesses said that Conchita knelt and put out her tongue to receive the Host. At first, nothing was visible. In a few moments, a white Host, thicker than usual, appeared on her tongue. It remained there for a few moments before being consumed. This *"little miracle"* was chosen to call our attention to the reality of the Real Presence of Our Lord in the Holy Eucharist.

The reception by Conchita of the Eucharist is a major part of the story of Garabandal. This mystical Communion of Conchita significantly highlights the main focus of the entire four years of apparitions is the **importance of the Eucharist and priesthood to the faith.** Even bilocation is more common than a mystical Communion given by an angel.

The Great Miracle Will be Eucharistic and Marian

Could the *"little miracle"* of Conchita receiving the Eucharist be the precursor to a bigger Eucharistic event?

The Miracle will be Eucharistic. The emphasis on devotion to the Most Holy Eucharist is so strong at Garabandal that a Eucharistic theme for the Miracle would be in perfect consonance with everything that happened in the village during the apparitions.

The Miracle will be ecclesial, that is, it will support the truth that through the Body of Christ, which is the Church, all graces come, and that all men and women are called not only to follow Jesus personally, but also to enter His Church and to submit to its discipline, teaching, and sacraments. For this reason, the Miracle will happen in connection with a great ecclesiastical event, and the Church's authority will be reinforced and authenticated by the fact of the *"ecclesiastical event."*

The Miracle will be Marian. It will assert the glory of the Mother of God, so that all Christians will give up their objections to her role in the Body of Christ and pay her the honor that God Himself gives her. The world will begin to give the Immaculate Heart of Mary the honor and devotion due her. Through this great miracle, many will begin to love *"Holy Mary, Mother of God."*

The Miracle is for the conversion of the whole world. This assertion was made by Our Lord Himself to Conchita at Garabandal. The Lord answered her question about Russia's conversion by assuring her that *"the Miracle was not only for the conversion of Russia,"* but *"for the conversion of the whole world,"* and that ***"thus, all will love Our Hearts"*** (the Hearts of Jesus and Mary).

It seems by His words that somehow **the Miracle will show us all how closely the Hearts of Jesus and Mary are united,** as a symbol of the peace-giving love that should unite our hearts. Perhaps the Two Hearts on the reverse side of the "Miraculous Medal" were a prophecy as well as a lesson. Reconciliation of hearts is what conversion is all about, and it seems that all authentic Marian appearances concern themselves with that message.

Unless the people heed the message of the Miracle, the punishment will come. There will be no escape from it. The Warning will set the fuse as we know the Miracle is within one year from the Warning.

Martyrs of the Eucharist — One Stands Out

A parlor game for decades has been to guess who is the *"little known martyr of the Eucharist,"* as the Miracle will happen on this individual's feast day. The Miracle is supposed to happen on a prescribed day, on a certain month and time, and on a Thursday. Many have thought it may be Saint Hermenegild of Spain whose feast day is April 13, and is a martyr who died in the year 586. Others have thought a good candidate, and validly so, is Saint Pancras (died circa 304 or 305AD), also a martyr at the age of fourteen with a feast day on May 12th.

But there is one little girl who falls in line with the mystical of the Eucharist like no other, and her name is seldom mentioned. Her named is **Blessed Imelda Lambertini.** She was born in Bologna, Italy in 1322. Imelda begged to receive the Eucharist at the age of nine and was denied because she was too young. One day at Mass the Eucharist was suspended in pure light and she was able to receive Our Lord without the aid of a priest. Imelda went back to her seat and died of ecstasy and pure joy. She was beatified in 1826 and is considered to be a Patron Saint of First Communicants.

Imelda died on May 12th, but her feast day is celebrated on May 13th. What is fascinating and rare by all accounts for mysticism in the Catholic Church is the extremely infrequent mystical appearance and reception of the Host. In the case of Conchita, she mystically received a Host on her tongue from Saint Michael, and for Imelda, the Host mystically appeared on her tongue as well. Blessed Imelda, a little-known saint of the Mystical Eucharist, fits all the criteria and framework of the spirit of the apparitions at Garabandal.

The Old Testament and Garabandal

If one were to be dropped to the Earth from outer space and had never read or known anything about the Bible, and read only the Old Testament (the Hebrew Scriptures to the Jewish people) one would ask where is the rest of this book? The people and the events of the Old Testament point to events predicted to happen in the future, that happened exactly as the Hebrew Scriptures said they would. Similarly, if that person just read the New Testament, there are many stories that speak of people named Jonah, Joel, David, Joshua, Noah, Moses, Elijah, and others, that refer to the first half of the book, because the Bible is broken up into two distinct parts — before the birth of Jesus Christ and after.

When the two testaments are read in their entirety, the New validates the Old, and vice versa. When one studies the Old and the New, there is an understanding of what God is asking of us. There is a completeness and fullness in the New that was prophesied in the Old. Jesus said, *"I did not come to abolish the law, but to fulfill it"* (Matt. 5:17). What messages might the New bring to the Old? Romans 9:4-5 speaks about the privileges of Israel. It reads: *"They were adopted as sons, they were given the glory and the covenants; the Law and the ritual were drawn up for them, and the promises were made to them. They are descended from the patriarchs and from their flesh and blood came Christ who is above all, God forever blessed!"* In Romans 11:26, St. Paul also foretells that *"all Israel should be saved, as it is written: there shall come out of Zion he that shall deliver, and shall turn away godlessness from Jacob."* The apparitions and messages of Garabandal are overflowing with Old Testament signs as part of Heaven's plan for the conversion of the world and a new Era of Peace, a New Jerusalem — New Times — which Heaven has promised.

Our Lady, A Jewess in Heaven

Conchita described Mary in her diary as a beautiful Jewish woman with dark and wavy hair, a perfect nose, full lips, and a rather dark complexion. In other apparitions Mary appears as a beautiful girl with the features of other beautiful girls of the country where she appears. Mari-Loli asked her one day if she was Jewish, and her answer was yes, and she said she was a Jewess in Heaven. It was the first time in the history of apparitions that the Blessed Virgin identified herself as such, saying that even in Heaven she belonged to the Jewish people. This was confirmed by the late Garabandal writer Father Laffineur.

Mt. Carmel

For the first time in the history of Marian apparitions, as announced by St. Michael, the Blessed Mother appeared under a title that refers to a Biblical holy place — Mount Carmel. The three holy mountains of the ancient people of Israel were Mount Carmel, Mount Sinai or Horeb, and Mount Zion or Jerusalem. Mount Carmel is the mountain made holy by Elijah the prophet. It is the mountain which Mary could see from where she lived in the village of Nazareth. Moreover, of all religious orders, the Carmelites are by far the closest to Judaism. Elijah is considered by Carmelite friars and sisters as their founder and model.

St. Michael the Archangel

A great deal has been written on St. Michael's role at Garabandal. St. Michael was the forerunner of Mary and her messenger to Conchita on several occasions. Might his appearance also have significance for the Jewish people? St. Michael is named three times in the Old Testament, each time as a guardian of Israel or as its Prince. Daniel 10:20 reads: *"He said then, 'Do you know why I have come to you? It is to tell you what is written in the Book of Truth. I must go back to fight against the prince of Persia: when I have done with him, the prince of Javan will come next. In all this there is no one to lend me support except Michael your prince.'"*

Daniel 12: 1-4 describes Michael again and his role in the latter times: *"At that time Michael will stand up, the great prince who mounts guard over your people. There is going to be a time of great distress, unparalleled since nations first came into existence. When that time comes, your own people will be spared, all those whose names are found written in the Book.... But you, Daniel, must keep your words secret and the book sealed until the time of the end. Many will wander this way and that, and wickedness will go on increasing."* Michael will *"stand up in a time of great trouble,"* and thanks to him *"thy people shall be spared."*

Daniel 10:13 tells about the apparition of Michael: *"The prince of the kingdom of Persia has been resisting me for twenty-one days, but Michael, one of the leading princes, came to my assistance."* His power is great as he is *"one of the leading princes."* Although the Church applies this passage to itself, it is not possible to exclude *"those who are Israelites,"* as they were the first to have Michael as their prince.

As Isaiah and others clearly pointed to the birth of a Messiah, Garabandal is pointing to something the world has never seen before. Those with a knowledge of Isaiah before the birth of Christ, were able to see the fulfillment of his prophesies. Jesus quoted Isaiah more than any other prophet for good reason — Isaiah was the most clear on who Jesus was, and what He would do — His mission. Only at the Lord's death did it all make sense. All things were fulfilled to the letter, exactly as it had been written by many in the Hebrew Scriptures with the birth of the Savior. Garabandal will make more sense after the events — and the events will validate what the Blessed Mother said in the early 1960s. It will be similar to what Isaiah prophesied about the coming of the Messiah, which happened exactly as was written.

The Blessed Mother is the prophetess of our age appointed by the Most Holy Trinity interceding for mankind. This is similar in the same way Queen Esther interceded to the Persian King Ahasuerus to save her people from destruction. Esther prayed and fasted for three days before meeting with the king. Approaching the king unannounced could have cost Queen Esther her life, yet she had the confidence and boldness to intercede for her people. As Queen Esther interceded to save her people, the Blessed Mother never ceases to be an advocate for all mankind. She acts as any mother would. Queen Esther is a precursor to the Blessed Mother's role interceding to the Most Holy Trinity for all mankind.

Is the Permanent Sign a Message to the Jews?

Conchita was told by the Blessed Virgin that a sign would remain at the Pines and it would remain there forever. It would be possible to photograph and televise it, but not touch it. It would appear as a thing not of this world, but it would originate from God. It would be miraculous, a permanent miracle. Is it comparable to a pillar of smoke, but also to rays of sunlight, insofar as it can be seen but not touched? It will be made up of an unknown substance. All the Hebrews who followed Moses out of Egypt saw the *"pillar of cloud by day and of fire by night"* (Exodus 13:21), saving them from the Egyptians (Exodus 14:24), accompanying the Torah at Mount Sinai (Exodus 19: 16-18,34 :5), remaining present among His people, serving as their guide *"wherever they halted on their journey,"* (Exodus 40:36), *"marking out their encampments"* (Deuteronomy 1:33). **The prophets announced it would come back, "a cloud and smoke by day, and the shining of a flaming fire by night"** (Isaiah 4:5). *"It shall come to pass that I will pour out my spirit upon everyone … and I will show wonders in the heavens and on Earth, blood, fire, and pillars of smoke"* (Joel 2: 30).

The luminous cloud has always been a choice subject of rabbinic thought and of Christian mystical theology. All Jews know what the pillar meant: a manifestation of God dwelling among His chosen people, tabernacling amongst them, guiding them, shedding light upon them, speaking to them. The other nations knew this (Numbers 14: 14). It is the Shekinah, the most sacred and mysterious sign of the deity. The Shekinah Glory is Heaven itself. It is God's physical presence that was with the Ark of the Covenant in the desert. A cloud by day, a fire by night.

Conchita has said that the Permanent Sign will be like a pillar of smoke above the pines. **On November 18, 1961, a column of smoke by day and fire by night was seen by a number of people between the nine pines.** Ramon Gonzalez, a shepherd about twenty years old, was tending his sheep and noticed a small fire about 50 centimeters in diameter. Again, in the Autumn 1962, this was seen by a number of people for a period of two or three months, all of whom provided written testimony. It was seen again on November 25, 1965, by four French witnesses. The column was seen at night, clear and luminous. The significance of this is hard to explain to the uninformed. This is just one event of the four years of mystical phenomena that surrounded Garabandal from 1961-65.

Those who return from the mountain in Garabandal will have seen the glory of the Lord and be eager to sound His glory to all the world. The glory of Zion, the glory of the New Pentecost prayed for by Pope John XXIII as he opened the Second Vatican Council and again by Pope Paul VI when he drew it to a close, will flow over the whole Church and the entire world.

The third event promised by Our Lady is a Permanent Sign that will remain forever as a result of the Great Miracle. It will be of supernatural origin and something that has never been seen before on Earth. Conchita has written: *"A sign of the Miracle, which will be possible to film or televise, will remain forever at the pines."*

A permanent, visible supernatural sign will remain at the pines until the end of time. It has been likened to a column of smoke or a ray of sunlight but is not either one. As a result of the Miracle, Russia and other countries will be converted. The Permanent Sign that the Blessed Virgin promised will remain at Garabandal after the Miracle at the nine pines at the base of the surrounding mountains. Little has been revealed about the nature of this sign, but we know the following details: it will remain at the pines until the end of the world.

It will remind us forever of the Great Miracle, which will center on that very spot. Anyone who wishes, will be able to go to Garabandal after the Miracle and see the sign. It will recall to our minds that God summons the world to repentance and holiness. The Israelites were continually reminded by the fiery cloud called the Shekinah Glory hovering over the Meeting Tent that God was with them, leading them to holiness and to the Holy Land. The sign will be with us like that cloud of God's glory, reminding us that the Lord is leading us to holiness and Heaven and that He will not tolerate idolatry among His people. Because it will remain there until the end of time, it will also insist by its presence that the world will indeed one day end, and that Jesus will come again, *"but they will have to give an account to Him who is ready to judge the living and the dead"* (1 Peter 4:5).

Mystical Numbers — Our Lady is Planning on Saving the World

Numbers can also be a sign, a marker for an event. For the Hebrews of the Old Testament, numbers were important to understand God's will. As the New fulfills the Old, Our Lady also would use numbers as signs to mark an event. Numbers are often a signpost to the faithful, and meaningless to the uniformed. Might numbers also be prophetic for future dates? No one can deny the numbers 12 and 40 are important numbers in Scripture, and you would not be into a hysterical numerology thought process.

Fatima is just one example of that. Everything that was told to the Fatima children happened, and her appearances were on the 13th of the month. It was on the 13th of the month of Adar Queen Esther interceded to save her people from annihilation (Esther 9) and that number 13th is still an important date to send signal graces for those willing to listen.

Also of importance is the significance of the number 18. The 18th is a number that has meaning to the Jewish people. It signifies life, and many observant Jews tithe in increments of eighteen as they feel the number will bring blessings and good fortune if they acknowledge God in their giving. The 18th of the month is when several important messages were given at Garabandal. On October 18, 1961, Our Lady said, *"already the cup is filling,"* and on June 18, 1965, she said, *"before the cup was filling up, now it is flowing over."*

In a book written by Mirjana named *My Heart Will Triumph*, that was released August 15, 2016, Mirjana states that March **18** will be a date of great significance that we will only understand when the events prophesied at Medjugorje start to happen. She also mentions specifically August 2 as another important date. The Church celebrates August 2nd as the feast day of Our Lady of the Angels. The Blessed Mother used to appear to Mirjana on the 2nd of every month, when she regularly received messages she conveyed to the world, and annually on her birthday of March **18**th. However, during the Covid pandemic, the 2nd of the month appearances ceased.

Our Blessed Mother appeared **18** times to Bernadette Soubirous at Lourdes, France. These apparitions began February 11, 1858 when the Blessed Mother prayed the Rosary with Bernadette. On February **18**, the Blessed Mother spoke for the first time and said, *"I do not promise to make you happy in this life, but in the next."* It was at Lourdes where the Blessed Mother said: *"I* *am the Immaculate Conception.*" The **18**th and final apparition occurred on July 16, 1858 on the Feast of Our Lady of Mount Carmel, a sacred site to the Jewish people as well as Christians.

Mirjana said, "*only when the things contained in the secrets start to happen will the world understand why she chose the 18th of the month... When everything starts happening, then you will be able to understand why the 18th of March, why every second of the month, and why Wednesdays and Fridays are days of fasting. The significance of the date will be clear.*"

Are these dates connected throughout these apparitions? Again, only when these events happen, will we fully understand the importance of the numbers 2 and 13, and possibly the 18th, as having some sort of great significance. It could be presumptuous to say the dates of the 18th, and the 2nd are directly linked at Garabandal and Medjugorje, and also foolish to say they are not. The honest answer is, maybe they are. It is obvious there are many similarities since the number 2 and 18 have such a common thread in both apparitions.

The Likely Reaction From the Rabbis

For cultured Jews and Rabbis, a thorough knowledge of the Scriptures is a large measure of their religious life. In Israel, whatever their beliefs, all citizens have studied the Hebrew Scriptures as a text of Hebrew classical literature. Whether or not they consider it as divinely inspired and obey it, they still know it. Signs from Heaven are a staple for Heaven to communicate with people. If one were to just indiscriminately open the Bible, we would see in many stories how the Lord is using either signs and wonders or just signs as a marker for an event, something to look for to validate what He is saying for the people to understand. The Warning, the Miracle and the Permanent Sign, are such events where something is foretold and then it happens.

Jews know that it has been prophetically announced that, "*your sons and your daughters will prophesy.*" (Song of Songs 3:6; Joel 2:28; and Acts 2:17-21). Thanks to the media that will cover the event, they will know at once that Catholic girls have announced in advance that in a Catholic village in Catholic Spain a Permanent Sign will remain "*para siempre*" — forever. They will be interested, especially the Sephardim, the Spanish Jews. Their interest will be extreme and lasting, because the Miracle will be a sign for them.

They know if the Permanent Sign is a pillar of smoke by day and a fire by night, this will be prophetic sign of enormous impact. During the apparitions a burning bush and a pillar of smoke has appeared. Many pilgrims who have visited Medjugorje and other shrines have seen a large white luminous cross appear on the mountain. These phenomena may be factors in the Miracle or Permanent Sign. It is interesting to note that at Medjugorje, there are ten secrets which allegedly deal with warnings, a miracle, a permanent sign, and preannounced events. Conchita will announce the day of the Miracle eight days in advance.

Consistent Themes

There are important links between LaSalette, France; Fatima, Portugal; Akita, Japan; and Medjugorje, Bosnia, and others to Garabandal. There are similar themes: the importance and power of the Rosary and of the priesthood; the emphasis on the Eucharist; the presence of angels the emphasis placed on the sacraments; the secrets given which will be revealed at later dates; the urgent calls for prayer and penance; the emergence of a main visionary among the children; and visions of coming calamities unless there is repentance. Garabandal is yet another instance where the Blessed Mother points to the absolute basic fundamental tenets of the faith.

The Miracle of Garabandal is different from any event at any other apparition site, yet similar in some respects. We do know a Permanent Sign of some sort will be left at valid apparition sites around the world, and whether it is the same sign would be speculation on anyone's part. To connect them as the same event may be valid and possibly not. Each apparition site has to stand on its own to be authentic after a thorough investigation by the Church.

Understanding the heart and mind of God, and what He is doing in our day enables one to absorb more freely without constraint what Heaven is doing now at this point in history. It appears we are seeing the confluence of world-wide phenomena culminating in events people are barely able to comprehend. But then again, God is a God of the supernatural, and the Lord said, *"My thoughts are not your thoughts, neither are your ways my ways*" (Isaiah 55:8). The major apparition sites that are Church approved, amplify one another and build on each other for a clearer understanding much in the same way knowledge of Scripture does for a person. In time, you get the mind of the Blessed Mother and understand her ways, and her appearances become like modern day epistles to edify and exhort the people of God. You see patterns in her appearances based on enormous amounts of information. As Saint Thomas Aquinas said in Summa Theologiae, *"Grace does not destroy nature, but fulfills its potential."*

We are literally on the threshold of events prophesied at Garabandal that have never been seen before in all history. Overflowing with signs where the New validates the Old, and vice versa, the events are so fantastic no one could deny they come from God when they happen. The events are very plausible if one bundles all the cogent facts together, and the events at Garabandal will be the only thing in the world that can turn mankind around from self-destruction.

The Chastisement

A Chastisement, is contingent upon the world's response to the Warning and the Great Miracle which has been prophesied. During July of 1962, Conchita, Mari-Loli, and Jacinta were shown a vision of the impending chastisement. This is often referred to as *"The Night of Screams."* Our Lady told the visionaries that, if we do not heed her warnings and mankind does not change after the Warning and Miracle, God will send the Chastisement. In a note Conchita stated: *"The punishment is conditioned upon whether or not mankind heeds the messages of the Blessed Virgin Mary."* Conchita said in her diary: *"If the world changes, the Chastisement can be averted."* In describing the vision of the Chastisement, Mari-Loli said that she saw people throwing themselves into the sea, but instead of putting the fire out, it *"would be worse than having fire on top of us—fire underneath us and fire all around us. It seemed to make them burn more."* The blood curdling screams of the three seers during **the Night of Screams** prompted the entire village of Garabandal to go to Confession the following day.

Conclusion

What is it in an individual that makes him or her open to all of the Blessed Mother's phenomena? After decades of observation, I think it is that the people who gravitate to her messages are open to what God is willing to freely give, and they simply say — YES. Since Mary as a young girl from Nazareth gave her yes, her fiat to the angel Gabriel that she would be the Mother of God, then God was able to accomplish His will for the salvation and redemption of the world. By saying YES, the Lord can work in our life. When there is surrender, there is growth. Surrender brings openness, and thus growth. Your YES is surrender. As Jesus said, *"Unless a grain of wheat falls into the ground and dies, it remains alone; but if it dies, it bears fruit"* (John 12:24). Only when our ego submits to the will of Heaven, is there growth.

The prophesied events at Garabandal will change history like possibly no other event since the Incarnation of Jesus. Msgr. Eugenio Beitia Aldazabal (deceased 1985) who was bishop of San Tander, Spain from 1962-1965 when the apparitions took place, said after reading a letter that Conchita gave to him, and then told his secretary, *"if these girls are not insane, this event alone (most likely the Miracle) is comparable to the death of Christ."*

The story of Garabandal is unlike any other apparition in history. Although the Blessed Mother seldom speaks in Scripture, her words, *"Do whatever He tells you"* (John 2:5) at the wedding feast of Cana are most significant. She is always pointing to her Son, and that is her most common theme of authentic apparition sites globally.

No one can doubt that the confluence of events in the world has pushed us beyond the tipping point. The world is out of control, and many people are anxious and discouraged, bordering on despair. Uncertainty, stress, and anxiety grip households. However, as Mirjana says in her book, *"Our Lady is preparing us for everything that is going to take place in the world. She is training us for victory. When the events in the secrets begin, everything will be clear."* Heaven has a plan and needs our cooperation to fulfill that plan. Garabandal is a big part of that plan, and those following it world-wide know it. God spoke to His people in the past, and He does so today. *"God is the same yesterday, today, and forever"* (Hebrews 13:8).

As predicted, there has been confusion and controversy in regard to the spread of the message of Garabandal. Jesus told Conchita on February 13, 1966: *"Don't worry yourself with whether people believe or do not believe…. I shall do everything. But I will also give you suffering. I will be with whoever suffers for me…. You will have much to suffer for few people will believe you."* Both the suffering of Conchita and the other visionaries, and the lack of belief in the apparitions were foretold by Our Lady. The Lord said, *"they hated me before thy hated you"* (John 15:18). We are now in a period of waiting and expectation in regard to the prophesied events of Garabandal. During this time let us all, in faith, while living and spreading the message, pray and make sacrifices and place all in the hands of Our Lord. Keep up your courage and remember there is nothing that so enlarges the capacity of the heart for God as does suffering and putting our trust in Him. He is the King of Love, Mercy, and Peace. One who finds God, finds peace.

Prepare for the great supernatural events that will change the world.

JESUS I TRUST IN YOU

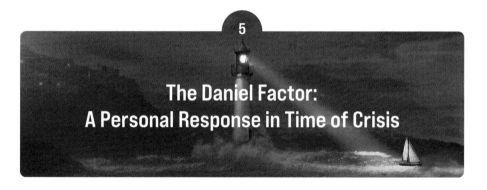

5

The Daniel Factor: A Personal Response in Time of Crisis

The king ordered Ashpenaz, his chief eunuch, to select from the Israelites a certain number of boys of either royal or noble descent; they had to be without any physical defect, of good appearance, trained in every kind of wisdom, well-informed, quick at learning, suitable for service in the palace of the king. Ashpenaz himself was to teach them the language and the literature of the Chaldeans. The king assigned them a daily allowance of food and wine from his own royal table. They were to receive an education lasting for three years, after which they were expected to be fit for the king's society. Among them were Daniel, Hananiah, Mishael, and Azariah, who were Judaeans. The chief eunuch gave them other names, calling Daniel Belteshazzar, Hanianiah Shadrach, Mishael Meshach, and Azariah Abednego. Daniel who was most anxious not to defile himself with the food and wine from the royal table, begged the chief eunuch to spare him from this defilement; and by the grace of God Daniel met goodwill and sympathy on the part of the chief eunuch. But, he warned Daniel, "I am afraid of my lord the king: he has assigned you food and drink, and if he sees you looking thinner in the face than the other boys of your age, my head will be in danger because of you." At this Daniel turned to the guard whom the chief eunuch had assigned to Daniel, Hananiah, Mishael and Azariah. He said, "Please allow your servants a ten days' trial, during which we are given only vegetables to eat and water to drink. You can then compare our looks with those of the boys who eat the king's food; go by what you see, and treat your servants accordingly." The man agreed to do what they asked and put them on ten days' trial. When the ten days were over they looked and were in better health than any of the boys who had eaten their allowance of food and the wine they were to drink, and God favored these four boys with knowledge and intelligence in everything connected with literature, and in wisdom; while Daniel had the gift of interpreting every kind of vision and dream.

Daniel: 1:3-17

The hourly onslaught of negative news reaches our senses through social media devices on a continual basis. It is every day if we are plugged in. With the digital/internet connection, the profound, bold, perverse, and the illicit continually increase. Yet, the demise of cultures, societies, and civilizations is not new in history. The world has experienced calamities before. However, the rapid decline of Western civilization is on our watch. It is especially hard for the older folks to observe having seen the best of the 1950s — 1970s. Cultures collapse slowly, then suddenly. It takes generations of scriptural abuse to reach where we are at this point. Mass goers and daily communicants largely remained silent as the gradual abuses were normalized, and through their polite silence, they lost their Church, and are now losing their country. A big mistake people will make going forward is thinking things will be normal and return to the past. They will assuredly not return. The new normal will be chaos due to a civilization no longer tethered to the Divine.

Is a nation that has killed over sixty million babies in a mother's womb worthy of the mercy of God, or His justice? Abortions are promoted with tax payer dollars. Can America afford to mock God with abortion any longer? The demise in society is judgment in various ways. It is God who raises up those who honor Him, and brings those down who seek to implement a world without Him. Yet historians ignore this glaring deficiency and are illiterate and ignorant on the subject as they study civilizations. The success of a country is proportional to its fidelity to God. Those with power most often assume they are correct with their endeavors and world-view. Even while violating the laws of God, they adamantly thrust forward with their agenda. That is precisely what the left is now doing. Behind the evil of progressive social programs, is their belief there are too many people in the world. An underlying concept in the implementation and execution of laws is population control. When that concept is fully understood, many things fall neatly into place. Population control is at the root of abortion, climate change, Covid 19, and other programs as well. The global elites simply believe there are too many people on the planet and they must eliminate people to sustain life the way they see fit. The experimental gene therapy has been their weapon of choice. People of good will find this too hard to believe because it is not remotely possible in their earthly way of thinking.

A Question We Must Ask Ourselves?

This begs the single most important question we can ask ourselves — **What is my role at this point in time?** Or asked another way. **What precisely am I being asked by the Lord to do? What is my response?** Are we spectators versus participants of those in the battle likened to Teddy Roosevelt's *Man in the Arena? "It is not the critic who counts; not the man who points out how the strong man stumbles, or where the doer of deeds could have done them better. The credit belongs to the man who is actually in the arena, whose face is marred by dust and sweat and blood; who strives valiantly; who errs, who* *comes short again and again, because there is no effort without error and shortcoming; but who does actually strive to do the deeds; who knows great enthusiasms, the great devotions; who spends himself in a worthy cause; who at the best knows in the end the triumph of high achievement, and who at the worst, if he fails, at least fails while daring greatly, so that his place shall never be with those cold and timid souls who neither know victory nor defeat."*

The fact is for every person working toward a **Solution**, 4,000 people are sitting at home and in coffee shops talking about the problems. Jesus was very clear in His mission. He searched in the thicket for the one lost sheep leaving the ninety-nine. Jesus didn't talk abstract or theoretical theology. He taught about the repercussions of virtue and sin alike. He walked the roads in the hot sun among the people offering a better way based on good choices. He spoke about amendment of life, forgiveness, self-donation, salvation, heaven and hell, and a joyful and contented life if you follow His ways. There is war in the streets because there is first war in men's hearts, thus the tensions we witness daily. There is no order or peace unless it is on the tenets prescribed by God's statutes and commands. All else is a castle built on shifting sand.

The United States is in a new place unlike any other time. Yes, without question there have been tough times in the past, but due to an organized global evil, it is the end of the world as we know it. (TEOTWAWKI). Not a hysterical end of the world cry as the unschooled will surely say, but, we are entering a New Era of time. The way we have lived in the past will change dramatically. It has already changed. Culture changes, and civilizations change with it. It is the evolution of societies as they shift gears for many reasons, and then a new paradigm begins. Time intersects eternity in a new place. What could have been defined as normal, will no longer be so. The days of unlocked doors and tranquility is in the rear-view mirror. We have come to a point where we have passed the last exit on the highway, and we are navigating New Times heading into a New Era. Heaven has been clear in its laments and messages, with an outcome predicted due to man's sin. We are reaping what we have sown for the last several generations.

Given Over to Depraved & Reprobate Minds

The answer to why the left acts the way they do is found in Romans chapter 1. When Paul arrived, Rome was immersed in great sin and pagan idolatry. Writing toward the end of his life, Saint Paul understood this principle and articulated the **HOW** and **WHY** people act the way they do. What St. Paul wrote in Romans 1 is close to what we are seeing today. Darkened intellects are promoting all types of vice, confusion, tensions, chaos, and anxiety. It is what darkened intellects do because they know no better. St. Paul writes,

"In other words, since they refused to see it was rational to acknowledge God, God has left them to their own irrational ideas and to their monstrous behavior. And they are steeped in all sorts of depravity, rottenness, greed and malice, and addicted to envy, murder wrangling, treachery, and spite. Libelers, slanderers, enemies of God, rude, arrogant, boastful, enterprising in sin, rebellious to parents, without brains, honor, love, or piety. They know what God's verdict is: that those who behave like this deserve to die — and yet they do it; and what is worse, encourage others to do the same" (Romans 1:28-32).

Other Scripture translations speak of *"reprobate lives and minds."* Paul wrote this toward the end of his life and was a mature believer. The description of a godless life is described above with graphic, clear, and emotive language. He does not mince words on what he is thinking.

Another answer why people think like they do is found in the gospel of Luke. It reads, *"Jesus said to his disciples: 'A good tree does not bear rotten fruit, nor does a rotten tree bear good fruit. For every tree is known by its own fruit. For people do not pick figs from thornbushes, nor do they gather grapes from brambles. A good person out of the store of goodness in his heart produces good, but an evil person out of a store of evil produces evil; for from the fullness of his heart the mouth speaks'"* (Luke 6:43-45).

Evil is strong today because people have been away from any faith for so long, there is very little resemblance to virtue or God-like thoughts and habits. It is for this reason it is hard to find common ground on so many issues. It is often like communicating with a brick wall. The chasm year by year is broadening as people are further cemented in with their ideologies. **The left has an ideological possession where logic eludes them.**

Opinions often called political, are not political; they are moral issues that have everything to do with what is best for the individual, the family, the community, the country, and the world. Truth must be articulated to the present generation to be preserved for the next.

Communism and paganism/barbarism are not first cousins, but brother and sister. Because communism is not Christ-centered it will eventually lead to pagan practices. State sanctioned abortion is Satanism. It is the same Baal and Moloch worship that demanded child sacrifice over 4,000 years ago. Judgment and chastisement await those regions of the United States that have violated the rights of the defenseless unborn. It is historical and scriptural. **God will not be mocked.**

All light to our hearts, minds, and souls comes from the inspiration of the Holy Spirit. Reasoning with a person who has little light or goodness is very difficult today. The culture in Hollywood is a morally toxic place akin to a cesspool. Lost people are generally attracted to Hollywood precisely for those reasons. It is where many, seeking distraction, go to feed their carnal appetites. So many Hollywood aspirants trying to break in the business barely graduated high school and are looking for the self-esteem they never received at home. Yet, they seem to have counsel for all America. A moral movie today is as rare as the stable family that the actors never came from. We have recently seen people like Angelina Jolie, Lady Gaga, Katy Perry, Bob Dylan, and others openly talk how they gave themselves over to Satan in ritualistic form to achieve fame and wealth.

However, Heaven always operates to give the world answers, whereas political and news media pundits define the problems but offer no relief. The money is in their talking up the commotion, not providing solutions.

Some cardinals, bishops and clergy are in open dissent against some of Pope Francis' views and the direction of the Church, while others dissent in silence. Many clergy live in fear of their bishop, because it can be dangerous to have a different world-view than your boss. Many clergy are frustrated and in near despair as they watch the troubled Church, and don't really know what to do. Support the good clergy, encourage and help them.

Life in Captivity—Or Another Word, Slavery

With the rapid diminution of free speech and rights, don't think for a minute the long reach of the State cannot make you a modern-day captive. Who would have thought only a few years ago just voicing an opinion on sin could land you defending yourself in court — or worse. We shouldn't wonder why people are using nom de plumes in their writing, or saying nothing at all. Believers world-wide are being charged with hate crimes for voicing a scripturally Christocentric based opinion.

Consider Australia. It historically has been a giant petri dish for globalization in Oceania, the same way Argentina has been for the Americas. The bankers and globalists use Australia to see how far they can push the people with their agenda. Australia first came after the guns, then free speech, and finally descended to trampling any human rights that conflicted with state goals. Government officials threatened to enforce mandatory vaccinations. They arrested a reporter for merely being at the scene of a protest reporting on what he was seeing. They arrested a pregnant woman in her home in Melbourne, wearing pajamas and in front of her children, for organizing a rally on Facebook against lockdowns.

Consider Europe. Just wearing a crucifix can get a *child beaten* where Muslims co-congregate. Up until recently the assault on Christianity has been relentless, persistent, and gradual. Now it is extremely aggressive and in the open. Not only has Europe hastened to undermine free speech with laws that are used to charge believers with hate crimes, they are being arrested if speaking against the government narrative.

This is a form of captivity that is now galloping toward our own country with more serious consequences. The left is primarily out to remove the First and Second Amendment, because when they are removed, the rest will fall like dominos. Free speech and the ability to defend yourself from a tyrannical government were paramount to the Founding Fathers, and remain so today. The principles of self-governance and freedom of faith are identical.

The goal of the left is to completely eradicate God in the culture. Once that happens, all other rights are gone. It is that profound, and yet that simple to understand. God has to be removed for communist rule of the masses. The mistake of believers is they want to believe the left operates in good faith. They do not operate in good faith. Once they get a concession, they immediately push for more. They are pagan, godless, and antichrist, and do not think as a believer. As Jesus said, *"My kingdom is not of this world"* (John 18:36).

Circulating around the internet is the following:

The Bizarre Becoming Normal:

- If a man pretends to be a woman, you are required to pretend with him.
- Russians influencing our elections are bad, but illegals and others voting in our elections are good.
- It was cool for Joe Biden to "blackmail" the President of Ukraine, but it's an impeachable offense if Donald Trump inquires about it.
- Twenty is too young to drink a beer, but eighteen is old enough to vote.
- Sexualizing children is bad, but 11-year-old drag queens are good.
- Illegals aren't required to show ID, but citizens can't buy cough medicine without it.
- Citizens are fined if they don't buy their own health insurance, and then they are forced to buy it for illegals.
- People who have never owned slaves should pay slavery reparations to people who have never been slaves.
- Inflammatory rhetoric is outrageous, but harassing people in restaurants is virtuous.
- People who have never been to college should pay the debts of college students who took out huge loans for useless degrees that will never train them for a job.
- Illegals with tuberculosis and disease are welcome, but you'd better be able to prove your dog is vaccinated.
- Irish doctors and German engineers who want to immigrate must go through a rigorous vetting process, but any illiterate Central-American who jumps the southern fence is welcome.
- $5 billion for border security is too expensive, but $1.55 trillion for "free" health care for illegals is not.

- If you cheat to get into college you go to prison, but if you cheat to get into the country you go to college for free.
- Politicians who say that the President is not above the law put illegal immigrants and themselves above the law.
- Leftists who say there is no such thing as gender are demanding a female President.
- We see other countries going Socialist and collapsing, and yet it seems like a great plan to our young people.
- Voter suppression is bad, but not allowing the President to be on the ballot is good.
- Some people are held responsible for things that happened before they were born, and other people are not held responsible for what they are doing right now.
- Criminals are caught then released to hurt more people, but stopping them is bad because it's a violation of THEIR rights.

Pointing out all this hypocrisy somehow makes us "racists."

Through modern forms of technological social engineering, we are already captives to the "cancel culture." It wouldn't take a lot more for the State to eliminate more freedoms. Year after year, decade after decade, and law after law legislated in Congress, we have come to boiling in the pot of hot water like the frog. For those who have sought to pin their hopes on a President that may hold their view, remember that no one lasts in that job forever. Parties alternate power. Expect chaos from here on out no matter who wins because neither side tolerates the views of the other. Not even a little bit. We now resemble the Hunger Games series where a few elites lord power over the masses. It was a struggle, but it took just one Catnip to revolt and change the direction of the fight.

The elusive dream of a world without God has always been pursued by the rich and powerful with all their sordid policies. From now on you will either be **IN or OUT** of the circle of influence depending on what you promote. If you follow the teachings of God in the current culture, you will be **OUT**. A properly formed conscience will not allow one to participate in the political and social agenda being thrust upon believers. As time moves on, it will be difficult to straddle the fence without making a commitment to decide on which side of the fence you stand. The turtle on a fencepost just observing will be taking the side of evil. The middle will be where the lukewarm gather without any conviction one way or the other, and the Lord has some harsh words for those who do so. *"You who are lukewarm I will spit you out of my mouth"* (Rev. 3:16).

To visualize captivity, which is actually slavery, think of waking up tomorrow morning, and having a foreign power running all administration of your life. For instance, Russian or Chinese troops outside your front door rationing what you eat, where you live, how you live, your new work assignments, choosing your employment, allocations for metered water and electricity, how you go about worship, where you can travel, and a myriad of other day-to-day experiences. Nothing is the same under captivity. That is just a sampling of captivity, as all of your work is for the benefit of your captor's national interest. That is how Daniel and the Hebrews lived under Nebuchadnezzar and Babylonian captivity. Under a totalitarian and tyrannical godless state, the individual is stripped of their God given rights. *"It has been your sin that has separated you from God"* (Isaiah 59:2). The Lord does not punish; it is our sin that allows the devil to maneuver in our lives. When man falls from grace through disobedience, a portal opens for the devil to enter.

The Two Principal Reasons for this Behavior in the United States

1. ***Who is Your Authority?*** At a personal level, this is the basic question confronting man, and it is not a new thought. Satan said, *"I will not serve."* This is the first disconnect of man from God. *Who Do You Serve?* You either serve God, asking Him to take over and direct the affairs of your life, or you are doing it through your own self-reason, in the house of self-knowledge. There really is no in between. Planned Parenthood represents the extreme example of self-reason unwilling to surrender a will to God. *"I've gotta be me"* is the daily mantra. Until a person surrenders one's will to God, he or she will never find peace of soul. There will always be another "ism" to confront, and an agitation in their spirit.

At a corporate level, the socialist/communist is always trying to direct the affairs of others to his or her own world-view. Unbelievers seek vindication and acceptance for their sin by trying to normalize their behavior through state sanctioned programs. LGBTQ is just one ideology that does this. Many on the left are no longer Christian, nor believers, nor traditional American democrats of old, but communists: they want a world without God. If one considers the current lack of civility, normalcy, and virtue, the West is looking more like Rome under the brute emperors before it fell. We have a controlled and propagandized press presenting lewdness and corruption on a daily basis and minimizing the good that believers are doing. At the senior level it is the cabal of the deep state running the show. The reality is the left is in control of the public relations industry, press, and many influential positions in government.

2. **What Exactly is The Role of Government in Our Lives?** The daily fight at the food court or café and yes, in nearly every home, revolves around what exactly is the role of government in our lives. Think of the origin of the arguments. Many communists want a cradle to grave government approach. They want the social services and goods from the state distributed evenly EXCEPT for those who are on the top who portion them out. In short time, they become a ruling class of their own under totalitarian rules for all but themselves. For them, with the unbridled human nature that exists in the lower nature of man, it is about stealing as much as they can for themselves.

When a nation's government continues to use invasion and mass migration to increase voter rolls and give away free goods for their votes, that nation is hanging by a thread for survival. It is actually doomed at that point. Under an unrealistic and idealistic agenda, the appeal is to the senses for change. **Leaders championing godless causes who call themselves Catholics need to be feared as sheep in wolves clothing because they have abdicated their first responsibility to God.** When elected officials ignore their conscience, legislating godless public policies, they lead the nation to chaos.

Many leaders have operated under the adage of *"Tell a lie often enough and people will believe it."* Who would have ever thought the LGBTQ and Planned Parenthood agenda could have garnered so much momentum years ago? When the United States Supreme Court removed prayer and the Bible from the classroom in 1962/63, did anyone see this coming? Did people speak up? Did the Church speak up? Some good people did speak up then, but they were too few. Many believers have consented with their silence. What else could the outcome be? There are now thousands of examples like this in America. Halloween can be celebrated as well as Islam in public venues of all sorts (not just public schools), but Christian based themes cannot. Try having an Easter or Christmas celebration in a public high school and watch the flurry of letters to the school board. That is an assault on Christianity, and totalitarian communism is their agenda going forward.

At the moment things look bleak to the believers as they read and watch the news. Satan seems to have the upper hand as many believers are being smashed to the rocks like a dinghy in a bad storm. Most families are enduring a trial of some sort. Some trials are small, others not. We ask ourselves, **"What is the Lord's Prescription for Peace of Soul in Troubled Times?"** We have an example rooted in faith. As we see the onslaught of filth and the mass of corruption around us, there is a 2,500 year-old letter where the Lord prescribed to the Prophet Jeremiah an antidote for what ailed His people, and how to live in the midst of a trial. The Lord tells Jeremiah obedience to the Commandments is necessary for the continuation of their culture, and residual blessings.

The Prophet Jeremiah Tells the Jewish People How to Live in Exile. The Lord Gives a Prescription for His People on How to Live In Captivity for Seventy Years and Have Victory from the Experience.

The more things change, the more they stay the same. The Jewish people throughout history knew what exile meant with all its repercussions. In two places (among others), we can find major Old Testament prophets providing instruction for being in captivity by a conquering nation. They are in the Book of Daniel as foretold by the Book of Jeremiah. Daniel gives an example of action under pressure, and Jeremiah tells the Hebrew nation how to endure seventy years of captivity. The crime the Hebrews committed? Not obeying the Sabbath. Think of how serious not obeying the Sabbath is in the eyes of the Lord. Today Sunday, the Lord's day for most, is a day of chores, errands, sports, entertainment, and inane activity. It is seldom thought of as a commandment. The observance of the Sabbath is increasingly rare.

In chapter 29 of Jeremiah, the prophet writes to those who had been exiled from Jerusalem and had to live under the tyrannical king Nebuchadnezzar. We can see time and again over a thousand years that the Lord reigned in His Chosen People often through a bad king. Weather and moral deterioration caused social problems from within, bending the will of His people to come back to Him. For us, like for the Chosen People, at this time in our history the blessing and protective hedge has been removed from America because America is under judgment. Nerves are tender and frayed everywhere we go, and it will continue. To give a blanket "no" to this thinking would make one scripturally illiterate. Now, the question is, how do believers conduct themselves and live a joy filled and peaceful life as we are asked to do amidst the moral depravity? Even though this story is an old one, the same principles apply as *"God is the same yesterday, today, and forever"* (Hebrews 13:8).

As Jeremiah wrote, due to disobedience, through His permissive Will the Lord prescribed 70 years of exile. The false prophet Hananiah predicted the exile would only last two years and he died shortly thereafter for *"preaching apostasy"* (Jer. 28:16). From the beginning, it was Yahweh who had ordained that Israel live in exile. **"When seventy years are completed for Babylon, I will come to you and fulfill my good promises to bring you back to this place. For I know the plans I have for you."** It was Yahweh who allowed exile for the good of His people in the long term, yet it could not be seen at that time. The present is often the most difficult to discern. Seeing things in hindsight is a wonderful teacher.

Jeremiah 29:5-14 provides instructions for His Chosen people and how they should live in exile. He reminds them of their ultimate authority while under the yoke of an oppressive government. He also lays out their role and what they are being asked to do. Yahweh said,

"Build houses, settle down, plant gardens and eat what they produce. Take wives and have sons and daughters; choose wives for your sons, find husbands for your daughters so that these can bear sons and daughters in their turn: you must increase and not decrease. Work for the good of the country to which I have exiled you; pray to Yahweh on its behalf,

since on its welfare yours depends. For Yahweh says this, only when the seventy years of Babylon are over, will I visit you and fulfill my promise in your favor by bringing you back to this place. I know the plans I have in mind for you — it is Yahweh who speaks — plans for peace, not disaster, reserving a future full of hope for you. Then when you call to me, to come to plead with me, I will listen to you. When you seek me you will find me, when you seek me with all your heart.... I will restore your fortunes and gather you from all the nations, and all the places where I have dispersed you...." In the vernacular: go about the business of life and do what you need to do not only to survive, but prosper and come out victorious. This prescription is from the Lord Himself, and it is timeless. It is as relevant today as it was thousands of years ago.

It was during this period of exile that the birth of a nation with its cultural and ancestral norms took root. It was during the Babylonian captivity that Israel moved away from the single temple concept in Jerusalem to a local community-based synagogue society — a local expression of faith lived in community. What they learned in exile sustained them for several thousand more years — prospering and thriving in the midst of trials as a wandering people.

We have a mandate of our own. Pray through Jeremiah 29 carefully, and see how the Lord speaks to your heart. God has a plan and we must see that He is in control. The Blessed Mother gave birth to her Son in a cold dung heap only warmed by the heat of barn animals. The Holy Family left in the middle of the night to live in exile in Egypt for several years to avoid adverse circumstances, and chose the safe but arduous route for the protection of their new-born Son Jesus. We can't see the future, so we have to trust the plan the Lord prescribes for us.

Heaven knows the trials we are enduring, and it is not abnormal in Church history. We have reached the point in our history as a nation when we will see the separation of the sheep and the goats, and the wheat from the chaff. It is now unavoidable. Covid 19 let the laity see which priests were fearless for the good of the people. We have crossed the Rubicon and sticking to the fundamentals of our faith will sustain us peacefully and joyfully. Reject the noise around you, and go about your business. Prayer and quiet will be the key to our spiritual health. The Lord is in control. Jeremiah's words are from the Lord Himself instructing us how to endure difficult times. We cannot improve on this advice. Credentialed and wealthy people will be looking after their own self-interests, not yours. Going forward you will need community, faith, self-reliance, and the holy boldness of Daniel.

The Prophecy of Jeremiah is Fulfilled as Daniel and the Hebrews are in Babylonian Captivity under King Nebuchadnezzar

The Book of Daniel is fourteen chapters, and offers a cogent and concise example of conduct for believers in times of State domination of a people by a foreign power. It is not the way most people will read it as they focus on the dreams of the kingdoms to come among other historical supernatural occurrences. It is the prophecy of Jeremiah fulfilled in the flesh among a persecuted and captive people. It is Daniel, his friends, and ten thousand of the best and brightest King Nebuchadnezzar took into captivity. Studying how Daniel, living in captivity and struggling with all of the issues of being a slave of the State, came to find favor with the king is how we can find an answer to living under a cruel and pagan state.

Chapter one sets the stage for the life Daniel and his three close friends, and how they ultimately endure captivity.

Upon arrival Daniel, which means in Hebrew *"God is my judge,"* has his name changed to Belteshazzar, which means *"Lady protect the king."*

Hananiah means *"Yahweh has been gracious,"* and has his name changed to Shadrach, which means *"I am fearful of God."*

Mishael means *"Who can compare to my God? No one,"* has his name changed to Meshach, which means *"I am despised, contemptible, and humiliated."*

Azariah means *"God has helped,"* and his name is changed to Abednego, which means *"the servant of Nebo."*

Several things have taken place with something as simple as a name change. The intent is to break their captives down through humiliation by taking away their identity and with Daniel even gender. They have had their names changed to take away their self worth as men, where the Lord has bequeathed them a Jewish identity rooted in their faith. What was once good is now evil in their eyes. When the name change took place, they knew what their new names meant, as it was an overt attempt to demoralize them. The goal was to make them submissive in their new environment with an agenda to serve the king and all of his requests. In the eyes of their new captors, their sole reason for existence was to please the dictates of the State. The king ruled on a whim with life and death, and no opinion was necessary other than the king's.

The early part of the book sets the stage for the need to survive spiritually and physically. Daniel and his companions were closely connected to each other (community), and had the trust of each other. They knew the prophecy of Jeremiah 29, and had a plan for not submitting to eat defiled food, serve pagan idols, and worship graven images. We can see the shrewdness of Daniel and his companions going to the head eunuch of the king asking to be excused from eating from the king's defiled table (Dan. 1:8). Daniel asks for a period of ten days to eat just water and vegetables so the head eunuch can see for himself if there is a negative change in appearance. The eunuch fears for his own life if the king finds out about the exception he has made for Daniel and his companions. The head eunuch says if they do not look any different from the others it will be permitted. After ten days of eating healthy food, and not the rich foods from the king's table, their complexion is satisfactory to the head eunuch.

Chapter 1:17-21 says, *"And God favored these four boys with knowledge and intelligence in everything connected with literature, and in wisdom; while Daniel had the gift of interpreting every kind of vision and dream. When the period stipulated by the king for the boys' training was over, the chief eunuch presented them to Nebuchadnezzar. The king conversed with them, and among all the boys found none to equal Daniel, Hananiah, Mishael, and Azariah. So they became members of the king's court, and on whatever point of wisdom or information he might question them, he found them ten times better than all the magicians and enchanters in his entire kingdom. Daniel remained there for the first year of King Cyrus."*

Fidelity and Trust in Times of Trial

The first chapter established Daniel and his companions' past, rituals for survival, and holy boldness in their belief in God and His promises, and called out Daniel's personal attributes leading to his ultimate spiritual prosperity. Daniel's companions were later thrown into a fire pit (Daniel 3) for directly disobeying and saying to the king they would not bow down and worship pagan gods. In his anger the king ordered the furnace to be heated seven times normal. The men were spared when the king saw a fourth person walking in the furnace and all of them came out untouched by fire. Not a hair or a robe was singed. The king then said, *"Praised be your God who sent his angel to rescue you. You were willing to give up your lives to serve your own God. He has sent his servant to rescue you.* **Therefore, I decree whoever speaks against Shadrach, Meshach, and Abednego, I will cut into pieces, and his house turned into rubble, for there is no other God who can save in this way"** (Daniel 3:28-29).

"When the time was over, I, Nebuchadnezzar, lifted up my eyes to heaven: my reason returned. And I blessed the Most High, praising and extolling him who lives forever, for his sovereignty is an eternal sovereignty, his empire lasts from age to age. The inhabitants of the earth count for nothing: he does as he pleases with the array of heaven, and with the inhabitants of the earth. No one can arrest his hand or ask him, 'What are you doing?'" (Daniel 4:31-32)

Time and again, the court of the king sought to find fault with Daniel due to jealousy and hate for what he stood for. It was a repetitious cycle he had to endure. Daniel was thrown into the lions' den (Daniel 6), and *the king asked how nothing had happened to him. Daniel replied,* **"'My God sent his angel and shut the lions' mouths so that they would not hurt me, because I am blameless, and I have never done you any wrong either, O king.' The king was overjoyed and ordered Daniel to be released from the pit. Daniel was released from the pit, and found to be quite unhurt, because he had trusted in his God. The king sent for the men who accused Daniel and had them thrown into the lion pit, they, their wives and their children: and they had not reached the floor of the pit before the lions had seized them and crushed their bones to pieces"** (Daniel 22-25).

There are many biblical stories like this where evil people plotted against the people of God. The book of Esther provides just one vivid example of how often when people are accused unjustly, the Lord comes to their defense and the tide turns in their favor. Daniel's response was one of trust and faith in God that he would be rescued from the trial. Daniel in time was asked to interpret dreams no one else could for the king and again found favor much to the chagrin of his detractors.

The four friends are a testament to fidelity to God's promises and to stand on them no matter how adverse the circumstances. **They sang psalms of praise under duress.** In times that were unimaginable for us today, they defied death through faith. They figured out how to deal with a despotic leader living in a tyrannical state. They lived the prescriptions of Jeremiah 29 while in captivity for seventy years. In these times, the average age for a young women to marry was as early as fourteen or fifteen. If you were to look at a generation at this time as fifteen years, then that is 4.7 generations living in captivity by a foreign power. Think back on your own life for nearly four generations, and how far back that really is.

Jeremiah told the people to plant, harvest, have children, grandchildren, nurture them in the faith, and stick to the rubrics and essentials of the faith. This plan will get them back to Judea and their homeland. Sticking to the fundamentals of faith brings long term fruit.

Judgment Begins First in the House of God

In the Old Testament, the Lord always chastised and exposed the Levites (priests) on account of their sin before He made any form of judgment on His people. We see this in Ezekiel 44:10-14; Isaiah 10, Leviticus 10, Numbers 16, and many other places in Scripture. He would remind them of duties of obedience and fidelity to His statutes and commands as leaders of His people. If they did not comply, the Lord would then ramp up the punishment for disobedience. In essence, the Lord doled out a Divine Spanking, or as some may say, a Divine Pruning, which is a merciful chastisement. The Lord held HIS LEADERS responsible for the actions of His people. In Scripture, it was the responsibility of the Levites (priests) to proclaim sin first and bring it to the open, because as priests that was their job. They would be judged more harshly if they did not.

After warning (or warnings) the priests, the Lord would then inform them of the consequences for disobedience. If there was compliance to His Law, the Lord showed mercy. If the people were still stiff-necked and hard of heart, the Lord never suffered from any lack of imagination in ways to rein in His people. We reviewed this trend in the banishment of the Jews to Babylonian captivity for seventy years in Jeremiah 25:29 and in 2 Chronicles 36:21 for disobeying the observance of the Sabbath. Something as seemingly innocuous and innocent as the lack of observance of the Sabbath could bring judgment. Time and again His chosen people had been warned, but they ignored what was required of them as leaders.

In the year 2000, judgment came to the house of God in the Catholic Church with the homosexual agenda that was first exposed in Boston under Cardinal Law. *"The time has begun for the judgment to begin at the household of God; and if we know now what is only the beginning, what will it be when it comes down to those who refuse to believe God's Good News?"* (I Peter 4:17)

The Lord judges the Levites (priests) first because it is their job to speak the truth. They are not politicians; they are supposed to be victim souls speaking the gospel void of public opinion. They are supposed to speak outside the temporal order. The issue of clergy abuse had been festering for generations, but it exploded on the world scene and spread like the bubonic plague throughout the rest of America. Hollywood was ecstatic. The problem then spread to nearly every diocese in America costing the Church well over $4 billion to settle claims from the abused. Church doors were shuttered due to lack of funds as people voted with their wallets, and then their feet. As of today, dioceses are closing schools by the dozen(s), and this too will escalate more rapidly due to Covid 19 and lack of funds. In the early 1960s Catholic school enrollment peaked at 5.2 million students. The U.S population in 1960 was less than 50% what it is today. In 2019/2020 that number has dwindled to 1.7 million enrolled, and falling fast. The next generation of Catholics will remain largely un-catechized, and then largely un-churched leaving more of a moral void in the culture. The number of children born out of wedlock in 1960 was 5%. In 2019 it was 40%.

The movie *SPOTLIGHT* released in 2015 was about an undercover investigative team from the Boston Globe exposing the lies of the clergy in Boston covering up the immoral agenda inside the Church. It was revolting to watch because it was true. Hollywood has contempt for the Church, and they now had the opening they needed to expose the hypocrisy inside the Church, and they jumped on it. A friend of mine's son who had attended Catholic schools from elementary grades through high school said he would never enter a Catholic Church again after seeing the movie. While it may have been an immature position to take, it continues to be the young man's position to this day. Families that sacrificed to send their kids to Catholic schools K-12, saw them come home from college near atheists, and at best agnostic voting democrat. It became common for them to espouse Charles Darwin and Karl Marx, leaving their parents and grandparents in tears.

Maybe keeping colleges closed helped stop the spread of students indoctrinated with communist ideology. It may have been an unintended consequence of Covid 19, and a beneficial one at that. There is nothing like a student living at home with a break from being brain-washed by a professor who is trained in Marxist philosophy. The professor and the student may have never done an honest day of work in their lives. Bringing out the garbage and cutting the lawn may bring a little reality to the now home-bound budding communist. Karl Marx and his manifesto had to wait a few months for a global utopia, or at least until school resumed.

Father Joseph Ratzinger & His Prophetic Utterance

In a very powerful prophetic talk given by Father Ratzinger (Pope Benedict XVI, Emeritus), in 1969 at Regensburg, Germany, he weighed in with keen insight as to what our Daniel response in our crisis must be.

"The future of the Church can and will issue from those whose roots are deep and who live from the pure fullness of their faith. It will not issue from those who accommodate themselves merely to the passing moment or from those who merely criticize others and assume that they themselves are infallible measuring rods; nor will it issue from those who take the easier road, who sidestep the passion of faith, declaring false and obsolete, tyrannous and legalistic, all that makes demands upon men, that hurts them and compels them to sacrifice themselves. To put this more positively: The future of the Church, once again as always, will be reshaped by saints, by men, that is, whose minds probe deeper than the slogans of the day, who see more than others see, because their lives embrace a wider reality. Unselfishness, which makes men free, is attained only through the patience of small daily acts of self-denial. By this daily passion, which alone reveals to a man in how many ways he is enslaved by his own ego, by this daily passion and by it alone, a

man's eyes are slowly opened. He sees only to the extent that he has lived and suffered. If today we are scarcely able any longer to become aware of God, that is because we find it so easy to evade ourselves, to flee from the depths of our being by means of the narcotic of some pleasure or other. Thus our own interior depths remain closed to us. If it is true that a man can see only with his heart, then how blind we are!…

"And so it seems certain to me that the Church is facing very hard times. The real crisis has scarcely begun. We will have to count on terrific upheavals. But I am equally certain about what will remain at the end: not the Church of the political cult, which is dead already, but the Church of faith. It may well no longer be the dominant social power to the extent that she was until recently; but it will enjoy a fresh blossoming and be seen as man's home, where he will find life and hope beyond death."

One must not neglect these words from a philosopher, theologian, historian, priest, Bishop, Cardinal, the head of the Congregation for the Doctrine of the Faith (CDF), and then Pope Benedict XVI. The ramifications of today's proclamations from Rome will have a profound influence on future generations. We can be sure that changes will be staggering in all spheres of the social milieu, similar to what happened after Vatican II when many within the Church took it upon themselves to implement their own interpretations of the Vatican II documents, and watered-down Church teachings for a confused laity. Yes, the Rhine still flows into the Tiber. Rather than the most prominent churchmen upholding Magisterial truth with a mandate to protect it, often hierarchy are the ones leading the charge against it from the very interior of the Church. It is difficult to fight a foe when there are powerful, organized, and influential enemies inside the gates. Many in the hierarchy have been intentionally undermining the laity and faithful priests for a long time.

Stand Firm as Daniel Did on the Promises of Scripture

To withstand these assaults, both within our country and within our Church, we will need to devise a strategy to adhere to the essentials and precepts of the faith like Daniel. We will need many of the same attributes he used to overcome an awful situation with a hostile king, living as a captive slave, being tempted to dishonor God by eating unclean foods, and having idolatry and paganism around him. Yet through fidelity to the prescription of the Lord through Jeremiah, Daniel not only endured, but in the end he thrived.

One thing is certain. We have been told that the Church will never perish. The Blessed Mother said that we will know we are in the times spoken of by seeing the events themselves. She has been speaking at numerous apparition sites around the world warning us about this day and how to avoid catastrophic consequences. The Third Secret of Fatima is about the apostasy of the faith, and the auto-demolition of the Church from the highest levels within. Is there a mother who would not warn her children of impending danger if given the chance? The events spoken of at the major apparition sites are all around us, and are often ignored to the peril of the individual refusing to listen. The Blessed Mother has told us repeatedly where we are headed, and it is now obvious to those who have paid attention that the future is here. We are deep into the events that have been prophesied for a long time. We are in the time of trials. In 1997 she told the Marian Movement of Priests in the very last message, *"All has been revealed to you"* (MMP #604). To those following the messages, there is little guesswork where we are headed. Like Daniel and his Jewish people, we know the path forward and are called to live joyfully no matter the circumstances around us.

Saint John Bosco (1815-1888) saw in his vision of the future of the Church, how the barque of Peter would be tossed from stem to stern, nearly capsizing. As the boat went through the **Twin Pillars** of the **Eucharist** on one high pillar, and the **Blessed Mother** on the pillar of less stature — the Church was saved and calm was restored. As Mediatrix, Co-redemptrix, and Advocate of mankind, we seek to follow the Virgin Mary's directives for safe passage, sustained by the Bread of Life, Our Eucharistic Lord.

At Medjugorje, the Blessed Mother said, *"I have a great plan for the salvation of mankind."* These apparitions have been occurring now for more than forty years, commencing on June 24, 1981. Our Lady has told us **prayer and fasting** can stop wars, and can alter natural law. How many fight the evil around us on that level with the tools Heaven has told us will defeat evil?

Trust the plan. Trust the Queen of Heaven and Earth. Trust the Daughter of the Father, the Mother of the Son, the Spouse of the Holy Spirit. We will never go wrong. At every valid apparition site on earth, she points to her Son. Here it is impossible for us to go wrong. They will direct our path.

JESUS I TRUST IN YOU

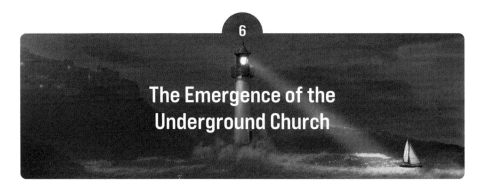

Keep Calm and Carry On.

A British motivational poster in 1939 England as they prepared to enter World War II

In the last several years we have seen a severe disruption in the cultural fabric of the United States in nearly every category. There are few exceptions. Every generation has its challenges, but this generation is experiencing a seismic shift. Generation Y (Millennials) are roundly in their 30's and Generation Z are about to come of age. Economic hardship gives rise to maturity and forces people to do things they would not ordinarily do. The U.S. is presently in the midst of a ferocious battle to determine the way America goes forward into the 21st Century. There will be only one victor, and it is the primary reason the battle is so intense. Both sides know only one ideology can win that will steer policy for the next generation(s). At stake are innumerable metrics of whom and how we govern ourselves. If the present tide is not turned, we will soon have a Marxist atheistic communism envelop the land. Years ago it was the talk of those in the know; now it is more widely understood. Who will be chosen as a justice of the Supreme Court is most important to the left because the battle at the court level is nearly exclusively about abortion and LGBTQ rights as Justice Brett Kavanaugh found out.

A recent poll indicated forty-three (43) percent of Americans saw some good in their lives come from the lockdown due to Covid 19, while others were in depression, or near despair. The lockdown showed chinks in the armor, such as who had parented well and those who had not, and many other things. In adversity, flaws and good character both blossom. People were running to the medicine cabinet for antidepressants that were in short supply, and prescriptions were dispensed for high blood pressure at a record clip. Marriage counselors had a great few months via Zoom and other similar technologies. Many people took the time to reflect on their lives at a far less hectic pace, and bicycle sales and repair shops had a banner year. Bible sales and spiritual reading were far greater than previous years according to book-sellers. Many felt that the Lord was saying *"slow down,"* and this was the healthy aspect of the lockdown. Many people reflected on what mattered most in life, albeit circumstances forced it. There is good that can come from hardship and suffering.

Over forty million people without work is no small thing. If we get a second wave and a more severe strain of Covid 19 at a later date, that number may swell far above forty million. Those businesses that survived the first wave may not have the financial stamina to survive the second wave. Think of a prize fighter needing to go in the ring in successive weeks. You don't have much strength in the body immediately after the first fight.

The fear mongering worked to perfection as the global elite took the temperature of a church populace willing to submit their constitutional rights of freedom of worship and assembly even after the data was coming out. Covid 19 was nowhere near as severe as health scientists had originally said. One meme said, *"Church service will now be held in the plumbing department of Home Depot."* Churches were held to strict compliance, but not other institutions. Some in the Church hierarchy were in lockstep with godless governors. The left had an opening and they drove a truck through it with little resistance, and with the full support of the democratic party. As the saying goes, *"Never let a crisis go to waste."*

Events in the Church were no exception. There were states completely locked down where some dioceses complied with governmental policy and never opened doors at all for any reason. Other priests had Mass in parking lots while people stayed in their cars. Other priests had drive-in confessions; some had Adoration attended by no more than ten people in the church; other priests held confessions on a regular basis only missing the first week or two for things to settle down as some models showed several million deaths in the U.S. alone was a possibility. Some churches streamed the Mass over the internet and people were able to choose a Mass regardless of the state they lived. What evolved is that few of the government models were any where near accurate early on with the expected mortality rate. With the Phase 1 openings, blue states and red states opened according to party lines. The battle to reopen was seen for what it was — political. Red versus blue states aligned like the north and the south in the U.S. Civil War. Once President Trump and his administration were defeated, the chaos continued. Violence even escalated in other directions. Expect no peace. It is a modern day political game of *"Whack a Mole."*

Archbishop Vigano, Cardinals Gerard Mueller, Joseph Zen and Janis Pujats and other prelates wrote an appeal in which they called into question a total lockdown that strongly restricted freedoms as a result of the Covid 19 outbreak particularly as the data emerged calling into question the justification for such measures. They as many other believers feel the Church became a primary target of the left to further a political agenda to weaken it. These prelates and others asserted that, *"The Covid 19 pandemic is being used as a pretext by world leaders to control people, strip them of their fundamental rights, while providing a disturbing prelude to the realization of a world government beyond all control. The Catholic Church firmly asserts her autonomy to govern, worship, and teach."*

Archbishop Vigano goes further than most in exposing the plans of a global elite wishing to subject the world to their leadership. In years past it was only a select few that saw the dangers coming from several fabulously wealthy individuals and their goals of having the populace serve their whims and fancies, and how they wish to rule the world according to a godless atheistic ideology. Depopulation was paramount for this agenda to take place. Once it is understood that depopulation and infertility injected into vaccines is the primary goal of an elite few, data points fall more neatly into place on the overall plan to control people. Archbishop Vigano has said, *"Plans for a New World Order must be unmasked, understood, and revealed."*

Several leading Cardinals saw the pandemic for what it was. Cardinal Gerhard Muller, former head of the Congregation for the Doctrine of the Faith (CDF), rejected the thought he was a "conspiracy theorist" as the data became obvious. He said, *"The concept of a forced vaccination is unacceptable and abhorrent to many in the Church violating basic freedoms."* He denounced world governments as using the pandemic to promote world government. He said, *"Certain powers want to instrumentalize this situation to suppress the Catholic Church. It is no conspiracy theory where governments wish to implement questionable measures."* He also said about forced vaccinations, *"The threat has been made publicly that 7 billion people will be forcibly vaccinated even if the drugs have not yet been sufficiently tested, and that if people are not complying, fundamental rights will be taken from them. No one can be forced to believe that a few philanthropic super billionaires have the best programs for world improvement just because they have succeeded in accumulating a huge private fortune."*

Many American bishops were too quiet about more than the loss of freedoms for their flocks. The woke, atheistic and socialistic demonstrations that defied the lockdowns when churches were closed netted no similar freedoms for Catholic churchgoers. George Floyd's death was inexcusable by any means. However, the chaos of the godless anarchists kicked into high gear looking for social change through violence and destabilizing society. These groups repeatedly said this was a once in a lifetime opportunity for change. The godless got a break and took full advantage of it. Pallets of bricks, baseball bats, and glass bottles appeared in the streets near the riot sites and needed to be given more press — and who did it? Just days previous the pandemic was the focus. In hours it became the residual effects of Minneapolis. Meanwhile many democrats fueled the fire. We have learned that Antifa is well organized, well trained, and well funded.

Then riots spread to multiple hundreds of locales and cities across the country; there were more challenges going forward as they continued. A lot more. The riots were orchestrated by a virulent leftist political agenda. It is impossible to justify what the police did in Minneapolis. However, the left used the perfect timing of this circumstance to advocate and promote a far larger and godless plan for social upheaval. George Soros and his Open Society with about two hundred organizations under that umbrella used that crisis as a springboard to promote goals they have wanted to implement for several generations. Saul Alinsky was the first to implement by name the Open Society, and Soros is the extension of it. The repercussions coming out of this will be substantial. Events will come at us like box cars now — one after another, and they will leave us dizzy and punch drunk.

How is a Church, already weakened in her faith by modernism, and then cut off from the fullness of her sacraments, going to be able to respond? So far, the agenda to weaken the Church has succeeded. The Roman Catholic Church is the single impediment in the way to bring in a New World Order according to Marxist principles. The goals of the left are to completely dissolve a resemblance to the past of the Constitution and Christianity. It is the work of a maestro choreographer. George Soros and men like him are like James Bond villains petting an exotic looking cat on their laps while plotting world domination in real time using a script of social engineering to bring it about. It has been through Covid 19, with people home watching videos on You Tube and other media, where more people are waking up to how real this diabolical agenda is.

Between Covid 19 and the riots back-to-back, governmental control looked like the USSR under Stalin. In the parking lot at a Lowe's Home Improvement near me two high towers broadcasted rules of conduct in the parking lot with cameras and loud speakers telling people how to act in and near the store. At a tennis facility in a town nearby (a democratic stronghold) town employees watched people play tennis making sure they obeyed the rules set up by the town. Reminds one of what it must be like living in North Korea with mandatory messaging from the Hermit Kingdom blaring propaganda into homes several times a day giving instructions on how to live — and how to think. A true mass psychosis to rule the people.

A plan of something similar to **The Hunger Games** is increasingly looking more like the streets we inhabit as it concerns state control. No matter the means or the end, it is about control and making the individual a tool for the state. To control, the state must subjugate the individual, and the biggest prize of all is to eradicate Christianity. Then Cardinal Ratzinger explained it in a 1969 German radio broadcast: *"How does all this affect the* *problem we are examining? It means that the big talk of those who prophesy a Church without God and without faith is all empty chatter. We have no need of a Church that celebrates the cult of action in political prayers. It is utterly superfluous. Therefore, it will destroy itself."* It is here where are the beginnings in which the Church will be renewed and will blossom like it has in ages past.

But, the remnant will be the new underground voice. We are witnessing the emerging seeds of an underground church. As Jesus said, *"My sheep hear my voice and I know them, and they follow me"* (John 10:27). The Church will shrink in size but it will become stronger in faith, and the gates of hell will never prevail against it. The liberals may get the properties, but the true believers will keep the faith.

The faithful know each other and which clergy stepped up to the plate on their behalf as victim souls rather than careerists. At annual fundraising events for conservative Catholic causes, it is the same people contributing year after year. It is the same few at daily Mass providing philanthropy and time to these causes.

Also, it is only a few bishops speaking out globally. One can take heart that when Saint Thomas More was under attack for not capitulating to the demands of King Henry VIII (the state) to break with the Catholic Church for not granting him a divorce, only one Bishop in all of the British Isles came to his defense—Saint John Fisher. The Lord is separating the wheat from the chaff and the sheep from the goats. America and the world are at a tipping point. At valid apparition sites throughout the world we have been told this day is coming. It is here now and it is not time to be lukewarm.

Do not look left, nor right, but up. Our refuge is in Her Immaculate Heart, so look or travel no further to find peace of heart and soul.

JESUS I TRUST IN YOU

7

As the Church Moves to the Underground— The Lord Instructs How to do it

My people perish for lack of knowledge.

Hosea 4:6

Is anything new today that has not happened before? The answer is no, because as civilizations decline, there is a geometric increase in confusion, lack of discipline, chaos, marginalization against beliefs, and then violence. That is the history of mankind for millennia. Class warfare is a part of that declining process.

I think the partial solution to our confusion may have been given to us through our elder brothers in the faith by Yahweh Himself. In Jeremiah 29, the Jewish people had disobeyed the observance of the Sabbath, and Yahweh was clear that disobedience to the Sabbath was a serious grievance. Moreover, the Jews were worshipping the gods of their neighbors. Therefore, as a result, Yahweh told His people through the prophet Jeremiah that their punishment would be seventy years in exile living in a foreign land. Seventy years is three and half generations that they would have to endure for disobedience. Exile was a Divine spanking or a nicer way of saying it, a Divine pruning. Their disobedience cost them dearly.

Yahweh told the Jews how they would endure the trial, and He gave them very clear instructions to follow. He was telling them this is what you must do; this is how you will conduct yourselves; and this is how you must live above all the noise for you to return from exile in Babylon. Yahweh said this is your prescription to survive as a people and as a nation. The beautiful thing here is that Yahweh didn't send them off without any instructions. He gave them a manual for how to return from captivity to normalcy — again governed by His laws to restore the lost years.

Jeremiah writes, *"These are the words of the letter which Jeremiah the prophet sent from Jerusalem to the elders of the exiles, and to the priests, the prophets, and all the people whom Nebuchadnezzar had taken into exile from Jerusalem to Babylon.*

"Thus says the Lord of hosts, the God of Israel to all the exiles whom I have sent into exile from Jerusalem to Babylon. Build houses and live in them, plant gardens and eat their produce. Take wives and have sons and daughters; take wives for your sons, and give your daughters in marriage, that they may bear sons and daughters; multiply there, and do not decrease. But seek the welfare of the city, where I have sent you into exile, and pray to the Lord on its behalf, for in its welfare you will find your welfare….For thus says the Lord, when seventy years are completed for Babylon, I will visit you, and I will fulfill to you my promise and bring you back to this place. For I know the plans I have for you, says the Lord, plans for welfare and not for evil, to give you a future and hope. Then you will call upon me and pray to me, and I will hear you. You will seek me and find me; when you seek me with all your heart, I will be found by you, says the Lord, and I will restore your fortunes and gather you from all the nations, and all the places I have driven you, says the Lord…" (Jer. 29: 1, 4-14).

We as a country have committed abominations far worse than the Jewish people for abdicating our spiritual responsibility of worship on the Sabbath. We are fast approaching a land of desolation due to sin before God. We will have a price to pay. What is cited above describes Yahweh's plan for the Jews so they could weather the storm while in exile and be restored. **Plant, harvest, have a family, marry, be good grandparents, or in the parlance of today's language: commute to work, go to little league, take your children to catechism, teach them faith in your home at the dining room table, live according to your station, build your family, live in a community of fellowship, and do the things you need to do to be in fidelity to the gospel — and avoid the things that are unhealthy and not wholesome. Maintain your identity as believers where you have been placed.**

In a world that is seeking solutions, I find few people or institutions providing answers. Don't just be the person always providing an analysis of the problems in our midst, but be the person building viable solutions for your family, and be the alternative for a culture to gravitate to find peace of soul. Wherever Jesus walked He cured, He healed, He consoled the down and out, and He gave answers to man's woes. It is no longer time to act as the talking heads or political pundits defining the problems: **provide solutions, God's solutions.**

JESUS I TRUST IN YOU

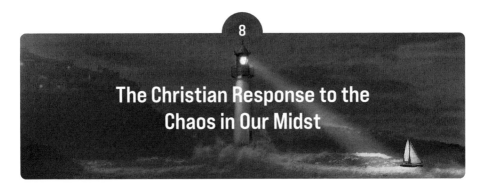

8

The Christian Response to the Chaos in Our Midst

In the beginning was the Word, and the Word was with God, and the Word was God.

—John 1:1

I, like everyone, have struggled with a wide range of emotions since the presidential election of 2020. If there is a human emotion to be had, I have had it. As a life-long student of history, I know well, that things can easily get out of control with a mob mentality and manipulation of the masses through disinformation campaigns. Do you take to the streets, retreat, start throwing things, or say to the Lord, *"This is your mess, you figure it out?"* People are asking two things. What is going on, and what should I do? People are trying to figure out which way the fox is going to go, and our personal anxiety is really about our welfare going forward. Will I have a job, will my financial safety net be there to catch me, or will the country frankly go broke? Profligate government spending and the horribly destructive domestic and foreign policies of government cannot go on much longer before we fall into a heap of ashes. At the moment we are on the precipice. We are at a critical juncture in world history. These are valid issues that concern all of us.

Is anything new today that has not happened before? The answer is no, because as civilizations decline, there is a geometric increase in confusion, lack of discipline, chaos, marginalization against beliefs, and then violence. That is the history of mankind for millennia. Class warfare is a part of that declining process.

The American Civil War was North v. South, and fought primarily over the perennial issue of state rights. The South didn't want to be told what to do by a North looking to take away their state rights as they saw fit for self-governance. Slavery was the vehicle for war. The upcoming conflict that is escalating is going to be Blue State v. Red State. Communism versus the principles of a Republic. We will shortly see a bifurcated country along the ideological lines of the role of government and enforcement of its laws. The ramifications of these differences will be more profound than most people think.

Relationships are fracturing at an alarming rate now. Believers and conservatives in general feel as if they have been pushed too far and are simply not bothering with liberal friends who shoved their ideology down their throats for years. No one is listening to the other now, and that too, will escalate, further breaking apart families and friends. Neutral or middle ground is now hard to find. Neutrality has ended, and that is troublesome for societal stability.

The Example of Jesus

This begs the question, what is the response of the believer to navigate the shoals that are now roaring in our hearts at close range? The answer is found in many places of Scripture. One that is most poignant is when Jesus was captured by Roman soldiers in the Garden of Gethsemane, due to the betrayal of Judas (John 18). Jesus came to the earth to die. He was the only person in the history of the world to fulfill a mission to die for the redemption of all mankind. Jesus said several times, *"My hour has not yet come."* Hour always refers to evil. Until Jesus was ready for the completion of His mission, He was untouchable. Going to Gethsemane, He knew the final act of His mission was about to unfold, and His apostle Judas was about to betray Him with a pre-arranged sign of a kiss on his Savior's cheek.

All of the apostles were with Jesus in the Garden but Judas. Prayer was absent from his life as he never grasped the true mission of Jesus. The other eleven fought staying awake, and Jesus rebuked them for not giving Him one hour of prayer. Jesus sweat blood while in agony knowing Calvary awaited Him. His hour had now come. At the moment of arrest, Peter drew a sword, and showing himself a swordsman, struck the high priest's servant Malchus, cutting off his ear. Jesus restored the man's ear then said to Peter, ***"Put your sword into its sheath. Shall I not drink the cup which My Father has given to Me?"*** (John 18:11) Literally hours away from death, Jesus tells Peter if you live by the sword, you will die by the sword. Violence begets violence. That is not the prescription for peace that Jesus came to give.

Before His trial, Jesus prayed alone and asked others to be with Him in prayer. Their human nature and lack of resolve got in the way, and they failed to be with Jesus in His darkest hour, falling asleep. Jesus was all alone. To a great degree, many of us are alone today. The overwhelming majority of humanity is insensitive to the cry of prayer, the power of Eucharistic Adoration, the rosary, the Mass, confession, redemptive suffering, fasting, building of local community, and understanding what Jesus wants from us. The greatest sin of all may be our indifference.

Now is the time to double down on spiritual exercises. It is not a time to be a doormat and lay down in surrender, but we are asked to be the light on a hill. Echoing the words of Jesus, *"Put your sword into its sheath,"* it is a time of **nonviolent, noncooperation** with tyranny and a state hell bent on pagan practices with an overt agenda to crush the believing population. Your silence is consent to tyranny, and for your own welfare, you must now speak up or you will be involuntarily silenced. We have lived for millennia without social media, and maybe Heaven is saying, it is time to put it away. Six plus hours a day staring at a screen for anyone is excessive. Most of the information traded on social media is insipid, inane, and banal anyway. It is a giant time sapper from what is most important in life. Is Jesus asking now, *"Can you not pray with Me one hour?"*

One of the brightest stars in the ecclesiastical world is Archbishop Vigano. He recently said, *"The Kingdom of Satan is upon the world."* That is an amazing statement from a man with his pedigree as a voice of reason in a world gone mad.

We are told through the Marian Movement of Priests the Blessed Mother said, *"My secrets will be revealed to you by the very events through which you have been called to live"* (MMP #561p). She also lets us know what a gift it is to be aware: "I am consoled by the littlest, by those who live truly as little children, whom Jesus forms and guards with the heavenly garden of his divine love. With what tenderness I carry them in my motherly arms, that they may be consoled by me. *To them alone do I reveal the secret of my Immaculate Heart, the light of my design, the battle plan and the moment of my victory* (MMP #512)." Repeatedly, we are told the refuge is in her Immaculate Heart. You will find safety no where else. Does being a believer in times of crisis and turmoil mean you turn into a mouse, or a swordsman? There is great room in between those two concepts to show your dissent from tyrannical rule, and your ability to do something spiritually constructive.

If you think we have reached a crescendo of evil you would be wrong. The possibility of a forced vaccine, or whatever ill of the next pandemic, will separate the men from the boys, and the girls from the women when various forms of commerce are precluded, such as flights, entry into buildings, shopping at your local grocery store, credit card use, the paying of your water and electric bill, the ability to register and drive your car, entry into schools, to name just a few lifestyle changes. Unless you can show your **Digital or Immunity Passport** you will be barred from many things. The passport is about the size of a credit card, and will show if you have all the necessary vaccines required by the state to show compliance and good standing with the state. It will be the same as the social credit score that is used by the Communist Party of China to determine if someone is in compliance.

In a world that is seeking solutions, I find few people or institutions providing answers. Don't just be the person always providing an analysis of the problems in our midst, but be the person building viable solutions for your family, and be the alternative for a culture to gravitate to find peace of soul. Wherever Jesus walked He cured, He healed, He consoled the down and out, and He gave answers to man's woes. It is no longer time to act as the talking heads or political pundits defining the problems: **provide solutions, God's solutions.**

Be a voice; time is short. Evil exists because good people do nothing. The silence of many believers has brought us to this place at this very moment in history. If you continue to live in fear of what others think of you, you will not have a voice that can bring a remedy to this mess in which we find ourselves. If not you, who? If not now, when?

"For the power of the wicked shall be broken, but the Lord supports the just." (Psalm 37:17)

JESUS I TRUST IN YOU

I have told you beforehand of the times which await you...
precisely in order to help you live in trust and in a great confidence
in your heavenly Mother.

Message #486u, the Blessed Mother to the Marian Movement of Priests, January 1, 1993

On March 18, 2020, Mirjana Soldo, the visionary of Medjugorje, during her annual birthday apparition was told by the Blessed Mother that she would no longer be receiving a message on the second of every month. This is significant because since 1987 (33 years total) she had been receiving a message on the second of every month that were heavily disseminated throughout the world. In many respects, she has been the most public mouthpiece for Medjugorje all of these past years. In June of 2021, Medjugorje celebrated its 40th anniversary since the apparitions began. The message read,

"Dear children, my Son, as God, always looked above time. I, as His mother, through Him, see in time. I see beautiful and sad things. But I see that there is still love, and that one should endeavor to make it known. My children, you cannot be happy if you do not love one another, if you do not have love in every situation and in every moment of your life. Also, I, as a mother, come to you through love to help you know the true love, to help you know my Son. This is why I am calling you, always anew to thirst all the more for love, faith and hope. The only spring you can drink from is the trust in God, my Son. My children, in moments of peacelessness and renunciation all you have to do is to seek the face of my Son. You just live His words and do not be afraid. Pray and love with sincere feelings, with good works, and help that the world may change and my heart triumph. As does my Son, so I also tell you to love one another for there is no salvation without love. Thank you my children."

The word **LOVE** is mentioned nine times in this very brief statement. After all of these years the second of the month has ended. The question is, what happens next? What should we expect? What should we make of this? What is our role?

The very next day, on March 19, 2020, the Feast of Saint Joseph, the Patron Saint of the Universal Church, Conchita, the lead visionary of Garabandal issued a brief statement in the midst of a stock market meltdown and the Corona virus (Covid 19) pandemic that read,

"God is detaching us from the securities of this world. In the silence of the Church or in our house we are now able to make an examination of conscience so we can clean what prevents us from hearing the Voice of God clearly. With sincerity we can ask God to tell us what He wants of us today, and continue to do that every day. And spend as much time as possible with God at church or somewhere in your home or where you find the silence. He is all we need."

From 1961 to 1965, the Blessed Mother appeared at Garabandal Spain over two thousand times to four young visionaries. Three of the girls married Americans and one remained in Spain. Conchita, the only visionary who knows the day of the Great Miracle, emerged as the leader of the four, and has always been known as reserved and respectful. When asked why she doesn't speak about Garabandal, she gave a very good answer. She said, *"I was only 12 years old when the apparitions began, and I was always concerned I could give the wrong answer as it was so long ago. Go back to what I said then to get the answer you are asking."* I can say, I don't remember much of what I did or said at twelve years old either. No one can remember Conchita ever giving a statement like her few sentences on March 19, 2020. She once did a television interview in Ireland when she was in her mid to late twenties. That would put the interval of time approximately forty-two to forty-four years that she never issued a public statement until the above, and just over a year away from Garabandal's 60th Anniversary. Is this another sign of the times, a coincidence, or something more?

Also, on October 6, 2019, Sister Agnes Sasagawa, the seer of Akita, Japan, was given a private message just for her by her angel, and then told to read another message that was to be given to the world. It read, *"Put on ashes and pray a repentant rosary (a rosary of repentance) every day. You must become like a child and make sacrifices every day."* Two days later the first Mass reading was from the Book of Jonah 3:1-10. This is the story of Jonah walking through the City of Nineveh saying it was going to be destroyed if it didn't repent from its sin. Nineveh put on sackcloth and ashes and did repent. October 6 was also the day the controversial Pachamama idol was brought onto Vatican grounds. The messages of Akita Japan are approved by the Church. Cardinal Ratzinger as Prefect for the Congregation of the Faith (CDF) stated on numerous occasions that *"the messages of Akita and the Third Secret of Fatima are essentially the same."* Both messages are severe for the world, with the weightiest and bulk of the Akita messages given in 1973, and only several beyond. There was a gap of silence for forty-seven years since 1973. Again, this is another rarity where a visionary hasn't spoken in such a long time, yet issues a public message. For the visionaries it is out of character to have such a change in behavior. Is Heaven communicating to us in their language that only a believer can understand?

What does this mean with so much going on in the world right now? Covid 19 caused stock market fluctuations that hadn't been seen since 1933, and people are legitimately insecure where this may bring us. It has caused havoc and a change in lifestyle and habits like nothing since World War II, or the Spanish Flu of 1918. With both of those events the world changed forever. The apparitions of Fatima were in 1917 just prior to the outbreak of the flu. Sister Lucia was told Russia would spread her errors throughout the world, and then came the prophesied aurora of 1938, where Sister Lucy knew the outbreak of World War II was on the immediate horizon. Heaven writes straight with crooked lines, and Heaven's children know signs the world doesn't know, and the world ignores them at their own peril.

Former Governor Cuomo of New York implored the help of God as Covid 19 brought devastation to his state. Yet, only months earlier he gleefully and near giddily lit up New York in rainbows, signing an abortion bill into law stating prolife people have no place in New York State. Yet, in one of the most inconsistent statements a person can make, on March 24, 2020, Governor Cuomo facing what to do about Covid 19 said, *"We must do all we can to preserve life, as human life is not disposable."* This is a galactic, incongruent, hypocritical statement for such a person's moral outlook on life. Cuomo is a confused soul.

The question must be asked, "Can America afford abortion?" With the killing of the innocent amidst a culture of death as the law of the land, the hedge of God's protection is removed. Churches were mandated to close by state governments and bishops, yet the killing centers of abortion mills, pot dispensaries, and liquor stores were permitted to remain open and deemed "essential services." Former Virginia Governor Ralph Northam, an open advocate for infanticide, made it a crime for more than ten people to attend a church service.

There is an advancement under these directives by a coordinated communist ideology to close churches and gun stores. Several mayors threatened if entities did not close as directed, water and electricity will be cut off. Drones were also being used for enforcement. If this was the nuclear option of the Deep State, it worked — temporarily. Be forewarned: government will continue to expand from crisis to crisis, and individual constitutional rights will incrementally get usurped.

It was at this moment the Church should have been doubling down keeping Churches open all day in Adoration, and mindful of prudent cautious distance. Many clergy lived in fear when they should have been proactive for their parishes imploring prayer. The Mass is the source and summit of the faith, and Saint Pio (Padre) said it would be easier for the world to exist without the sun, than without the Mass. The Lord slowed us down so we could focus on what is Most Important in life — Him.

If you think it was only the Medieval Ages that were relegated to two popes and a plague, think again. We are living in a time of *A Great Transition* where we have been told to expect the Triumph of the Immaculate Heart. To have a New Time, we have to have the old pass away before the New can be ushered in. Unless there was Good Friday, there would never have been the Resurrection. The Blessed Mother said at Medjugorje, *"I have a great plan for the salvation of mankind."* Are these events precursors to what awaits us? I think the case is building where we may see great spiritual events in our future. God will not be mocked. There have always been two cohorts in battle, those of God versus Satan. Good versus evil has always been the battle, and is still the battle. The more things change, the more they stay the same. To prevail know your enemy, and know his tactics.

Beautiful words from a hymn by St. Ambrose below.

> *Now that the daylight fills the sky,*
> *We lift our hearts to God on high,*
> *That He, in all we do and say,*
> *Would keep us free from harm today.*
>
> *May He restrain our tongues from strife,*
>
> *And shield from anger's din our life,*
> *And guard with watchful care our eyes*
> *From earth's absorbing vanities.*
>
> *O may our inmost hearts be pure,*
> *From thoughts of folly kept secure,*
> *And pride of sinful flesh subdued*
> *Through sparing us of daily food.*
>
> *So we, when this day's work is o'er,*
> *And shades of night return once more,*

Our path of trial safely trod,
Shall give the glory to our God.

To God the Father glory true,
The same, eternal Son, to you,
And to the Spirit glory be,
Both now and for eternity.
Amen.

JESUS I TRUST IN YOU

10

The Hour and the Day Life Changes for Tens of Millions of People

If you do not live what you believe, you will end up
believing what you live.

Archbishop Fulton Sheen

At some point in the recent past, a decision had to be made in households across the nation whether you and members of your family took a mandatory vaccine for work or school. If you did escape taking the jab, in a matter of time you may very well face the decision again over a new jab for a new pandemic crisis. Whether it be called an **Immunity Passport** or any other name, the United States Government in all of its many forms, and many state governments, pushed for a Covid 19 Vaccine ID system for identification and control. Tens of billions of dollars have been spent to find a vaccine that can stop the transmission of Covid 19. Many credentialed respected health experts doubt any will be effective. Yet, others promote it not knowing precisely the harm it may cause. This article is not how Covid may come back in a more virulent form, or any drug treatments. It is singularly focused on the fact we are heading rapidly into governments' mandating a forced vaccine.

If someone were to have a bushel basket filled to the brim with apples, and each apple were a social issue of some sort, just one of those apples, if it were labeled VACCINE, would be more explosive at many dinner tables and cafés than the rest of the bushel basket combined. If you bring up the word VACCINE in mixed company where a person doesn't know where other people stand, the waters may part like Moses raising his staff. Nothing is as divisive today especially for young families as vaccines. Millions of families feel the plethora of vaccines mandated by government has been a contributing factor to their children being on the autism spectrum.

The extreme volatility of vaccines is on several levels. First, is the distrust of government from a concerned populace on the reasons for the vaccines, what is in them, and the general efficacy for its intended purpose. Years ago, those who questioned the motives of Big Government and their plans were considered conspiracy theorists and the far right. Media portrayed these people as ideological extremists. The strategy was and still is to take away their voice. But, the facts over the last several years have shown that this group is far more literate than the rest. Years ago, this group was considered fringe, but the truth is they were more aware of the insidious plans of government than the rest of the gullible public. Now, people have seen the whites of the eyes of the left and the destructive policies of the communists operating in stealth for decades. Second, millions of people have an inherit distrust of government more broadly that has been verified in the last several years as legitimate. Their many lies are now in the open for all to see.

Since Donald Trump was elected President of the United States, a lot of information about the nefarious machinations and deceit of the Deep State and Deep Church has come to light. Not just in medicine and the National Institutes of Health (NIH), and its affiliated agencies, but in law enforcement, the intelligence community, executive agencies, the U.S. Congress, non-governmental organizations (NGOs), and a host of other socialist and communist organizations. While many believers slept, evil worked around the clock. It took a long time for the truth to come out on the plans of the Deep State, but there has been an agenda across the board to control the masses for decades.

At this point, people have drawn swords and taken sides on who and what to believe about Covid 19. A place where one can see this is how people talk and implement a mask policy. It is often an explosive situation because so many believe that the government used the mask as a method to soften the beachhead as a precursor to a mandatory vaccine. Others believe there is honorable intent by government. The mask is the ultimate psychological operation (psy-op) and conditioning towards the ultimate goal of forcing the vaccine. The mask through social indoctrination gets people ready for the next step of voluntarily accepting a mandatory vaccine. People will not question its content. In 1968 there were 200.7 million people living in America. An estimated 1-4 million die from the flu worldwide every year, and there was never hysteria from governments to lock down countries.

Bill Gates is on the record that it will take at least two shots, and probably more for the elderly to be ready for clearance of their **Immunity Passport.** MIT has been working on a handheld device that can detect if people have received the required shots before a person can be accepted safely into the general population. It is something that resembles a *"passport tattoo"* that can be scanned. An App in the form of a QR Code will also be available on your phone to detect if all immunizations have been covered according to Federal and State protocols. But to believers who see a more insidious agenda, having aborted fetal and animal cells injected into their body will be unacceptable. Science has shown that injecting an individual's DNA into another person has been the genesis of many illnesses. There is substantial empirical data with autoimmune disorders, autism chief among them.

Where the Rubber Meets the Road

Crunch time is going to come when Federal and State governments mandate an Immunity Passport before people can be admitted into their place of employment, classroom, government building, favorite restaurant, Department of Motor Vehicles, and anywhere the Governor says you can or cannot go. Unless you have the clearance that you have been vaccinated, you will at some point in the near future be precluded from entry to buildings and receive public or private funds. If you are in a blue state you will have little option but to comply. In only but a few red states you may have a fighting chance as long as you don't travel across borders. What will people do if a co-worker demands that unless everyone receive the vaccine and can prove it, they won't go to work? The classroom? Church? Sports venues, a pharmacy, supermarket, Home Depot or Lowe's?

The list gets long very fast, especially if a more virulent form of Covid comes back, which it may according to many predictions. The very nature of a virus is to mutate. Robert Redfield, the head of the CDC, said *"Expect the Fall (2020) to be the worst public health time in American history — surpassing 1918."* AIDS was first discovered in 1981, and there is still no cure. It can be managed, but there is no cure.

A recent poll said forty two percent of the population said they will not take a mandatory vaccine. Will they still stick to that if their kids cannot go to school unless they can show their **Immunity Passport**? If the reach of the STATE says Medicare, Medicaid, Social Security, and health care costs are denied to a person who refuses the vaccine, they will submit to government demands. People will bow under pressure when jobs are at stake.

A gym owner in New Jersey opened for business when the Governor said not to open. Atilis Gym in Bellmawr, New Jersey then had the locks changed by the police. The owner then took the doors off. The STATE then shut his electricity off, so he then installed his own generator. The next day they shut his water off. On August 11 by a vote of 5-1 the City Council found the owners of the gym in contempt for violating court ordered limits on indoor operation under emergency orders as ordered by Governor Phil Murphy and the New Jersey Health Commission. The City Council then revoked their license to operate. If they operate in defiance, will they suspend driving licenses? If so, will the owners of the gym be able to drive? Can the owners then be arrested and put in jail? How big will the fines be to penalize the owners? The reach of the state has few limits and can impose draconian measures to force compliance. Meanwhile states allow casinos to open. Is a casino or liquor store an essential business? Is a bus seating 64 people with 340 square feet? The state can say what is essential, and you can rest assured if you are in a blue state, it will be an anti-Christian policy.

Bill Gates, founder of Microsoft and world crusader for vaccines as a form of population control, took part in an online question and answer session. One user asked, "How should we determine which businesses stay open?" Gates replied, "The question of which businesses should keep going is tricky.... Countries are still figuring out what to keep running. Eventually we will have some digital certificates to show who has recovered or been tested recently or when we have a vaccine who has received it." Gates is saying *digital certificates will be used to verify and track those who have received the Covid 19 vaccine. Is he further inferring those certificates will be used to determine who can do business, who can travel, and who can get services?* Did he mean the term "digital certificate" to include microchips? They are certainly a kind of digital certificate. The enzyme that will make the Gates vaccine microchip implant work is named, LUCIFERASE, and its patent number is 060606. This sounds a lot like biblical prophecy to me, and if not, it is a first cousin.

There is a lot of rhetoric with people saying what they will or will not do, but when it comes to finances and the inability to pay bills, hearts and minds will need to make a big decision — and millions of families will be forced to make difficult choices. If history is our teacher, it will be a small percentage who will do what is right because most people will act to protect self-interests. What percentage of the people in Germany rose up against Hitler? Ninety-seven percent of the people of Austria embraced Hitler when he annexed it in March of 1938, and he was greeted by joyous crowds. From the heritage of Strauss, Mozart, Haydn, Wagner, Schubert, and many others, brutes were bred in time of stress among an educated and civil society. The people welcomed a despotic economic ruler with open arms.

For those wishing to dive a bit deeper into the back stories of the National Institutes of Health, The National Institute of Allergy and Infectious Diseases (NIAID), Dr. Anthony Fauci, big pharmaceutical companies using the NIH as a tax payer funded agency and a wholly owned subsidary, they should get the book, *Plague of Corruption, Restoring the Faith in the Promise of Science,* by Dr. Judy Mikovits and Kent Heckenlively, 2020, 221 pages. It has a Foreword by Robert F. Kennedy, Jr. and Signs of the Times (Sign.org) carries the book.

If one wants to see a guaranteed conflict of interest, look no further than the *"Bayh-Dole Act which allows federally funded scientists to patent discoveries"* under their own name, Page 184, Mikovits. Dr. Mikovits has accurately titled her book.

11

Birth Pangs and a Divine Mercy Promise

My secrets will be revealed to you by the very events
through which you have been called to live.

The Blessed Mother to Father Stefan Gobbi,
Milan Italy, the Marian Movement of Priests (MMP #561p)

If there has been a long-term relationship with a group of people that share the same values and past history, there is generally some sort of similar thinking. We like being around people with our views, and it is where friendships are forged. Whether it be people in corporate life or war buddies, they often share the same bond and outlook.

When people gather and talk of the Blessed Mother's apparitions, they instantly identify with each and become fast friends. At the level of their soul, they share the same ideology and outlook on life. Yes, there may be nuances and some differences, but generally they see the world through the same lens disbursing its light to the world. Believers share a bond past the human condition that goes to the eternal. They see the Blessed Mother as the North Star directing us to our eternal reward. They also know that if the words come directly from Her through an approved and reliable source, they will never go wrong.

With the Coronavirus firmly in our midst, we again see major differences many believers have with so called *"government experts."* During the early stages there wasn't distrust of people like Dr. Anthony Fauci and other *"health experts."* As President Trump gave his press conferences on a daily basis, people began to do research on the health team by his side, and unsavory data came to light about their previous relationships and projects. People have begun to realize that the CDC is essentially a privately run corporation controlled by Big Pharma under the auspices of a government agency in the National Institute of Health.

What they found was a cabal of people with the same ideology. Big Government run by Big Pharma tied to both political parties looking to have greater government control over civil liberties and all for profit. At the center of that cabal were people like Dr. Fauci and Bill Gates who have been in collaboration for decades. Flags started going up that they seem to have an agenda under a perfect storm scenario, and believers instantly became skeptical of what they were hearing again from *"the experts."* Believers are aware that aborted fetal cells are in many vaccines that have ruined many families, and they have a legitimate distrust of government. So when they hear that government will mandate another vaccine it is like a red flag in front of a raging bull. To mandate a *"digital certificate"* or *"immunity passport"* for maintaining any status in society has played into their worst fears. Believers worldwide know it can lead to ominous consequences if they do not comply with a government that has an antichrist mentality. With this virus, it is plausible to see a Nazi like enforcement coming into reality under an umbrella saying, *"This is good for you, this will protect you."*

The reason for the radical divide with ideologies at its root can be summed up with the answer to the question: *"What is the role of government in our lives?"* Liberals want more of Big Government; conservatives less. With the open architecture of the internet, someone can now get as smart as they want, as quick as they want on just about any subject. What believers have come to know and understand is there is a nefarious evil agenda from an evil cabal in high places in government to enslave mankind and make people a ward of the state from cradle to grave. They have been embedded in government now for generations perpetuating evil programs.

Some liberals don't want God anywhere in the State, the Family, the Culture, or the Church. Once a believer begins to understand that, the bread crumbs are easier to follow and this enables us to discern where they lead.

Of all days, it was on Good Friday former Governor Ralph Northam (D-Virginia) signed an extreme abortion bill legalizing infanticide into law — a Good Friday signature even though the Bill had been drafted and agreed upon months before.

Of all days, the experts said the virus was to peak was Easter Sunday. The virus had been around for several months, and the medical experts determined it was to peak Easter Sunday. A day premeditated as an excuse for law enforcement to keep people away from church to minimize its role. Yet, liquor stores and Planned Parenthood were deemed "essential services" and allowed to remain open. This was a giant step for the globalists to further erode civil liberties, force a vaccine, and then require people get a *"digital certificate"* before they can return to schools and work.

If people are not realizing how intense this spiritual battle is, they better become more engaged before all rights are completely stripped away. First, a forced vaccination, and then *"show me your papers"* reminiscent of Lenin, Hitler, Stalin, and Mao. Many believe there is also an agenda to insert a chip in the vaccine to track people through Big Tech. Scientists at MIT in cooperation with Big Pharma and Big Tech have developed a hand held device (it will be done with your phone) to scan an individual to determine if they have received vaccines. No vaccine, no entry.

Here is the big disconnect on the most important issues of our times. We presently have an economic collapse leading to the biggest unemployment since the 1930's. Civil unrest awaits us. Blue states are now aligning with other blue states working on agendas in unison much like the North and South each aligned for the Civil War.

We are in the midst of a transition in the world that happens only a few times a century. There are events that cause a civilization to involuntarily pivot in another direction. The last pandemic was 1917-1919, and it altered the landscape of the world economically and socially. World War II set up the United States as a superpower. America was then firmly enthroned as the reserve currency of the world with the ability to print money for any reason, for any project, with size of the project of little concern.

With this virus, the globalists played their hand brilliantly looking to simultaneously destroy the Church, and the economic systems of the world at the same time. Evil genius. If the virus subsides, they will say it was due to containment that worked through their efforts. If it spreads, they will blame Trump and the red states that they jumped the gun not isolating people long enough, or the unvaccinated. Either way, they win — for the short term.

The liberal agenda is to silence the pulpit of all denominations because **the Church is the last obstacle to world government**. A percentage of the populace is educated now on just how evil this embedded bureaucracy (the deep state) is in our government at all levels, and know they can't be trusted. *They ask if this is another ruse to crush individual liberties telling the people it is for their best interests to socially isolate while bankrupting them?* Is this another calculated evil agenda to usurp more rights while growing government at all levels and increasing taxes and bankrupting families? The question being asked by a disbelieving percentage of the public, *"Is this real?"* We are now in real time watching the perfect storm of an evil cabal to gain more control.

Heaven Has a Plan

However, the end result of this mess that we can't clearly see at the moment, is Heaven is exposing evil throughout the world. It is painful to go through, but necessary to get what Heaven has planned for humanity. Much good will come from this difficult time. All of the data points to a transitional spirituality now. Marian believers are largely of one mind: major changes are on the horizon. We are presently headed to a New Era, a New Pentecost, New Times, and a New Jerusalem. Each of these words indicate a change, and each has a slightly different meaning. It is not the end of the world as a skeptical detractor would say, but the end of an era. The collapse and restructuring of the world economy coupled with the desecration of the Church will have profound and long-lasting implications. This is all part of the Great Reset globalists have worked for generations. Out of chaos will come their new order.

The Blessed Mother through Father Stefano Gobbi of Italy as head of the Marian Movement of Priests on November 15, 1990, from Malvern, PA., gave a message to America called **The Hour of the Great Trial.** It partially reads, *"And now I announce to you that the hour of the great trial is on the point of arriving. The great trial has arrived for your country. How many times, as a concerned and sorrowful Mother, have I endeavored to urge my children to follow the path of conversion and of return to the Lord.... **You will know the hour of weakness and of poverty, the hour of suffering and defeat, the*** *purifying hour of the great chastisement. The great trial has arrived for your Church…. The great trial has arrived for all humanity."* (MMP #437)

We may get a glimpse of where we are now headed recalling that very powerful prophetic quote from then Father Ratzinger (Pope Benedict XVI, Emeritus), when he was teaching theology and philosophy in 1969 at Regensburg, Germany. The quote that follows was a commentary he made four years after the final session of Vatican II. It may have been an insight based upon his knowledge of history, a prediction as a philosopher, or a prophetic utterance. Nonetheless, here is what the young theologian said fifty years ago based upon what he saw.

"From the crisis of today the Church of tomorrow will emerge — a Church that has lost much. She will become small and will have to start afresh more or less from the beginning. She will no longer be able to inhabit many of the edifices she built in prosperity. As the number of her adherents diminishes, so it will lose many of her social privileges…." Father Ratzinger said that he was convinced the Church was going through an era similar to the Enlightenment and the French Revolution. He continued by saying, *"We are at a huge turning point in the evolution of mankind. This moment makes the move from the medieval to the modern times seem insignificant."* Professor Ratzinger compared the current era to that of Pope Pius VI who was abducted by troops of the French Revolution and died in prison in 1799. The Church was fighting against a force which intended to annihilate it definitively, confiscate its property, and dissolve religious orders.

"Today's Church could be faced with a similar situation, undermined by the temptation to reduce priests to social workers and it and all its work reduced to a mere political presence." Yet he also gave hope that *"a great power will flow from a more spiritualized and simplified Church."* This church, he said, *"will be a more spiritual Church, not presuming upon a political mandate, flirting as little with the Left as with the Right. It will be hard going for the Church, for the process of crystallization and clarification will cost her much valuable energy. It will make her poor and cause her to become the Church of the meek."*

Divine Mercy — The Hope — The Promise

As turmoil on many levels affects our lives, we are encouraged by the Lord through Saint Faustina in the prayers of the Divine Mercy Novena. On day seven in the Novena it reads:

"Most Merciful Jesus, whose Heart is Love Itself, receive into the abode of Your Most Compassionate Heart the souls of those who particularly extol and venerate the greatness of Your mercy. These souls are mighty with the very power of God Himself. In the midst of all afflictions and adversities they go forward, confident of Your mercy; and united to You, O Jesus, they carry all mankind on their shoulders. These souls will not be judged severely, but Your mercy will embrace them as they depart from this life."

In the concluding prayer of the Novena we are reminded where our trust is placed:

"Eternal God in whom mercy is endless, and the treasury of compassion inexhaustible, look kindly upon us, and increase your mercy in us, that in difficult moments, we might not despair, not become despondent, but with great confidence, submit ourselves to Your holy will, which is Love and Mercy itself. Amen" (Diary #950)

JESUS I TRUST IN YOU

12

I am the Mother of Mercy

There are decades when nothing happens,
and then there are weeks where decades happen.

Vladimir Lenin, Russian Communist

We have reached a point of a near lack of any civility toward those with opposing opinions from our own. It is uncertainty that breeds anxiety, and at the moment we have a heavy dose of uncertainty in the state, the Church, the family and the culture. When a man masquerades as a woman and calls himself a woman, and the Church and the state accept it, the culture has reached a new level of depravity. Tensions are high, and people are going to become more frayed in the coming months and years as we watch the demise of institutions that have worked reliably for a long time. Albeit, not perfect, but they functioned and served an intended purpose. On every issue, ideological sides are firmly dug in. Neither party will concede an inch to the other, and that is a recipe for civil unrest that could soon explode. One in three people feel a civil war is in our future. In addition, a recent poll says people are the most unhappy they have been in over fifty years. Gun sales have never been so brisk at nearly two million a month since Covid 19 hit.

The U.S. Supreme Court (SCOTUS) landmark decision (June 12, 2020) on granting LGBTQ rights based on sex discrimination is a further erosion of morals legislation and the Judeo-Christian heritage in the United States. GOP appointed judges Gorsuch and Roberts ruled with the liberals. It is very rare indeed to find a liberal justice go with a conservative decision on morals, but it is often the GOP court appointed judges swinging to the left. That itself is another topic on how and why this happens. There will be a renewed and venomous assault on Christian values with backing from this SCOTUS decision. Filings of liberal sex discrimination law-suits will soon explode. It will be relentless and formidable, and will further marginalize believers in all society. The ramification of this decision is another ugly chapter of American decline.

This is another extension of the June 26, 2003 United States Supreme Court decision of Lawrence v. Texas that ruled American laws prohibiting private homosexual sodomy acts between consenting adults are unconstitutional. Justice Antonin Scalia said, *"This was the end of morals legislation in America."* He was proven right.

What is the path forward for believers? How are we to navigate a society that is moving to darkness? Again and again we turn to Jesus through Mary. Jesus said, *"My kingdom is not of this world"* (John 18:36). A devout believer lives in a parallel universe from someone with no faith perspective. As believers, we can defy and suspend the laws of nature due to prayer. Heaven has given us the prescription for peace in troubled times, and at this point, we better jump on board and take prayer and quiet times more seriously if we are to keep our sanity. The tension in the air is palpable everywhere, and we need to apply spiritual principles we know to be true that work for peace of heart, mind, and soul. If we let others take our peace away, it is often our fault. Stress is a normal human emotion, but not letting interior peace dissolve is something we control through spiritual disciplines.

I am the Mother of Mercy

Many believers are presently paralyzed with fear due to recent world events. The single most common lament I hear believers say is they don't know what to do. Questions are asked, *"What am I to do? What is my role in these times? Do I take to the streets like Black Lives Matter and shout the gospel? I feel like nothing I do matters, so why bother? Do I shrivel up and just let the drama play out?"* There is a wide range of emotions about the times in which we live, so people are asking where to turn for the peace the Lord promises.

No one has done a better job at giving us a soothing balm for our path forward than the **Marian Movement of Priests** (MMP) from the messages of the Blessed Mother to Father Stefano Gobbi of Italy. Father Stefano Gobbi, founder of the MMP, was pressured from Vatican Cardinals to say his messages were only his reflections and/or personal meditations. It was a way to discredit him before the general public and fellow priests and take away the supernatural nature of his locutions. Father Gobbi would never say even at his death they were his own imaginations. The messages of MMP are a light in times of dense darkness to the world and to the Church. The messages of the MMP reflect the spirit of the age, and how people of God should spiritually respond.

Archbishop Carlos Vigano has spoken openly about the *"deep church"* and the insidious role of Freemasonry in the hierarchy having an agenda for a One World Church, and One World government. This is a herculean battle of the destiny of the Church going forward into the 21st Century. The **Deep Church** is the ecclesiastical version of the political **Deep State** and its entrenched bureaucracy. The Deep Church is at war with the people of God with an agenda of words and actions to undermine orthodoxy.

Archbishop Vigano and his writings are a breath of fresh air. People have been starving for a person in the Church to speak the unadulterated truth. The movement to discredit Father Gobbi was successful to some extent, but not with the *sensus fidelium* that were on sure footing with the authenticity of the Blessed Mother's messages to the world. Those that are Consecrated to the Immaculate Heart know what is true, and what is not. An individual consecrated and living the messages has a hedge of protection around them, and are secure they are under the Blessed Mother's mantle.

The weak from the strong are being filtered like the wheat from the chaff. Small communities are the next step for the faithful to congregate. House churches and small gatherings is where we may end up. We will see a remnant of approximately 3% stay in fidelity to Magisterial teachings in the coming years. We are seeing signs of this with Covid 19 as many people are not returning to church at all. As hardships increase, many on the margins will abandon practicing faith altogether. Those that do not understand the Divine Plan, will question God during this trial and many fall away as well. The Consecrated Soul sees this for what it is, and will endure the trial with much greater fortitude.

Below is a very succinct and cogent solution for a person struggling to find their place in the mystical body of Christ, and to feel assured they are on the right path going forward. The words are from the Blessed Mother concerning this exact point in history. Topics addressed are specific to dealing with events and trials of our time. She is saying, "Here is my prescription for peace of soul." The Blessed Mother speaks to us through the messages given to the MMP.

Rely on Me Alone, (MMP #37), February 10, 1974

"Rely only on me and not on human means; entrust yourself only to me. There is one thing that you can always do, and which is the only thing I want you to do at each moment, because it is so useful to me for the Movement: your prayer, your suffering, your trust in me.

*"This is what I ask of you: that you let yourself instead be divested of all other preoccupations. **This is not one of many movements, but it is my Movement,** my son. So then let me act!…*

"But I want the priests of my movement to be mine alone.

"If they do not accustom themselves now to seek me alone, to listen to me alone, and to entrust themselves to me alone, how are they going to find me at the moment of the great tempest when everything will be plunged into darkness? Let them accustom themselves as of now to see me as the light of their very action!"

Over the last several years those following the messages of the Blessed Mother are aware that embedded in the Third Secret of Fatima is the apostasy of faith. One does not need to look far to observe the free fall of morals and doctrine over the last generation. It has also greatly accelerated in just the last few years. Part of the confusion and anxiety people feel is the loss of a stable structure that has carried them forward in previous history. There are severe cracks in the foundation with doctrine that has never been questioned for two thousand years now in question from leading clergy and hierarchy. In addition, the public disagreements among hierarchy is a central message of Akita, Japan. It is the Woman Clothed with the Sun of Revelation 12, speaking to the Marian Movement of Priests that provided the solutions for the ills of the world.

The Pope of My Secret, (MMP #449), May 13, 1991

"When this Pope will have completed his task which Jesus has entrusted to him, and I will come down from Heaven to receive his sacrifice, all of you will be cloaked in a dense darkness of apostasy, which will then become general.

"There will remain faithful only that little remnant which, in these years, by accepting my motherly invitation, has let itself be enfolded in the secure refuge of my Immaculate Heart. And it will be this little faithful remnant, prepared and formed by me, that will have the task of receiving Christ, who will return to you in glory, bringing about in this way the beginning of the new era which awaits you."

This is in reference to Pope John Paul II who was a strong supporter of the Marian Movement of Priests. Father Gobbi concelebrated Mass with the Pope for many years on December 24 while both were living.

All Has Been Revealed to You, (MMP #604), December 31, 1997

After twenty-five years of public messages, this was the last public one ever given.

"In order to give the suffering and crucified Church of your time my motherly help and a safe refuge, I have brought the Marian Movement of Priests into being and have spread it through every part of the world by means of my book, which traces out for you the road along which you must journey in order to spread my light. With this book, I teach you to live the Consecration to my Immaculate Heart with the simplicity of children, in a spirit of humility, of poverty, of trust and of filial abandonment.

"I have now been guiding you for twenty-five years, with the words which I have spoken to the heart of this, my little son, whom I have chosen as an instrument for the realization of my maternal plan. During these years I myself have carried him several times to every part of the world, and he has allowed himself to be led with docility, small and fearful but totally abandoned to me, like a baby in the arms of his Mother.

"As of now, all that I had to say to you has been said, because all has been revealed to you.

"Therefore, on this night, there comes to an end the public messages, which I have been giving you for twenty-five years; now you must meditate

on them, live them and put them into practice. *Then the words which I have caused to come down from my Immaculate Heart, as drops of heavenly dew upon the desert of your life, so threatened by snares, will produce fruits of grace and holiness.*

"*From now on, I will manifest myself through the word, the person and the actions of this, my little son, whom I have chosen to be your guide and whom I am now leading to the painful summit of his mission....*

"**All has been revealed to you....**

"*I invite you to repeat often in the cenacle, the prayer that I have asked of you: 'Come, Holy Spirit, come by means of the powerful intercession of the Immaculate Heart of Mary, your well-beloved Spouse.'*"

You Will Have Them Walk Toward Me, (MMP #79), August 23, 1975

"*For my Movement of Priests, I will manifest myself through you; you are the instrument chosen by me for this mission. This must be understood by everyone in order to avoid any confusion whatsoever with which my Adversary will attempt to obscure my work. Those who will accept it through you will receive the gift of my most pure light....*"

The Task Entrusted to the Church, (MMP #337), October 27, 1986

"*[I]t is necessary that all men come to a knowledge of the truth and to accept and to follow the Gospel of Jesus.*

"*This is the task entrusted to the Church.*

"*That is what her ministers, her consecrated ones and all her faithful must do today: with the courage of martyrs and the strength of confessors of the faith, there is need to announce to the whole world the good news that Jesus Christ alone is your Savior and your Redeemer.*

"*Only Jesus Christ can bring you to Peace....*

"**The attempt to bring together all religions, even those which adore false and lying gods, with the prospect of forming a world-wide religious union for the defense of human values, is vain, dangerous and not in conformity with the desire of my Immaculate Heart. It can on the contrary lead to an increase of confusion, to religious indifference and even make the attainment of true peace more difficult.**"

Be Joyous, (MMP #83), October 18, 1975

"My adversary will one day think that he is celebrating a complete victory: over the world, over the Church, over souls.

"It will be only then that I will intervene — terrible and victorious — that his defeat may be all the greater when he is certain in his conviction that he has conquered once and for all.

"What is in preparation is so extraordinary that its like has never happened since the creation of the world. That is why everything has already been predicted in the Bible....

"First of all, it is necessary that my enemy have the impression of having conquered everything, of having everything now in his hands....

"Be serene: be joyful!!

*"This is not the end of my Church; what is in preparation is the beginning of its **total and marvelous renewal!**"*

There is tremendous hope in this message. The Lord never abandons His people, and the Scriptures are clear that the gates of Hell will never sink the Church. No matter how small the remnant, the Lord is faithful to those faithful to Him. That is the story of the Bible, whether it be about the 1% who fought with Gideon after being winnowed, just twelve apostles changing the world, or Saints Francis, Dominic and Ignatius as men starting world-wide movements in the dark ages of the Church on a vision and a prayer. God plus one is a majority, and we are called to be joyous at all times spreading the Gospel. The Gospel means the Good News. The Lord knows our situation, and He had difficult times when He walked the earth with people not believing His message either. Jesus said, *"If the world hates you, know that it hated Me before it hated you"* (John 15:18).

The awareness of the Consecrated Soul — A Soul of Faith

A person with a consecrated soul to the Immaculate Heart of Mary and Sacred Heart of Jesus has a heightened sense of spiritual awareness far beyond the person who has no faith. This is the yeast of goodness which brings an elevated sense of awareness with a deeper understanding of the times in which we live, and how we are to respond to the world around us, as God would ask. The physical world is subordinate to the spiritual realm. The person of faith sees the effects of sin in the culture, and where it brings us, through spiritual eyes, rather than just the eyes of intellectual reason. This is because a person of faith sees more of God's plan in the redemptive process of mankind. A person who lacks faith is blind to this reality. Therefore, they have a humanistic view, which lacks clarity to the wider circumstances of life. It is the person of deep faith or a consecrated soul that will understand more of these messages than one not consecrated. To the soul lacking spiritual formation, these messages are folly, and the hobgoblin of small minds. There is less fear and anxiety in a believer's life, because of the grace from consecration. Peace of soul is seeing God in all things, and dealing with the outcome.

The Prayer from the Blessed Mother to Cure Our Ills

There is nothing as effective as prayer to calm the nerves. It is the single most important part of our day to maintain a spiritual equilibrium balanced against the chaos surrounding us. The prayer of the rosary given to us is time tested as an exorcism prayer. Multiple hundreds of saints and scholars have recognized it as the prayer given from Heaven.

Your Rosary, (MMP #184), October 7, 1979

On the Feast of the Most Holy Rosary, October 7, 1979, at Lourdes, France, the Blessed Mother gave the Marian Movement of Priests a message titled, *Your Rosary.* It reads, *"By this prayer, you offer your heavenly Mother a powerful force in intervening for the salvation of many of my poor straying children and in disposing the painful events of your time according to the motherly plan of my Immaculate Heart.*

"Your entire rosary, which you recite in the cenacle in accordance with the urgent request of your Mother, it is like an immense chain of love and salvation with which you are able to encircle persons and situations, and <u>even to influence all the events of your time.</u>

"Continue to recite it, and multiply your cenacles of prayer, thus responding to the invitation which the first of my beloved sons, the Vicar of Jesus, has so urgently made to you.

"*I am now able to make use of the power that comes to me from your prayer and I want to intervene as a Mother* **to shorten the time of the trial** *and to comfort you in the sufferings which await you.*

"**Everything can still be changed** *if you, my children, listen to my voice and unite yourselves, through prayer, with the unceasing intercession of your heavenly Mother.*

"*For this reason, here, where I appeared as the Immaculate One, I ask you again to continue with greater generosity and perseverance in the recitation of the holy rosary.*

"**The rosary is the prayer which I myself came down from heaven to ask of you.**

"*By it you are able* **to lay bare the plots of my Adversary;** *you escape from many of his deceits; you defend yourselves from many dangers which he puts in your way; it preserves you from evil and brings you ever close to me, because I am able to be truly your guide and your protection.*

"*As has already happened in other critical situations, so also today, the Church will be defended and saved…through the power which comes to me from you, my little children, by means of the frequent recitation of the holy rosary.*

"**Take courage, beloved children! Pray, have confidence and enter into the refuge of my Immaculate Heart, that you may form part of my victorious cohort.**

"**This is my hour and soon the whole Church will be brought to a new splendor by her whom you invoke as Queen of Victories.**"

Heaven has given us the prayer for peace of soul, yet few do it as instructed. Countless hours are spent in restaurants, coffee shops, and iPhones discussing the plight of our times, but very few pray and provide solutions.

A Glorious Future Awaits Us — The Hope

On the Feast of the Solemnity of Pentecost, Our Lady gave us a glimpse of the new life that will become the Church. In the first Cenacle of Jerusalem, the Apostles and disciples were transformed by the descent of the Holy Spirit at Pentecost. The second Pentecost will be accomplished in the spiritual cenacles of Mary's Immaculate Heart.

Tongues of Fire, (MMP #546), June 4, 1995

"Tongues of fire will bring heat and life to a humanity which has now become cold from egoism and hatred, from violence and wars. Thus the parched earth will be opened to the breath of the Spirit of God, which will transform it into a new and wondrous garden in which the Most Holy Trinity will make its permanent dwelling place among you.

*"**Tongues of fire** will come down to enlighten and sanctify the Church, which is living through the dark hour of Calvary and being stricken in her pastors, wounded in the flock, abandoned and betrayed by her own, exposed to the impetuous wind of errors, pervaded with the loss of faith and apostasy.*

"The divine fire of the Holy Spirit will heal her of every malady, will purify her of every stain and every infidelity, will clothe her again in new beauty, will cover her with his splendor, in such a way that she may be able to find again all her unity and holiness, and will thus give to the world her full, universal and perfect witness to Jesus.

*"**Tongues of fire will come down upon you all, my poor children, so ensnared and seduced by Satan and all the evil spirits, who, during these years, have attained their greatest triumph. And thus, you will be illuminated by this divine light, and you will see your own selves in the mirror of the truth and the holiness of God. It will be like a judgment in miniature, which will open the door of your heart to receive the great gift of divine mercy.***

*"And then the Holy Spirit will work **the new miracle of universal transformation** in the heart and the life of all: sinners will be converted; the weak will find support; the sick will receive healing; those far away will return to the house of the Father; those separated and divided will attain full unity.*

*"In this way, **the miracle of the second Pentecost** will take place. It will come with the triumph of my Immaculate Heart in the world."*

"The One Who Prays is Not Afraid of the Future, And the One Who Fasts is Not Afraid of Evil."

Our Lady Queen of Peace at Medjugorje, January 25, 2001

JESUS I TRUST IN YOU

13

The Forgotten Lessons Of Nuremberg and The New World Order

We know they are lying.
They know they are lying.
They know that we know they are lying
We know that they know that we know they are lying.
And still they continue to lie.

Alexander Solzhenitsyn

I recently saw a favorite film again for the nth time (it is one of those films you have to watch when it comes on), and again it brought back lessons from history mankind unfortunately needs to relearn every several generations. The lesson is, if truth and virtue are skipped for a generation, vice will rear its ugly head the next generation to repeat the negative cycle of state abuse.

The film is the 1961 Oscar award winning classic *Judgment at Nuremberg*. It is a fictional account of the story of the trial in 1947-48 in Nuremberg, Germany of Nazi war criminals for their atrocities against humanity during World War II.

This film had an all-star cast with Spencer Tracy as the presiding American judge, Judy Garland as a wrongfully abused woman at the hands of the Third Reich, Burt Lancaster as the great German judge of his day, Richard Widmark as the allied prosecutor, Maximillian Schell as the German defense attorney, and Marlene Dietrich as the widow of an executed general, and other luminary actors. This film is a lesson of history.

The time prior to the rise of Hitler and the aftermath of the war has been well documented and little is left to tell as it has been told so many times before, but, there is one very poignant scene that has amazing relevance to

Americans today. At the end of the movie, Burt Lancaster, as the famous German judge Janning now found guilty of collaborating with the Nazis, asks to see the judge (Spencer Tracy). The judge reluctantly obliges the request going to Janning's cell with his hat in his hand as he is homeward bound. Janning says to him, *"By all that is right in this world, your verdict was a just one."* Referring to the mass murder of innocents, Janning asks him to believe that, *"I never knew it would come to that."* The judge then says, *"Herr Janning, it came to that the first time you sentenced a man to death you knew to be innocent."* Janning stares stone faced with simultaneous shock at the logic of the reply.

When America legalized abortion at the Supreme Court of the United States we sealed our fate as a nation. The blessing left America that very hour and day in the eyes of Heaven. Christina Gallagher was told by the Blessed Mother the sins bringing down judgment on the country are the killing of the innocents (abortion), the immoral abuse of the innocents, and the sacrifice of the innocents to Satan. They are sins against nature itself. When we legalized abortion we condemned our nation. The slaughter of the innocents is paramount to the destiny of a nation. It is like an umbrella blocking out the rain and sunshine, precluding God's blessings because of sin.

Solomon said, *"Nothing is new under the sun"* (Eccl. 1:10). The lessons of Israel and Yahweh's blessings and chastisements to His people are the biblical narrative over millennia. If Israel sinned in a modest way of disobedience there would be a Heavenly rebuke. If the sin continued in a more egregious fashion, the rebuke would be more dramatic with consequences for His chosen people. That is the mystery and the reality of the Jewish people throughout the covenanted history of the nation of Israel. The same applies to the gentile nations. Sin has consequences. *"It has been your sin that has separated you from God"* (Isaiah 59:2). God does not punish, but we enable the devil to intervene in our lives because of our sin. Sin clouds the intellect and graces are precluded from operating. Mortal sin is just that, it is mortal to the mind, body, and soul. **It has probably been some time since you have heard the words "mortal sin" from a pulpit.**

The battle we see today in the streets, classrooms, and in our neighborhoods is ultimately a spiritual one. Satan first said he would not serve. And so it plays out in the culture today. The numbers of those who are trying to adhere to a moral code according to scriptural dictates continue to shrink as the years go on. It is unbeliever vs. believer as so many times in history. The story today is a similar one just with different names and dates than the past, as history repeats itself. There is war in the streets because there is war in our hearts. *"Unless the grain of wheat falls to the ground and dies, it cannot bear fruit"* (John 12:24). Until there is submission of our will to the Will of God, we will not see fruit as a nation.

It is estimated that approximately 95% of the liberal press is unchurched. Being unchurched illustrates a mindset of who is your master. Going to church will not assure that person will sit at the right hand of the Father upon death, but it does show there is a disposition to God and His precepts and statutes — and an affinity for ideology to His laws. Who are you trying to follow? Many in the liberal press are at best agnostic and many are atheist. If they are not outright unbelievers, they are often practical atheists in their views and lifestyle. It is not consistent to call yourself a believer and vote for abortion or transgender acceptance. In 1922, five years after the Bolshevik Revolution it was asked of the babushka (in Russian this means old hat, but loosely translates to old woman) in the streets of Moscow, *"How did this happen?"* Her three-word response was as profound as it was simple, *"We forgot God."*

America is at the same point today as empires of the past, which is why we find ourselves in this moral quagmire. Historians with little knowledge of Scripture or philosophy, do not realize that it is the Lord who raises a nation up because of fidelity to Him, and brings a nation to its knees because of sin. That is the more accurate way to interpret the rise and fall of civilizations. Due to their lack of knowledge, it is an ignored fact of history to interpret it as just a mere historical cycle. That is the underlying ebb and flow of cultures and great civilizations.

The great historian Will Durant, and the author of the eleven volume *Story of Civilization,* opined in late age in his book Lessons of History, *"Great empires do not die from an enemy without, but they commit suicide."* The decline is always from within. America is presently committing suicide. People speak of democrats and progressives like Biden as bad moral leaders. The greater threat is the millions that walk among us who endorse their pagan policies. That is far more to fear for the general welfare of the nation knowing the threat of this immorality. It is actually being propagated by an unsuspecting, gullible and foolish electorate that have been so dumbed down, they believe these immoral leaders — and follow them blindly.

The biggest mistake conservatives make is thinking progressives will negotiate and act in good faith. They do not act in good faith for the best welfare of the nation. You can see just how aggressive the democrats are today. They are not socialists, but communists, and they want everything to do with the Divine completely removed from the culture.

Radical Changes in Our Midst

Believers are fighting for survival and must now stand up and be heard or we will end up like Nazi Germany or the former USSR under Lenin and Stalin. If that sounds extreme look at the progress they have made in recent years and especially since the Covid 19 state tyranny began. It is not a time to be passive in any way. Now is the last-ditch effort to proclaim the truth without fear. People must realize what is called the democratic party is not democratic at all. The most virulent of the agenda is by democrats, but many Republicans are on board with the agenda of global government. It is the 21st Century version of the American Communist Party (ACP). They are out to fundamentally destroy the United States as it has been in the past. The most fundamental goals are to deconstruct the U.S. Constitution and all that implies. This means the glue that kept the Constitution alive for two hundred thirty-four years is being destroyed at this moment in time. Their social agenda for years is saying there are too many people on the planet and the way to deal with it is to reduce the population of the world. Not understanding their goal of depopulation precludes someone from understanding plans like the Global 2020 Agenda, that is now the 2030 Agenda. Moving the date to 2030 enables a devotee to have a long-range vision for change.

Satan is out to destroy God's people and even creation itself. The kill shot planned years in advance was Covid 19 and all the plans implemented since its inception. The unseen enemy of a virus has given the State the ability to employ abusive tactics for more control. It is the perfect storm. Every day is another insane agenda item that gets traction because communists are relentless. Dr. Anthony Fauci is on record wanting to "give the jab" to children as young as six months! One day the goal is to pack the Supreme Court with four more progressives, then D.C. statehood, then to force vaccine shots on the mentally incapable. It won't end. This tyrannical agenda has police raiding churches but allowing sports and other special interests to gather in large numbers without interference.

The primary target of control from the beginning has been churches and the freedom of assembly to worship. All totalitarian regimes look to crush people of faith first because they are independent thinkers who do not look to the state for their salvation as secularists do. The United States has been the beacon of hope for the world as the longest living constitution in world history. A radical element in Congress has taken control pushing a godless heinous ruinous agenda hellbent to destroy the Republic and Christianity itself. The Vatican is far removed from historical orthodoxy and deeply complicit in promoting world government. As in ages past, it has lost its way. It has been deeply infiltrated by leftist communists and masonry for several generations. The Holy See is also making itself a servant of the godless New World Order. This must be understood if one is to know what we are fighting.

Words have meaning. The LGBTQ and migration/immigration movement have said they learned their tactics from the abortion rights movement to never give an inch and always be aggressive with goals. The globalists have an agenda to radically transform the landscape to a one-party system using immigration. Immigration is the weaponization of the political process to end a conservative vote ever having meaning. Its goal is to end all dissent for communist control by a cabal of evil elitists which is now called the Deep State. It is an organized masonic agenda to virtually collapse the country from within to bring in new godless global governance.

Judging by the political views of elected officials in Congress today, it is working. Billions are going to promote this agenda in the new $1.9 trillion stimulus bill. Hitler, Stalin, and other tyrants didn't appear overnight. There was silence in the land for decades before their rise. Nor has the tyranny in our midst today happened overnight.

Frederic Bastiat, the French philosopher and statesman who lived in the aftermath of the French Revolution summed it up best. *"When plunder* becomes a way of life for a group of men in society, over the course of time they create for themselves a legal system that authorizes it and a moral code that glorifies it."

Outside the Auschwitz prison camp was a sign that read, **"When they came for the mentally handicapped, I said nothing. When they came for the infirmed, I said nothing. When they came for the Jews, I said nothing. When they came for me, there was no one left to speak. Signed, a Catholic priest."** Either speak now, or you will lose your voice for several generations.

"Give ear to my words O Lord, give heed to my groaning. Hearken to the sound of my cry, my King and my God, for to thee do I pray. O, Lord in the morning thou dost hear my voice; in the morning I prepare a sacrifice for thee, and watch. For thou are not a God who delights in wickedness; evil may not sojourn with thee. The boastful may not stand before thy eyes; thou hate all evildoers. Thou destroyest those who speak lies; the Lord abhors bloodthirsty and deceitful men. But I through the abundance of thy steadfast love, will enter thy house. I will worship toward thy holy temple" (Psalm 5:1-7).

Psalm 5 — Trust in God for Deliverance from Enemies

RESIST.   RESIST.   RESIST.

JESUS I TRUST IN YOU

14

The Banality of Evil

Then Pilate said to Jesus, "So you are king, are you?" Jesus answered, "You say that I am king. For this I was born, and for this I have come into the world, to bear witness to the truth. Everyone who is of the truth listens to my voice." Pilate said to Him, "What is truth?" After saying this he went back out to the Jews and told them, "I find no guilt in Him."

John 18:37-38

It is difficult to participate in nearly any conversation today with several people or more when differing outlooks will arise quickly on nearly any subject. The group will soon have sharp differences, too often downright derisive and hostile. People of all backgrounds are now shaking their heads in amazement how the culture has devolved so quickly. But did it happen so quickly or was it generational? No one seems to have an answer to what can be done to turn the present situation around to a more civil discourse — with workable solutions. Problems appear so large right now, there doesn't seem to be an answer politically or spiritually. Or even a pathway to middle ground. Many leaders in all spheres of influence compromise quickly and are on the take, and will go with the highest bidder. It is how evil has flourished and been so widespread. How did we end up here where so many feel we are at a hopeless, depraved, and reprobate state of existence?

In January of 1838, when Abraham Lincoln was only 28 years old, he addressed a gathering in Springfield, Illinois with the following; *"From where shall we expect the approach of danger? Shall some trans-Atlantic military giant step the earth and crush us at us a blow? Never. All the armies of Europe, Asia, and Africa combined... could not by force take a drink from the Ohio River or make a track on the Blue Ridge in the trial of a thousand years. At what point then is the approach of danger to be expected? I answer, if it ever reach us, it must spring up among us. It cannot come from abroad. If destruction be our lot we must ourselves be its author and finisher. As a nation of freemen, we will live through all time, or die by suicide."*

Lincoln made that speech 13 years before the firing on Fort Sumter, Charleston Harbor, South Carolina on April 12, 1861, which is considered the start of the Civil War. What was a violent act on Fort Sumter released the pent up anger of people that had festered for generations. Founding Father John Adams said at the signing of the Declaration of Independence, the final act of the signing would be the abolition of slavery. It took another 89 years for the Civil War to end to have the abolition of slavery at least legislatively codified.

The pent-up anger and frustration was also seen in the explosion of the French Revolution and shortly after the Reign of Terror, as well as the Bolshevik Revolution. Out of that chaos came profound societal changes. None could argue the abuse of the monarchies of the Sun Kings of France and the Czars of Russia. Today, we have arrived at this point exactly like previous empires. A simple spark could ignite a conflagration like we haven't seen domestically since 1861.

The Banality of Our Times

The word banality means something devoid of the freshness of originality, trite, or commonplace. The most common phrase people use for the direction of the country is **insane.** Everyone says what it is happening is **insane.** There are also a hundred other synonyms for what is happening and they are all correct. Choose nearly any governmental policy and the word **insane** is applied by any person who is logical or rational. Maniacal thought would be another description of our times.

I have tried, especially since the onset of Covid, to come up with a common denominator for what types of people do not go along with the experimental injection (some call it vaccine) and other abhorrent policy programs. There are a few obvious possibilities. They would be conservative, believers in general, church goers, daily communicants, devoutly religious, Bible believing evangelicals, people who understand the U.S. Constitution, consecrated souls, etc. However, none of those fit the bill entirely, although they may be partially correct or even totally correct for some. There just doesn't seem to be a clean definition of why some people seem to **"get it"** and others don't see what is happening in front of them. It is as if the Holy Spirit informs people, and some listen. It is baffling why divergent opinions are so intense when data clearly supports that the "vaccine" is deleterious to health. Nothing is more evident than people who understand the experimental injection and its ramifications, and those who don't. It is a clear line of demarcation for nearly everyone and no family I know of is spared. A gas station attendant asked a patron coming in to put on a mask, and the person shot him. Yes, there is tension in the culture, which will get far worse when there is more economic hardship from the permanent loss of jobs caused by ill-considered government mandates. This will foment a two-tiered economic system. Will the denial of services for those who have not gone along with the mandate increase? Will the experimental injection mandate in the military force out conservatives? Is it designed to do this? One size doesn't fit all, especially for those who have had the virus and now carry natural immunity.

The former head of the U. S. Food and Drug Administration (FDA) and Harvard Professor Dr. Herbert Ley said in 1969, *"The FDA protects the big drug companies, and is subsequently rewarded, and using the government's police powers, they attack those who threaten the big drug companies. People think that the FDA is protecting them. It isn't. What the FDA is doing, and what the public thinks it is doing are as different as night and day."* That was said in 1969, and today the FDA is far more compromised than it was then. Big Pharma runs the organization and dictates its policies. **The FDA and the CDC are wholly owned subsidiaries of Big Pharma,** gaining billions each year in patent royalties.

The common denominator for me has been reduced to people who **"get it"** are people who seem to have an innate understanding of evil and how it operates.

Those not going along with the mandate have an understanding there is a nefarious agenda in government.

There is also the flip side of that coin and the question could be asked, are the people advocating these policies evil? The answer for me is yes and no. I believe there are people on top of the hierarchy who are evil and have willingly given themselves over to Satan and other evil humanistic philosophies. We know many in the upper echelons of business and entertainment speak of it. In the Church it is more subtle. Many in the hierarchy are severely compromised and have been man pleasers, and became captive to power and political influence through high level masons. Over time they became bureaucrats rather than men of God. They wanted wealth and power and were willing to do what was necessary to achieve that end, following the path of the German populace in 1930's Germany. Compliance was consent.

However, for most all the rest, the road to perdition is more banal. I was sent an article by a friend that helped me come to the conclusion that evil nor good is a conscious choice for the vast majority of mankind. Hannah Arendt, wrote a series of articles for the New Yorker which became her book called, *Eichmann in Jerusalem: A Report on the Banality of Evil* (1963). Eichmann had been a chief player in what Germany called The Final Solution, which was the extermination of Jews in Europe during the war. Arendt was a German secular Jew who fled Germany in the 1930's, and went to live in New York City, escaping the carnage of World War II.

Upon the capture of Adolf Eichmann in Argentina by Mossad agents in 1960, Arendt went to the trial to see Eichmann in person to explore how such evil could exist. She said she needed to see it firsthand to try to understand it. Arendt, a world class political theorist, had written extensively on the origins of evil. She had taught at Princeton, Columbia, Chicago, and in California, among other schools. Some of her major works were *The Origins of Totalitarianism* (1951), about the roots of Stalinism and Nazism; *The Life of a Jewess* (1957), which is considered a semi- autobiographical story of the destruction of the German Jewish culture in Germany; and *The Human Condition* (1958), which researched social issues as they affect a society's actions.

She has many similarities to Ayn Rand in her background and perceptions, and few personal religious views were central to her formation and thinking. Her conclusions were surprising to many people, yet very insightful. Arendt said, *"The sad truth is most evil is committed by people who never make up their minds to be good or evil."* Even after seeing the totalitarian regimes in Germany personally this was her conclusion.

Arendt expressed how disturbed she was by Eichmann, but not for obvious reasons. She didn't see a man with smoke coming out of his ears spewing fire with a pitchfork in his hand. She said she saw *"A terrifyingly normal bland bureaucrat who carried out his murderous role with calm efficiency not due to an abhorrent, warped mindset, but because he had absorbed the principles of the Nazi regime so unquestionably. He simply wanted to further his career and climb the ladder of power. He embodied the dilemma between the unspeakable horror of the deeds and the undeniable ludicrousness of the man who perpetrated them. His actions were defined not so much by thought, but the absence of thought,"* convincing Arendt of the banality of evil. She concluded, *"Evil is perpetuated when immoral principles become normalized over time by an unthinking people. Evil becomes commonplace, it becomes the everyday. Ordinary people — going about their everyday lives — become complicit actors in systems that perpetuate evil. We live and think not in isolation, but in an interconnected web of social and cultural relations, a framework of shared languages, behaviors, and shared conventions and we are conditioned by them every single day."*

To understand the German thinking one would have to go back to what the youth had been fed in an endless program of godless ideology through the educational systems. From youth they were introduced to Georg Hegel (1770-1831) which bred in them the idea of a superman ideal. The German thought of the Aryan principle emerged and grew from that. Hegel greatly influenced Friedrich Nietzsche, Karl Marx, and Friedrich Engels. Coupled with the idolized German giant Nietzsche (1844-1900), there emerged the antichrist that helped birth the Nazi movement. The superman and the antichrist merged into a national outlook that became the ideal of the National Socialism (which was not socialism) of the Third Reich and the Nazi Party. Germany didn't happen in a vacuum, but over several generations of godless indoctrination. Nietzsche had greatly influenced Sigmund Freud, Jean Paul Sartre, Martin Heidegger and many other nihilists. The truth of Christ was absent from the people that most influenced the Germans as a prelude to the atrocities of the 1930's and 1940's.

In other words, Arendt, got a lot right, but didn't highlight sufficiently the origins of the mindset instilled in all German students from a very young age. Here is where Arendt is similar to Ayn Rand. Both were articulate on the culture, but couldn't hit the nail on the head of the quintessential reasons for the decline of thought that produces heinous behavior. And most importantly the cure. She herself was a product of that culture, but knew enough to get out before the carnage fully erupted. Eichmann and a nation of citizens like him had been programmed not to think anything other than that statism was the zenith of existence. *In times of mass conformity, it becomes a revolutionary act to speak the truth.* In our time the bizarre has become the normal, and is generally accepted by the electorate. People fall into line to avoid conflict, go along to not disturb employment, make lifestyles paramount, and never understand the government agenda of depopulation.

The United States and the western world are identical to the citizens of Germany in the 1930's. In the West, we are now at the point of state-run radical fascism like the Nazi Party in the 30's. Compliance of good people not speaking up and resisting from the beginning was the cause of Germany's downfall. In the United States, we are witnessing intentional acts to dismantle government for a new, godless, Nazi-like regime. Many have recently written how the United States is comparable to the fall of Rome, but at least in the end, Rome had good roads.

If one thinks this view is extreme, they have not been paying attention to the corrupt generational and incremental erosion of freedoms and liberty. Government in excess breeds fascism. The people have seen the corrupt practices of Congress when they legislate laws where they are exempt. Congress and their staff are exempt from Obamacare and the vaccine mandate. The Center for Disease Control (CDC), the FDA, and the judiciary, are also exempt from the vaccine mandate. When a governing body exempt themselves from laws they promulgate, the people are not governed but ruled. This is how communists govern. What's good for me is not good for thee.

When people see this duplicity, all reason to abide by law is lost as people perceive the double standard of "do as I say not as I do." If the policies are so good, why are they exempt from the laws they write? They exempt themselves simply because they can.

Our situation today is similar to the German Reich. Government today has an agenda to strip the truth of Jesus Christ from the culture. **It is no**

mistake we have so many mindless people blind to the truth. We arrived here the same way the German populace did and will end the same way unless there is a national repentance. The sinful nature of man can only be adequately articulated clearly though the truth of the cross. *"The lust of the eye, the lust of the flesh, and the pride of life"* (I John 2:16).

The root of the problem is the failure to correct the lower nature of man with the purity of the gospel message. *"My sheep hear my voice and I know them, and they follow me"* (John 10:27). To pursue true justice is to follow Christ and obey His commands. The godless utopia of the left is not attainable on earth as long as there is Original Sin. When the gospel is stripped from the culture, it is only a matter of time and degree when chaos becomes the norm. The bizarre becomes the new normal. The abnormal then becomes more bizarre day after day. Revolutions start when economic hardship is so prevalent the people see no way out but to go to the streets. We are increasingly approaching that day.

The totalitarianism of evil germinates when the population seeks safety in anonymity thinking there will be a refuge for them. It is the direct opposite. A great portion of the population is seeing the truth with the lies of government. Either join the people now speaking the truth or your liberty and freedoms will be a concept of the past. Time is short as the relentless push of the godless is so aggressive and virulent. Thomas Jefferson, who had witnessed the French Revolution while in Paris, said, *"When tyranny becomes law, rebellion becomes duty."* Also, an oft used phrase is, **"The only thing necessary for the triumph of evil is for good men to do nothing."**

St. John Paul II said on the advent of this current millennium: *"But let us end on a note of hope and call all Christian believers to beg the Lord Jesus **to save us from this present darkness."***

"The great Jubilee to be celebrated at the end of this Millennium and at the beginning of the next ought to constitute a powerful call to all those who worship God in spirit and truth. *It should be for everyone a special occasion for mediating on the mystery of the Triune God, who in Himself is wholly transcendent with regard to the world, especially the visible world"* (Dominum Vivifocantem #54).

As the Blessed Mother said at Fatima in 1917, *"In the end my Immaculate Heart will triumph."*

JESUS I TRUST IN YOU

15

I Just Followed Orders

Evil comes from a failure to think. It defies thought for as soon as thought tries to engage itself with evil and examine the premises and principles from which it originates, it is frustrated because it finds nothing there. That is the banality of evil.

Hannah Arendt, Eichmann in Jerusalem

My previous article, *The Banality of Evil,* when first published seemed to have hit a nerve and there was a great deal of response as I related Germany to the United States today. When Hannah Arendt's book *The Banality of Evil* was published on the Eichmann trial it became a firestorm of controversy, especially in the Jewish community, and she became a pariah in many Jewish circles. She was in essence excommunicated in many intellectual settings. It was the word banal that most objected to. However, many people missed the nuance of her message as they gave a cursory overview of the book without understanding her reason for the word in the title. Jews who had endured the holocaust from near or afar didn't see it as banal. Many felt she wasn't forceful enough. The fact was she got it correct. Her explanation of what happened in Germany, and what we are seeing in the United States today, have much in common, in my opinion. At the trial she expected to see Eichmann as a man with fire coming from his nostrils, smoke from his ears, and horns in his head, holding a pitchfork (my words).

However, what she saw was a **"bland bureaucrat"** who simply went along to go along, where he could climb the ladder of power for a good career. For him it was emotionless and career advancement. Eichmann saw nothing that he did as pernicious or evil. Many leaders in the Third Reich thought they would be memorialized in history as great statesmen with monuments constructed in their honor. They said so, and were that delusional. It is career advancement and the love of money that often turn men into such monsters as they abandon questioning the morality or ethics of their actions.

The Banality of Evil deals with many moral and social issues. It is striking how it resembles the moral side in the Christian West over the last generation. Arendt speaks about the relentless pursuit of efficiency of the German population, how the German Jews were often complicit to follow orders from a godless hierarchy of leaders, and how so few Germans in general spoke up to stop the tide of corruption many saw coming. The sense of normalcy blinded many from seeing where events were moving — then and now. Eichmann's accomplices in his crime were ordinary German citizens aiding the corruption. At trial, Eichmann said he *"felt guilty before God but not before the law,"* as before the Nazi legal system he had not done anything wrong. Eichmann stressed he had been an obedient servant of the state and didn't want to go against the mandates of the state. Arendt writes about Eichmann, *"What Eichmann failed to tell the presiding judge in cross-examination was that he had been an ambitious young man who had been fed up with his job as a traveling salesman even before the Vacuum Oil Company had been fed up with him. From a humdrum life without significance and consequence the wind had blown him into history, as he understood it; namely into a Movement that always kept moving, and in which somebody like him — already a failure in the eyes of his social class, and of his family, and hence in his own eyes as well — could start from scratch and still make a career"* (page 33).

Arendt writes what few will grasp in its significance and its ultimate pinnacle of power and authority behind the scenes. Operating in stealth and deception, it works by promoting recruits who will do exactly as they are told by superiors without questioning directives due to career perks that come with blind obedience. It is Freemasonry. Arendt seems to be saying that Eichmann's rise to power was loyalty to the State and Freemasonry.

She writes of this power, (*"Incidentally, an eagerness to establish museums commemorating their enemies was very characteristic of the Nazis. During the war several services competed bitterly for the honor of establishing anti-Jewish museums and libraries. We owe to this strange craze the salvage of many great cultural treasures of European Jewry).* **The trouble was that things were very, very boring, and he was greatly relieved when, after four or five months of Freemasonry, he was put into the brand-new department, concerned with Jews. This was the real beginning of the career which was to end up in the Jerusalem courtroom"** (page 37).

Again, for the readers of Signs of the Times and our articles, there has been a consistent theme on this subject for nearly thirty years. Arendt is clear, Eichmann's demise came about from his unquestioning loyalty to the authority of the state and his superiors. She makes the direct connection to his rise from the ash heap of a listless lackluster career with no future to one of promotions, prestige, authority, financial largesse, and stature. All was enabled and fast tracked by Freemasonry.

The most common phrase of the war criminals at trial was **"I was just following orders."** Therein lies the issue of our day. We see it all around us. It is all about career advancement rather than being a voice for truth. A robotic compliance with godless directives from a neopagan state. Being a voice speaking against the tide of filth, error, and moral injustice to go along, and not interfere with career advancement is the work of the weakling. The righteous with a conscience and virtue are being purged from the ranks of employment in industry, military, government, and other disciplines for non-compliance against a godless state in its many forms. The incompetent will see greater rise and promotion in this transition as moral talent departs. Left in the ranks will be mindless bureaucrats void of courageous free thinkers for freedom, and expressions of conscience. It is this compliant group that will now be promoted, and rewarded financially for "going along." The S.S. of Hitler attracted that person because they had already purged those who dissented, and the mediocre and depraved assumed, by attrition, positions of leadership. After the war the entire nation had a common cry. Citizens and military alike said they didn't know what was happening in their country. For those left in the United States will it be people saying, **"I just followed orders?"** The complicity is bigger than just an experimental serum that is a gene altering injection (many incorrectly call it a vaccine).

This lack of courage and ethics in our social policies has destroyed families at all levels of government, to our smallest institutions. It has been percolating now for generations. It is not just about this present hour of the injection of this experimental serum. It has been several generations of government overreach and abuse by tyrants in leadership positions pushing an agenda of godless policies. All the while many people sat back and didn't see where this would lead the nation. It has been everywhere at every level that has brought us to today, with government intrusions stripping personal liberties and freedoms.

Removing prayer (1962) and the Bible (1963) from U.S. schools by order of the United States Supreme Court sealed our fate as a nation. That is just shy of sixty years ago for an agenda to evolve, and we see what is happening now. Three entire generations of not wanting God in our culture. What we are witnessing today is a direct result of abandoning God. If one doubts that, look what we have become. This did not happen overnight. This demise has been incremental, where sin went unchallenged and the body became so diseased it lost all life. We have become desensitized as a nation because of sin. Whether it be critical race theory, gender identity, vulgar behavior in its many forms, family break up, the church and people refusing to speak with courage, or confusion in the culture as a whole, it **can be narrowed to one thing, and that is sin.** When we point a finger at someone who didn't speak up, remember three fingers are pointing back at us. We are here because the voice of silence has been tacit consent. Sin became a subject that was rarely addressed, but it is the root of the cultural depravity around us. We forgot God. It is that profound and that simple in those three small words. Pundits on TV will talk all day and night about the problems, but not a one will provide a solution. Any talking head can identify the problems, but it is only Jesus Christ who provides solutions to the sinful lower nature of man.

Words to describe the public and private policies of the United States today are tyranny, totalitarian, diabolical, Satanic, depraved, reprobate, dictatorial, maniacal, dystopian, godless, fascist, insane, lunacy, crazy, unbalanced, demented, bizarre, mentally deranged, irrational, psychotic, mad, and a litany of other words that no longer really resonate with our psyche since they are used so often. They don't seem to relate any longer to our intellect. The madness has now penetrated to our souls. Evil has taken on a new and much larger dimension. The state of depravity and reprobate nature of our slide to Sodom is picking up speed. If schools want to teach the history of LGBTQ in our classrooms, they may want to first study Sodom and Gomorrah and ask why it was destroyed.

I have heard on numerous occasions from friends that they never understood how the German and European populace stayed so silent in the rise and entrenchment of Hitler and the Third Reich. They say they now understand. They have watched many stay silent in light of such abuse by government with so many complacent, thus, complicit people. If you ever wondered if you would have spoken up in 1930's Germany, think no more if you have remained silent on the large moral issues of our day and not spoken against them. Sitting back and watching the decline in nearly every social milieu was more the norm than the exception.

Government is not an esoteric entity. It is made up of your neighbors, colleagues, and people in your church. The communists upon taking over, first took down the nation's symbols of its history and the church. They need to eradicate the past to bring in the new. This is exactly what we are seeing today. Liberty and freedom will most certainly be expunged unless you begin to speak — and act in righteous indignation before fascist tyranny makes the choice for you. The principal agent totalitarian governments use to incubate change is intimidation and fear. Public relations has taught us controlling the narrative is enough to have the desired result, and in this instance it appears to be in total control. The use of intimidation and fear are used to frighten the people to make a decision against their will. After generations of brainwashing children in government indoctrination centers (public schools) they now have an older population that bought the lie. The communists learned long ago, controlling schools was the key for long term change. They have largely succeeded. The globalists took over the U.S. education system in the 1930's with John Dewey using Soviet principles with great success. We are now in great peril, and close to the precipice.

The unbeliever is not able to discern spiritually where a nation is headed. Most don't have the spiritual sensitivity to understand what the Lord is saying to the culture. Unbelievers have darkened intellects and are largely incapable of shedding the light the Lord asks. It is for this reason Jesus said, *"You are the salt of the earth"* (Matt. 5:13). Salt in all history until the modern era of refrigeration was a valued commodity. It was more precious than gold and often used as money, as food would rot without it. Mariners couldn't sail without it. The believer creates stability in a society, not the pagan. Without believers, chaos would be the norm. Because the believer's voice has not been heard in the market square for so long, it is precisely for this reason we are watching deterioration and rapid decline.

The coronavirus lockdown made people take pause and listen more to alternative news. Many no longer subscribe to the globalist media campaigns of propaganda which has been a benefit. There is now greater involvement than in the past. It took a crisis for them to engage. People, having less alternatives for entertainment and socializing, have been enabled to evaluate their lives, and how they have been fed a steady stream of lies over the years. This was one positive aspect of slowing down. Absorbing information they would normally not have heard with busy lives made them more aware. A major benefit of study and silence in the quiet of corona being home more often was people saw evil being exposed on a more widespread basis. As a result, more people are speaking out fearlessly, and finding their voice against tyrannical mandates and abhorrent government policies of every kind. This is very encouraging and must continue.

JESUS I TRUST IN YOU

16

The Strategy that Destroyed the Church and State, but the Gates of Hell Will Not Prevail Against It

The American people will never knowingly adopt socialism.
But under the name Liberalism, they will adopt every fragment
of the socialist program until one day America will be a
socialist nation without knowing how it happened.

Norman Thomas, Socialist Party, and U.S. Presidential candidate in the 1940's

If history has taught us one thing, it is that words have meaning. Words then translate into movements, that in time often become policies of nations—whether they be good or bad. In previous generations it would have been unthinkable to imagine the national debates now taking place in the United States. Flagrant lunacy is now on the table as national domestic initiatives by the democratic party in the United States. We will discuss that it is not democratic in any way, but an agenda by another name.

The discussions among American people of all backgrounds today would have been in the past a script from *The Twilight Zone*. Narrated by Rod Serling in the late 1950's and early 60's, it was popular for several years on American television, and it was about the absurd and the bizarre. However, much of it was based on real stories. We are now living in real time, *The Twilight Zone*.

Since Machiavelli and Antonio Gramsci, few have been as effective for evil in our modern culture as Saul Alinsky and George Soros. Machiavelli gave the world a prescription for the means justifying the ends with his book *The Prince*. In other words, win followers, but have your goals and end game in mind. The philosophy is, *"Say and do what needs to be said no matter who you are with to further your agenda."* The left has penetrated all religious denominations in America using this formula. Antonio Gramsci was co-founder of the Italian Communist Party. After visiting Moscow in 1922, he was clear in his writings that the Bolshevik Revolution would ultimately fail because it was too violent for the Russian Christian soul.

Gramsci then devised another path to socialist control. He came up with a plan after being thrown into prison by Mussolini. Il Duce (Leader) feared Gramsci could become more popular than him, and a threat to his dictatorship so he incarcerated Gramsci on his return from Moscow. Writing in his prison notebooks, Gramsci made the plan for socialism more satisfactory than revolutionary communism, and easy to follow because it was not as violent. It was more palatable to the citizenry, along with radical revolutionary people wanting change in Italy. Gramsci's was a plan to infiltrate places of power from within, keep your agenda quiet, and overtake the system informing no one other than close confreres of your collaborative intent. Gradual incrementalism was his answer to violence in the street, and key to take over institutions of power and authority.

Gramsci's ideas spread. In England they were adopted by the Fabian Society. It is for this reason that the London School of Economics in Surrey, England, a hotbed of Fabianism, has as its symbol the turtle. One must remember, the turtle beat the rabbit in the race. Also, the library at LSE was gifted a stained-glass window featuring prominent Fabian society members of the early twentieth century hammering out a new world order beneath a wolf in sheep's clothing. To a believer, this is a despicable thought, but to a revolutionary, it is admirable, and a means to an end. To the socialist/ communist, it is a highly laudable plan of action, and for many generations now, followed by them. At this point in time this highly effective and virulent anti-Christian strategy has been effective in the takeover of academia, government at all levels, the Church, and the entire culture; all having been infected with communist thinking. The Judeo-Christian foundation of our country is gradually sinking due to institutional longitudinal rot and fighting for its life. Western Civilization and Christianity itself are hanging by a thread.

When a culture gets to this depraved and reprobate phase, the present era will pass away — and a new paradigm begins. When a man calls himself a woman and vice versa, and the government actually embraces and supports that ideology, and persecutes another who won't submit to its thinking, we have reached a low level of sanity. This has been the plan of the modern-day Bolsheviks, and what is known as the Democratic party. Their plans have been highly codified, organized, and well-funded by the radical left. America is swiftly moving towards communism, not socialism.

Archbishop Fulton J. Sheen wrote about communism and said, "*Whenever a civilization begins to die morally and spiritually, then there begins to appear vultures. Communism is a scavenger of a decaying civilization. It makes its way into a country and into a culture only when that culture begins to rot from the inside.*" The church has become so infected with this infiltration, it is a mere shell of its former majesty. Capturing the hierarchy was key for the communists as all clergy was subject to them under the vow of obedience.

Bella Dodd, Saul Alinsky, & George Soros – The Continuation of Evil

In the early 1950's Bella Dodd was a ranking official in the Communist Party of America, who had been raised a Catholic and was welcomed back into the Church by Archbishop Fulton J. Sheen. In her autobiography, **School of Darkness,** Dodd writes extensively about her thinking as a communist, and her transition to Christianity.

As an insider to the inner thinking and actions of the American Communist Party, (ACP), after the depression years of New York, she had a unique view, and was articulate on the agenda of the communist party. Speaking before the U.S. Congress in the 1950's she gave testimony how the Communist Party had infiltrated the Roman Catholic Church. She said, "*In the 1930's we put eleven hundred men in the priesthood in order to destroy the church from within. Right now they are in the highest places in the Church.*" In her autobiography she spoke about being expelled from the Communist Party. For something as simple as reading any book not approved by the Party, you would be watched. If a book was not in conformity to Party ideology, it would not be allowed to be read or on the shelves in New York headquarters. (See Sign.org for Dodd's book). Sound familiar with the tech giants of today censoring Christian books in all forms of social media?

In a lecture at Fordham University Dodd said, "*In 1944, there was a national convention for the Communist Party, which I was elected to the national committee openly in Madison Square Garden. During that convention there were many people that came from all over the United States. One of the social events I attended was a dinner given by Alexander Trachtenberg, who is a known socialist, graduate of Yale, millionaire,... who is head of the publishing firm for the communists. At the end of that evening, Trachtenberg rose and made a little speech. He said, 'When we get ready to take the United States we will not take it under the label of socialism. These labels are unpleasant to the American people, and have been spared too much. We will take the United States under labels we have made loveable. We'll take it under* **liberalism,** *under* **progressivism,** *under* **democracy.** *But take it we will.'"*

According to Dodd, a particular target the communists had to destroy was Senator Joe McCarthy because of his investigations into communist activities in the U.S. Hollywood then aligned with Saul Alinsky for a full-scale assault to destroy his reputation. A few years after the McCarthy hearings, the government released the Venona Files which substantiated and verified what McCarthy had said was correct. Hollywood and the U.S. Department of State had been at that time the most infiltrated with communist activity. McCarthy developed an alcohol addiction, and died prematurely at just forty-eight years old.

Saul Alinsky (1909-1972), a hardened atheist, in his **Rules for Radicals,** picked up where Machiavelli, Gramsci, and other communists left off. His book was a manual for creating chaos, and as Sun Tsu's *Art of War,* it is based on deception. It was precise in methods to be used, which was just one reason for its popularity. Alinsky's social programs were heavily funded by Catholic prelates who were deceived and thought they were helping the poor, but were in reality doing the direct opposite. The Catholic Campaign for Human Development (a USCCB Program) is a movement created by Alinsky that morphed very quickly into a social justice program void of Christian teaching. It was a Trojan Horse approach to infiltrate many Christian denominations, particularly the Roman Catholic Church on which Alinsky focused. The Catholic Church was too organized, too large, and too powerful to openly confront, so a page was taken out of the Masonic playbook of the French Revolution. Infiltration from within the Church became the method to remold it to their vision. The Catholic Church had to be eliminated to bring about their dystopian communist agenda, and the turtle, and not the rabbit, was their animal of choice.

The designers planned their coup using church hierarchy as Lenin's useful idiots. It was a horizontal approach to the gospel message of man to man without a vertical approach to God. The first three commandments became irrelevant to the left. To control the narrative, they did not want God in the discussion. The social justice programs we see so prevalent today are an outgrowth of how effective Alinsky and others have been with their stealth approach. Alinsky worked with close friend and confidante Monsignor John Egan of Chicago. For fourteen years Notre Dame University was their base of operations. Appearing as the sheep to help the poor in the Church, their agenda was to socialize the Church without Catholics being aware they had been taken over. A little sedation at a time was the prescription until they fall asleep.

In Jacques Maritain's *The Peasant of Garonne* (1966), the celebrated Catholic philosopher and theologian called Alinsky *"an authentic revolutionary and one of my closest friends... an indomitable and dreaded organizer of people's organizations, and an anti-racist leader with methods that are as efficacious as they are unorthodox."* Today, there are over 800 Alynskian type programs throughout the United States alone, wreaking havoc on the intellectual landscape of youth on what it means to be a disciple of Christ.

Alinsky's group think was called *The Open Society*. Continuing another iteration of chaos, and becoming the de facto standard bearer of chaos, confusion, and evil, was/is George Soros. Soros adopted the same name for his umbrella organization — *The Open Society*. Today Soros has several hundred leftist programs which he funds under the innocuous name of *Media Matters*.

Socialism and communism look good on paper to a college freshman philosophy student; however, there isn't a single success story in world history — anywhere. Communism brings destruction and ruin wherever it rears its ugly head.

To bring about change and end this thinking, people must understand words have meaning, and when nonsense is spoken, people must speak against it with prudence and calm. Proverbs says, "A gentle answer turns away wrath." It will be love and humility that will win people over. The battle we face is between good and evil, and we must recognize that, and use the tools Heaven has given us to defeat evil. Speaking against error is essential so others will have the courage to speak up.

JESUS I TRUST IN YOU

17

A Collision of World Views — Blessings or Cursings

The thief comes to steal, kill, and destroy, but I have come to give you life, and give it more abundantly.

John 10:10

America is under the judgment of God. The Transition that is taking place is bringing the world to a New Era, a New Epoch of Time, and that is a concept spoken about for many years by leading mystics and scholars in the Catholic Church. Not the end of the world as people would have it who often mock derisively an individual with a biblical belief, but a place it has never been before. Being a believer today is not acceptable in many venues. There is at present a global shift and transformation of how people view religion today, and the animus towards Christianity is becoming more virulent. Quite simply, Heaven has told us that we are living in the end times — the end of an evil era. Cardinals Sarah and Burke have also said this over the last several years. Emotionally charged, this concept, incredible as it is, divides people.

The word of God does not change, but some may say this is an Old Testament concept that is no longer relevant. However, Scripture tells us, *"Jesus Christ is the same today, as He was yesterday, and as He will be forever"* (Hebrews 13:8). One does not need to look very far in the Old

Testament, New Testament, or history, to see that nations, families, and people experience positive or negative repercussions as a result of virtue or sin. God does judge nations much to the chagrin of progressives and liberals who deny the very existence of God. Don't expect to get truth from the agnostic, unchurched press. It is impossible to avoid the onslaught of immorality we get bombarded with daily by these folks. Do we think we will get the wisdom of God listening to their views? Like it or not, this is where most people get information. If you want to know what a person thinks, you only need to ask where they get their news. Not that going to Church makes everyone a saint, but it does show there is a desire to first seek the things of God.

Due to our abysmal disregard for sin in today's culture, few can recognize the signs that a nation is even under divine judgment. The intellectual will often view events solely through the eyes that history repeats itself in cycles and this is true. What they fail to recognize, is that it is God who raises up a nation and brings another down. It is the blessings of God which bring forth fruit to a nation, and it is the Lord who commands its destiny.

The reasons for our anxiety are numerous, but there is one main reason why we lose peace of soul: it is because we have become separated from God. Isaiah says, *"It has been your sin that has separated you from God"* (59:2). As a nation, we have left the spiritual for the temporal in profound ways over the last several generations. Economics trumped spirituality much in the same way the people of Germany chose Hitler as leader because on paper he gave them a way out of the morass of what happened in World War I. The Weimar was a time of economic desolation for Germany, so they chose a leader with a vision, even a godless one. The entertainment craze in our midst is only one area that has led people to think they don't need God due to the continuous distraction it provides. Sports and entertainment has submerged the things of God to where faith and belief are no longer welcome in many places. The Sabbath is often ignored to provide more time for Sunday sports, errands, and chores. Has God turned His back on us? No, it is we who have turned our back on Him.

Your View of the World — Or God's Eternal View of the World

No matter where one turns, there is general discontent. Everyone knows in their gut something is wrong. The reason is quite simple — we forgot God. The ramifications of how God has been ignored, mocked, and vilified are playing out around us and wreaking havoc in our homes, neighborhoods, and workplace. The end result is that few of us feel safe anymore. The security of living under God's protection is not there, as there has been wholesale spiritual abdication of our responsibilities.

There are few topics or social indices today that are functioning as designed. No matter the profession today, many people see what is happening around them is not working. This is not a question of seeing the glass as half full; it is seeing the reality of what has happened in the last several generations and how we as a country have drifted so far from the Light of Divine Truth.

Few know what to do as they feel helpless against this Leviathan of reckless government. Many don't see a realistic solution for what ails us. Political pundits and writers of social commentary continue to look at the problems of the U.S. with great clarity and diagnosis. However, they rarely if ever see that the root issues to the problems are moral, not political. Few propose a viable solution. Some refuse to clearly see that adherence to moral guidelines is what makes a nation civil and good. Know this, it starts in our homes and schools. If you are in some Catholic high schools today (especially Jesuit run), you are probably learning more about Buddha and Islam than Jesus Christ. It is no wonder the kids are lost as they are not taught the rubrics and fundamentals of the faith. Some students are being taught to be social activists rather than disciples of Jesus, led by Scriptural doctrine. Social activism must branch out from the heart of what Jesus is asking of us to go make disciples, not social workers. Activism must be borne from a life of prayer and discernment. Saint Teresa of Calcutta was always clear that she was not a social worker, and the strength and growth of her sisters came from Eucharistic Adoration. She often said the work was not possible without a Holy Hour every day.

People now see the support groups and social structures that they have become so acquainted and familiar with over the last several generations disintegrating around them. If one looks for what may be a genesis when

America lost its innocence, it could be the day President John F. Kennedy was shot. Then came Viet Nam. The day of unlocked cars and unattended purses had passed. No one was safe from the onslaught of a nation on its way to control by a firmly embedded liberal bureaucracy hell bent on removing God — everywhere. People no longer see a safety net supporting them as families, schools, and neighborhoods experienced in previous generations. A sound nuclear family is now in the minority, and people do not have the support they once had. If one has been reading the financial news over the last several years, a major shift took place recently where the greatest financial gurus who have lived their whole lives in the financial sector are now speaking in language that was unimaginable for them to say in public years ago. They are using apocalyptic language as they describe where the world monetary system is headed.

This has taken place in previous civilizations and many have ended up on the ash heap of history. It is actually a very simple answer when broken down to the simplest element. When the Holy Spirit is extinguished from a culture, then it is left to its own devices. The culture is not sufficient to maintain order without God as its foundation. Jesus said about believers, *"You are the salt of the earth"* (Matt. 5:13). Salt is a preservative, and when the salt is not present, society collapses into disorder. When Jesus used the metaphor, people understood this as they would starve without salt as a preservative. Remove the believer from society, and you will have a breakdown quicker than anyone could imagine. This is precisely what we are seeing now as we slide so quickly into moral and civil chaos.

Saint Paul in Romans speaks how people are given over to depraved minds absent of God. He says, *"In other words, since they refused to see it was rational to acknowledge God, God has left them to their own irrational ideas and to their monstrous behavior"* (Romans 1:28). Once the light of the Holy Spirit is extinguished, there is no light, truth, or wisdom. Don't expect logical rational thinking from a government that is out of control and given over to depraved behavior. The believer must make a transition that it is not business as usual, and there is a huge shift taking place as the Lord is doing away with the old, to usher in the new. It will be disruptive.

Social Indices That No Longer Function as Designed

Governments at all levels are leveraged and broke. Social Security is being used as a giant Ponzi scheme by the Federal Government. Social Security Disability Income (SSDI) is being used as long term unemployment rather than a temporary program. Union and state pension plans are severely underfunded by billions, and the welfare program is so broken no one knows how to repair it. Job insecurity is at nearly every level. People on Food Stamps have formed a permanently unemployed class of people. An inordinate number of vaccines are being forced upon young children by a Federal government, and broken and godless public school system bullies young mothers. We have other issues including: the controversy of global warming, excessive government regulation destroying initiative in nearly every area of living, currency wars, drones, extreme weather and natural phenomena eroding Federal, State, and municipal budgets across the land. There are 100 year droughts, 100 year cold, 100 year rain depending on the part of the world you live. The elderly are losing all types of funding that were reserved for them after a lifetime of saving. Tax payers are forced to fund abortions as sanctioned and paid by the government. A prison system is bursting at the seams. A banking system is over $170 trillion in debt when one looks at derivatives and other fancy financial instruments no one understands, but the bankers are taking fees from them. There are approximately 100 million Americans not working for valid and invalid reasons, and Governor Cuomo of New York said that conservatives and pro life people have no place in politics in his state (yes, a Governor said it). We are a country that has lost its way.

The list will stop lest you look for a ledge to jump from, as the purpose of this article is to show clearly we have drifted so far from what the Lord is asking of us. As Dorothy said in the Wizard of Oz, *"Toto, I don't think we're in Kansas anymore."* The sooner we realize we need trust and hope in the Lord's plan, the sooner we will personally achieve peace of soul, and civility will be restored to the nation. Coming to this realization is a very difficult thing to do. Know this, the social and financial structures are not going to get better any time soon. It gets worse before it gets better, and making an adjustment in your personal and spiritual life is the key to grasp what Heaven has been doing during this time of Transition in the world.

As the babushka said, *"We forgot God."*

Much more could be said here, but the point is made that changes are coming at us due to disobedience to the commandments. In the near future they will come at us like box cars one after another, and if we don't have a well developed spiritual life, then we will at best struggle, and at worst perish. At this point, we must realize we are beyond human solutions for fixing these momentous societal problems.

Below is Chapter 28 of Deuteronomy in its entirety. It is called *The Blessings and the Cursings of a Nation*. It is not happy talk that all is fine, because things are not fine. There are several things to take note. The first 14 verses are the blessings. Notice how simple one blessing is and the benefit to all who receive it. There is a protective hedge around that nation that observes the laws and statutes of God. There are only 14 verses where all live in relative prosperity and peace — and quite simple to understand. In verse 15 there is a radical departure to the famous *"if then"* clause. There is a requirement to obedience for God's blessings. There are many preachers who teach the "prosperity gospel" that have a very good message on hope, trust and faith. However, with this repeated message of God's blessings and how we deserve them, little is ever mentioned about obedience or sin. This continual message soon becomes hollow. Very little is ever mentioned on how to deal with suffering, and its role in our lives.

Embracing the cross to endure the dark night of the soul is avoided and considered negative to this crowd. It is as if God is a cosmic bell-hop who is meant to send financial delights on a whimsical prayer to Heaven. Does God want us to live in a state of poverty? No, I think not. But living in extravagance is another matter. In this chapter we see the repercussions of sin and how every area of life is affected because of it. IF, there is repentance as when Jonah walked through Nineveh, then there can be restoration. But today, few speak of repentance. After King David sinned with Bathsheba and had her husband Uriah killed by sending him to the front lines in battle, the Lord said it would be the next generation that would cost his son the kingdom of Israel. Sin has consequences.

After verse 15 comes the cursing of a nation which then continues for another 54 verses. The blessings are so general and easy, yet the cursings are lengthy. The Lord's ways are always easy as Jesus said, *"My yoke is easy, and my burden is light"* (Matt. 11:30). Just 14 verses of blessings, and 54 nauseating verses of cursing. The Lord can be specific to correct His people if necessary as mankind has seen throughout history.

Do you see anything here that has happened to America as we have turned our face from God? You decide.

Deuteronomy 28

1. *But if you faithfully obey the voice of Yahweh your God, by keeping and observing all his commandments, which I am laying down for you today, Yahweh your God will raise you higher than every other nation in the world,*

2. *and all these blessings will befall and overtake you, for having obeyed the voice of Yahweh your God.*

3. *You will be blessed in the town and blessed in the countryside;*

4. *blessed, the offspring of your body, the yield of your soil, the yield of your livestock, the young of your cattle and the increase of your flocks;*

5. *blessed, your basket and your kneading trough.*

6. *You will be blessed in coming home, and blessed in going out.*

7. *The enemies who attack you, Yahweh will defeat before your eyes; they will advance on you from one direction and flee from you in seven.*

8. *Yahweh will command blessedness to be with you, on your barns and on all your undertakings, and he will bless you in the country given you by Yahweh your God.*

9. *From you Yahweh will make a people consecrated to himself, as he has sworn to you, if you keep the commandments of Yahweh your God and follow his ways.*

10. *The peoples of the world, seeing that you bear Yahweh's name, will all be afraid of you.*

11. *Yahweh will make you abound in possessions: in the offspring of your body, in the yield of your cattle and in the yield of your soil, in the country which he swore to your ancestors that he would give you.*

12. *For you Yahweh will open his treasury of rain, the heavens, to give your country its rain at the right time, and to bless all your labours. You will make many nations your subjects, yet you will be subject to none.*

13. *Yahweh will put you at the head, not at the tail; you will always be on top and never underneath, if you listen to the commandments of Yahweh your God, which I am laying down for you today, and then keep them and put them into practice,*

14. *not deviating to right or to left from any of the words which I am laying down for you today, by following other gods and serving them.*

15. **But if you do not obey the voice of Yahweh your God, and do not keep and observe all his commandments and laws which I am laying down for you today then all these curses will befall and overtake you.**

16. *You will be accursed in the town and accursed in the countryside;*

17. *accursed, your basket and your kneading trough;*

18. *accursed, the offspring of your body, the yield of your soil, the young of your cattle and the increase of your flock.*

19. *You will be accursed in coming home, and accursed in going out.*

20. *Yahweh will send a curse on you, a spell, an imprecation on all your labors until you have been destroyed and quickly perish, because of your perverse behavior, for having deserted me.*

21. *Yahweh will fasten the plague on you, until it has exterminated you from the country which you are about to enter and make your own.*

22. *Yahweh will strike you down with consumption, fever, inflammation, burning fever, drought, wind-blast, mildew, and these will pursue you to your ruin.*

23. *The heavens above you will be brass, the earth beneath you iron.*

24. *Your country's rain Yahweh will turn into dust and sand; it will fall on you from the heavens until you perish.*

25. *Yahweh will have you defeated by your enemies; you will advance on them from one direction and flee from them in seven; and you will be a terrifying object-lesson to all the kingdoms of the world.*

26. *Your carcass will be carrion for all wild birds and all wild animals, with no one to scare them away.*

27. *Yahweh will strike you down with Egyptian ulcers, with swellings in the groin, with scurvy and the itch, for which you will find no cure.*

28. *Yahweh will strike you down with madness, blindness, distraction of mind,*

29. *until you grope your way at noon like a blind man groping in the dark, and your steps will lead you nowhere. You will never be anything but exploited and plundered, with no one to save you.*

30. *Get engaged to a woman, another man will have her; build a house, you will not live in it; plant a vineyard, you will not gather its first-fruits.*

31. *Your ox will be slaughtered before your eyes and you will eat none of it; your donkey will be carried off in front of you and not be returned to you; your sheep will be given to your enemies, and no one will come to your help.*

32. *Your sons and daughters will be handed over to another people, and every day you will wear your eyes out watching for them, while your hands are powerless.*

33. *A nation hitherto unknown to you will eat the yield of your soil and of all your hard work. You will never be anything but exploited and crushed.*

34. *You will be driven mad by the sights you will see.*

35. *Yahweh will strike you down with foul ulcers on knee and leg, for which you will find no cure — from the sole of your foot to the top of your head.*

36. *Yahweh will send away both you and the king whom you have appointed to rule you to a nation unknown either to you or to your ancestors, and there you will serve other gods, made of wood and stone.*

37. *And you will be the astonishment, the byword, the laughing-stock of all the peoples where Yahweh is taking you.*

38. *You will cast seed in plenty on the fields but harvest little, since the locust will devour it.*

39. *You will plant and till your vineyards but not drink the wine or gather the grapes, since the grub will eat them up.*

40. *You will grow olive trees throughout your territory but not anoint yourself with the oil, since your olive trees will be cut down.*

41. *You will father sons and daughters but they will not belong to you, since they will go into captivity.*

42. *All your trees and the whole yield of your soil will be the prey of insects.*

43. *The foreigners living with you will rise higher and higher at your expense, while you yourself sink lower and lower.*

44. *You will be subject to them, not they to you; they will be the ones at the head, and you the one at the tail.*

45. *All these curses will befall you, pursue you and overtake you until you have been destroyed, for not having obeyed the voice of Yahweh your God by keeping his commandments and laws which he has laid down for you.*

46. *They will be a sign and a wonder over you and your descendants for ever.*

47. *For not having joyfully and with happy heart served Yahweh your God, despite the abundance of everything,*

48. *you will have to serve the enemy whom Yahweh will send against you, in hunger, thirst, lack of clothing and total privation. He will put an iron yoke on your neck, until he has destroyed you.*

49. *Against you Yahweh will raise a distant nation from the ends of the earth like an eagle taking wing: a nation whose language you do not understand,*

50. *a nation grim of face, with neither respect for the old, nor pity for the young.*

51. *He will eat the yield of your cattle and the yield of your soil until you have been destroyed; he will leave you neither wheat, nor wine, nor oil, nor the young of your cattle, nor increase of your flock, until he has made an end of you.*

52. *He will besiege you inside all your towns until your loftiest and most strongly fortified walls collapse, on which, throughout your country, you have relied. He will besiege you inside all the towns throughout your country, given you by Yahweh your God.*

53. *During the siege and in the distress to which your enemy will reduce you, you will eat the offspring of your own body, the flesh of the sons and daughters given you by Yahweh your God.*

54. *The gentlest and tenderest of your men will scowl at his brother, and at the wife whom he embraces, and at his remaining children,*

55. *not willing to give any of them any of his own children's flesh, which he is eating; because of the siege and the distress to which your enemy will reduce you in all your towns, he will have nothing left.*

56. *The most refined and fastidious of your women, so refined, so fastidious that she has never ventured to set the sole of her foot to the ground, will scowl at the husband whom she embraces, and at her son and daughter,*

and at the after-birth when it leaves her womb, and at the child to which she has given birth-

57. *she will hide away and eat them, so complete will be the starvation resulting from the siege and the distress to which your enemy will reduce you in all your towns.*

58. *If you do not keep and observe all the words of this Law, which are written in this book, in the fear of this glorious and awe-inspiring name: Yahweh your God,*

59. *Yahweh will strike you down with monstrous plagues, you and your descendants: with plagues grievous and lasting, diseases pernicious and enduring.*

60. *He will afflict you with all the maladies of Egypt which you used to dread, and they will fasten on you.*

61. *What is more, Yahweh will afflict you with all the plagues and all the diseases not mentioned in the book of this Law, until you have been destroyed.*

62. *There will only be a small group of you left, you who were once as numerous as the stars of heaven. For not having obeyed the voice of Yahweh your God,*

63. *just as Yahweh used to delight in making you happy and in making your numbers grow, so will he take delight in ruining you and destroying you. You will be torn from the country which you are about to enter and make your own.*

64. *Yahweh will scatter you throughout every people, from one end of the earth to the other; there you will serve other gods made of wood and stone, hitherto unknown either to you or to your ancestors.*

65. *Among these nations there will be no repose for you, no rest for the sole of your foot; there Yahweh will give you a quaking heart, weary eyes, halting breath.*

66. *Your life ahead of you will hang in doubt; you will be afraid day and night, uncertain of your life.*

67. *In the morning you will say, "How I wish it were evening!", and in the evening you will say, "How I wish it were morning!", such terror will grip your heart and such sights you will see!*

68. *Yahweh will send you back to Egypt, either by ship or by a road which I promised you would never see again. And there you will want to offer yourselves for sale to your enemies as serving men and women, but no one will buy you.*

69. *These are the words of the covenant which Yahweh ordered Moses to make with the Israelites in Moab, in addition to the covenant which he had made with them at Horeb.*

You be the judge if America is under judgment for disobedience.

JESUS I TRUST IN YOU

18

A Set Back for a Set Up — Finding the Silver Lining Today

A man does not yield when the mere universe has turned against him, he yields when his own heart has turned against him. We surrender, not when circumstances are miserable, but when we are miserable.

G.K. Chesterton

I was recently sent something that I have not been able to get out of my mind. I suspect after reading it, you won't be able to either. It is a story that few will know. It is from the book, *Reflections on Pearl Harbor* by Admiral Chester Nimitz.

After the December 7, 1941 bombing of Pearl Harbor, President Franklin D. Roosevelt paged and spoke to Admiral Nimitz. Roosevelt told Nimitz he would now become Commander of the Pacific Fleet and wanted him in Hawaii.

On Christmas Day 1941, Nimitz took a boat ride around the massive destruction of Pearl Harbor. Row after row he saw sunken vessels of every size. The entire fleet was in deep despair and discouragement. Nimitz later told the story there was so much depression that the people he spoke to felt as if the Japanese had already won the war. After the boat tour of the harbor, a young helmsman asked the Admiral what he thought.

The response shocked him and everyone else as it was not what they expected to hear. Nimitz said, the Japanese made three of the greatest errors an attack force could ever make. Nimitz explained:

Mistake Number One: *"The Japanese attacked on Sunday morning. Nine out of every ten crewmen of those ships were ashore on leave. If those ships had been lured to sea and been sunk — we would have lost 38,000 men instead of 3,800."*

Mistake Number Two: *"When the Japanese saw all those battleships lined in a row, they got so carried away sinking them, they never once bombed our dry docks opposite those ships. If they had destroyed our dry docks, we would have had to tow every one of those ships to America to be repaired. As of now the ships are in shallow water and can be raised. One tug can pull them over to the dry docks, and we can have them repaired and at sea by the time we could have towed them to America. And I already have crews ashore ready to man those ships."*

Mistake Number Three: *"Every drop of fuel in the Pacific theater of war is on top of the ground in storage tanks five miles away over that hill. One attack plane could have strafed those tanks and destroyed our fuel supply."*

"That's why I say the Japanese made three of the biggest mistakes an attack force can make. God was taking care of America." In the middle of disaster, Admiral Nimitz saw the silver lining.

No matter how you look at the above statements Nimitz was an optimist. Although he professed no outward religious affiliation, he had a view that God would work things out. Roosevelt had chosen the right man for the job. This is something we need more of today than ever before to see God's hand in our country. It is bleak at the moment as evil has such a stronghold, but it will take a person of faith to see God's hand in what is happening. We will only really see what God is doing in retrospect. The wheat is separating from the chaff and the sheep from the goats. We now know where people stand on many moral issues, and people of faith know who is with them and who is against them. There is little neutral ground on most social issues today. This is spilling over into who we congregate with, and where we spend our time, energy, and resources.

Covid Forced Us to Slow Down
and Think on a Deeper Level

The pandemic forced many people to sit more in silence at home and reflect where they are headed. The cultural demise has been a factor for many to reassess their lives and level of involvement and what they are open to read. Many who had not explored news outside the mainstream press, began reading alternative news. They are reading other reliable news stories outside the globalist controlled mainstream media fake news. The pandemic has forced people to slow down, and this is a good thing. It took a crisis for people to evaluate their spiritual priorities as yesterday's normalcy has slipped away to a distant thought. The evil being perpetrated on humanity by a global elite working on a depopulation agenda was unthinkable just a few years ago. But it was an agenda that was being carried out in stealth. If one is observant and open, it can no longer be denied. The chaos has made people choose which side of the fence they wish to fight, and fight for what they truly believe lest our way of life end as we have known it. Many have given greater thought to the spiritual part of life which is a fruit of Covid. The Lord can turn a negative into a positive as we have seen so many times in Scripture. Just one story is how Joseph became a slave after his bothers left him for dead in the bottom of a pit, and he rose to exalted heights in pharaoh's Egyptian kingdom. Joseph saved the Hebrew nation from starvation. **A major set-back became a set-up for the future, unknown at the time to Joseph and his brothers.** As a result of Joseph's position, the young Hebrew nation was saved. *The Lord can use negative circumstances for His greater glory, and I do think we will see the same in time with our present circumstances.*

At some point it has to come down to what is our response in this time of trial? Over the years I have become more interested in the subject of what we speak is what we get in life. The concept of *"speaking faith"* is talked about frequently by mature and young Christians alike. One can tell immediately what frequency the person is listening to depending on what they say. When a person speaks, they speak either faith or doubt as it relates to the word of God. Out of the abundance of the heart, the mouth speaks. There are two sides to this expression of faith—the false and the real, the genuine and the fraudulent imposter. One is real the other isn't, because the Lord sees the motives of the heart. Show me a person who is a hypochondriac (an excessive preoccupation with one's health), and you will often find a person who is frequently sick. This is entirely different than a chronic or serious illness. Yes, tending to your health is a necessity, but speaking negatively about your life all the time is the point. It is often the same with people who continually have bad fortune (some say luck). There is also a great deal of mystery around why some things happen and others don't, much like why some people are healed and others are not.

Much of the false teaching can be relegated to the television *"Pillow Prophets"* fund raising, giving the genuine faith dimension a bad name. The TV and mega church ministers often ask for a donation after telling the people they will get a hundred-fold in return to buy the new car, if they give right then, as they ask to pray over their wallets. Often these false prophets are living a lavish lifestyle at the expense of their congregation. However, there is a very real element of faith in action and how **we speak either Faith or Doubt.** Doubt and fear are Satan's domain, and faith and trust is when God works. Scripture is full of people speaking faith rather than doubt, and speaking faith is when seas part, and mountains fall into the sea. Miracles happen when faith is spoken.

The Scriptures have an enormous amount of material on this. Whether it be a major or minor prophet, the stories are similar as it concerns speaking faith to overcome natural circumstances. The biblical figures in Scripture are there because they acted in an extraordinary way. Laws of nature are suspended when the supernatural becomes a factor, and when God moves to alter an event for His glory. There is no end to the stories, but here are just a few reminders about how words matter in the faith realm.

Moses acted on the word of God to save a nation in exodus from Egypt, and parted a sea for safe passage because God told him to do it. Joshua came back from a scouting trip in Canaan speaking faith that the Israelites could conquer after the other ten spies reported, *"There are giants in the land."* Gideon won a battle with just 300 men after his army had been culled from 32,000. Yahweh was clear to Gideon that it would be Him who won the battle and not Gideon. Daniel was thrown in the fiery furnace and the fire did not consume Daniel and his three friends. Esther operated in faith to save her people from the wrath of an evil plot in the king's palace to exterminate her Hebrew people. With no food or water Esther and her companions fasted and prayed for three days, and her people were saved. *Natural law is suspended in times of great faith as it is subordinate to the supernatural and will of God.*

Chapter eleven of the book of Hebrews, I call the Hebrew Hall of Fame. It was written by Saint Paul and is forty verses in total. Verse after verse are brief descriptions or vignettes about major events in the lives of the giants of Scripture and their action. **By faith** Abel, **by faith** Enoch, **by faith** Noah, **by faith** Abraham, **by faith** Sarah, **by faith** Isaac, **by faith** Jacob, **by faith** Joseph, **by faith** Moses, **by faith** Elijah, **by faith** David, **by faith** Barak, etc. Note the language of *speaking events into existence by speaking faith.*

Moses is Told to Speak to the Rock

Scripture gives us the reason why Moses was not permitted to enter the Promised Land. It has been a source of confusion for many, but Yahweh gives an answer.

Moses had a unique distinction of seeing God fact to face and had an unusual relationship with Him. Towards the end of the forty years of wandering, in the Desert of Zin where there was no water, Yahweh instructed Moses to speak to a rock to bring forth water. Instead, Moses strikes a rock not once, but twice (Numbers 20:10-11, and Deut. 32:51-52). Moses did not do specifically as God commanded, and unjust as it may seem to us, it was a mistake that needed to be punished. God for His glory told Moses just to speak to the rock, not strike it.

The supernatural doesn't happen speaking doubt. Miracles, signs and wonders happen when people speak the supernatural. I am surely not putting Admiral Nimitz in the faith hall of fame, but he spoke faith and saw the silver lining of how God could prevail in a situation with his cooperation. There is a lesson in that for all of us about speaking doubt in times of stress like we are seeing today. God has a great plan; we just don't see at the moment how He will work. But, work He will for His glory.

Several verses on speaking faith are listed below. The bible is filled with this subject. The intersection of faith and speech are clear. You cannot express doubt and expect God to move in your life. **It is by faith God acts.**

The tongue has the power of life and death. (Proverbs 18:21)

As a man thinketh in his heart, so is he. (Proverbs 23:7)

If you claim to be religious, but don't control your tongue, you are fooling yourself, and your religion is worthless. (James 1:26)

Jesus Christ is the same yesterday, today and forever. (Hebrews 13:8)

The heart of the righteous weighs its answers, but the mouth of the wicked gushes evil. (Prov. 15:28)

But speaking the truth in love, we are to grow up into all aspects into Him, who is the head, even Christ. (Ephesians 4:15)

What goes into someone's mouth does not defile them, but what comes out of their mouth, that is what defiles them. (Matt 15:11)

A soothing tongue is a tree of life, but perversion in it crushes the spirit. (Proverbs 15:4)

From the mouth of the righteous comes the fruit of wisdom, but a perverse tongue will be silenced. (Proverbs 10:31)

I have made you the father of many nations — in the presence of the God in whom he believed, who gives life to the dead and calls into existence the things that do not exist. (Rom. 4:17)

Faith is the substance of things hoped for, on the evidence of things not seen. (Hebrews 11:1)

From Genesis 1:1 *"In the beginning"* to Revelation 22:20 *"Come Lord Jesus,"* the Word is speaking events into existence. It is the very story of the Bible narrative from beginning to end. The silver lining in difficult times is in your outlook and who you serve. **Obeying Our Lord and His commandments will bring you through any trial.**

In the book of Esther, there was a plot by Haman (his position was like a prime minister today) to kill all the Jews. Mordecai was an influential Jew in the king's court and Haman had erected seventy-foot gallows to hang Mordecai. Queen Esther fasted for three days and nights, and the Jewish people were spared. The Lord intervened to save the Hebrew people because he heard the cry of Queen Esther. The king saw the evil plot against Mordecai was false witness and the next day the king hung Haman on the very gallows he had built. Evil has a day, as we are seeing now. In the end God will win, and His people will be spared. We have to trust that God will hear the cry of His people against such an evil onslaught we are seeing today. Will the noose be turned on the evil doers of today as it was with Haman?

JESUS I TRUST IN YOU

19

A Battle of "The Time Of Times"

The true soldier fights not because he hates what is in front of him,
but because he loves what is behind him.

G.K. Chesterton

Since the Corona virus landed on the shores of the world and caused hardship to so many, I have been asked on numerous occasions, *"What do you think the Lord is saying?"* Not wanting to give a casual or cavalier answer to someone hurting, I start by saying there are only three ways to look at an issue. They are the way I see it, the way others see it, and the way God sees it.

There is only one truth that is indisputable and that is the light of the Divine Truth the way God sees it. Jesus said, *"I am the way, the truth, and the light, no one comes to the Father but through Me"* (John 14:6). He is true God and true Man. He was the only Man who came into the world with a plan to die for the salvation of mankind. He was also the only person who said he would rise from the dead — and did. Jesus is absolute truth, and there is never falsehood or error in Him. There are things we may not understand in their totality, but there is no error in the words of Jesus *"For now we see through the glass darkly"* (I Cor. 13:12). No man sees the totality of their being for our lives are a mystery no man can comprehend.

Over the last several generations, it is estimated there have been 50 million abortions, although no one really knows for sure. It is still estimated there are between 1,500 and 2,000 per day, and it must be remembered there are two people involved for every abortion. In recent years the number of surgical abortions has dropped largely due to chemical abortifacients, and the Plan B Pill. Anyone can go to their local drug store and get Plan B over the counter. We have thrown God out of the culture, mocked Him in every way imaginable in the public square, and by order of the United States Supreme Court, a Bible and prayer are not allowed in a public classroom. Now pornography is as ubiquitous for an eight year old with an internet connection as purchasing candy; heinous and diabolical curricula is taught to youth at all levels; an antichrist ideology is in the face of believers from waking to bedtime; moral corruption is at all levels of commerce and government; some clergy are so compromised that they are captive to the State; and a cabal of elites look to depopulate the earth and control people because they feel life is not sustainable with 7.5 billion people living on the planet.

Once a person understands there is a cabal of global elitists who have had a long term agenda for depopulation, then a lot of information can be properly assimilated to better understand the fierce battle in the news. The Coronavirus was A KILL SHOT to knock off the economy (and the currency) and the Church with a single event. It was a go-for-broke strategy. It was the nuclear option to remove President Trump from office after all else failed since the day he was elected to office. It was designed by a group of very evil people to destabilize life to such an extent that the elitist ruling class are able bring in their own agenda because *"Out of chaos will come a New World Order."* It is evil perfection. As the saying goes, *"Never let a crisis go to waste."* The Progressives in government and the Church are out in the open that this crisis will allow them to further their agenda of more intervention and control. They wish to remove God from every aspect of our lives through language and social engineering. This event fits the criteria to bring change for a New World Order.

On a rational level there is nary a shortage of opinions on what has been happening with the Coronavirus, and what the future may hold. The uncertainty has brought us to a frightful fear about our economic and spiritual future. In the lockdown, liquor stores, lotteries, pot dispensers, and abortion clinics were allowed to remain open. Other venues were allowed to remain open if social distancing of 6 feet was maintained. If that was so, why were churches singled out if abiding by the same set of guidelines as others? The answer is the State is out to decimate the Church and continue to weaken it to a thin veneer of the doctrines of old. Only a tiny handful of bishops speak against it. The Government's goal is to destroy and remove faith and religion because there can be no dissent from the goals of Statism. It is not socialism they are pursuing, but communism, and God is in their way. The Catholic Church and the United States of America are the last impediments to State Control.

Coronavirus gave government authorities the ability to exert another level of control like they haven't had since President Franklin D. Roosevelt's New Deal, and World War II. The pandemic, no matter the source nor the validity of cause of death, is the point of this discussion because it was fraud perpetuated on the American people. What is most troublesome is churches were targeted first to limit assembly. Evil people ploughed forward to see how far they could go before there was pushback. If there was a little pushback, progressives pushed more. As a result, democracy and capitalism itself are being threatened at this very time. Changes forthcoming will be catastrophic to political, moral, and financial structures of the past. The injection from the Federal Reserve/Treasury of $3 trillion plus in Covid relief, and unemployment exceeding the Great Depression, will alter life as we know it. Modern Monetary Theory (MMT) of reckless printing of the currency, now endorsed and supported by both parties, is new for America. We are in a different time now.

Evil is relentless in its pursuit to destroy the people of God at all costs now. It is a full court press to achieve global government. While many businesses were granted 6 feet of social distancing and others allowed to stay open, the question must be asked why did the leading Catholic ecclesiastical authorities capitulate to the dictates of a godless State so quickly, to only allow no more than ten people in a large venue? Their capacity is often up to 1,500 in many churches. It is not a situation of one size fits all. It is nothing but rational to abide by good health precautions, and during the 1918 Spanish Flu pandemic churches closed for a period of time.

But, and this is a big but, then there was nowhere near the hostility of the State with clearly articulated goals to destroy the Church as there is today. Lighthouse Fellowship Church on Chincoteague Island filed suit against Governor Ralph Northam (D-Virginia) because 16 people were arrested who attended a Palm Sunday Service. They had socially distanced to state guidelines, yet they were still arrested because there were more than 10 people in church. It is this kind of behavior that created so much animosity and distrust among believers. The emotional divide is escalating toward violence. If the State continues to find ways to single out believers, it is only a matter of time before there is civil disobedience — and worse. You can only push a person so far, and the dialectic of Karl Marx wants class warfare. The divide of ideologies is so vitriolic today because believers have virtually no trust in the motives of progressives.

We are now looking at the battle of the ages as the **Woman Clothed with the Sun** of Revelation 12 is battling the serpent for the soul of man. We have been told this in countless reliable and other Church approved sources over the last one hundred years. We were never meant to live in this immoral cesspool we see today. As the frog has grown acclimated to the boiling water, man has lost his way living in a dystopian engineered disaster. We arrived at this place because some believers feared the opinion of man more than the truth of the Word of God, and as a result evil advanced.

The relentless pursuit of efficiency through materialism in the 20th Century through today has dulled our senses to the Gospel message. As the

East lost its faith under communism, the West lost it through materialism. Collectively, the world is lost. The Lord is purifying His people. These events will bring us back to some resemblance of normalcy, civility, and Godliness. In the end, the Church will see much good come from these times.

We were being slowed down to focus on Him. The question is how many did? It only takes thirty days to form a habit. When the opportunity came to go back to church, many said why bother? It is estimated overall church attendance is down 30 percent from pre-pandemic levels. The economic fallout of the pandemic will be another large nail in the coffin of the Church going bankrupt. The lack of donations will crush budgets and forcibly close social welfare programs which will hurt the needy. Will the people continue to give when their own household budget is limited? When this debacle is over we will see a cleansing in the Church. It will be painful for many, but it is necessary and good to bring us back to what is most necessary in life.

Donations will continue to drop, some churches will close, consolidation of parishes will take place, and the Church will be purified as they do with less and lose their voice in civic affairs. Each person's character will be tested by adversity, which brings out the best and worst in people. In wartime and plagues, people are stretched and their character is in full view. Some alleviate pain and suffering in times of stress from dawn to dusk looking to lend a hand while others have been seen taking gold from the teeth of dead bodies for their own gain.

Virtue and vice are accentuated for all to see in difficult times. We are seeing some of that now. Chinks and strengths in the armor of spiritual, financial, and psychological/emotional stability are surfacing.

It is best to be reminded, the Blessed Mother said, **The Refuge is in my Immaculate Heart.** Evil has a season, and in time will boomerang on the perpetrators. In the end, good always prevails. *"But you, O wicked and of all men most criminal, be not lifted up without cause with vain hopes, while you are raging against His servants. For you have not yet escaped the judgment of the almighty God, who beholds all things"* (2 Maccabees 7:34-35).

The Hope — Heaven's Intervention

On May 1, 2020, at 3:00 pm EST, on the Feast of Saint Joseph the Worker, the Patron Saint of the Universal Church, the United States Catholic Conference of Bishops (USCCB), renewed their Consecration of the United States and Canada to Mary, Mother of the Church. Archbishop Gomez, head of the USCCB composed a prayer to Our Lady of Guadalupe. He said that as one family under God we turn to our Mother for protection from the threat of the Coronavirus. Hopefully, this was a prelude to the bishops' processing Our Lady of America into the Shrine of the Immaculate Conception in Washington, D.C., as Our Lady has asked.

As the Blessed Mother has told us, *"Right when it appears Satan is the victor, I shall snatch his victory away in a trice."* Trice means "in an instant." Come Lord Jesus.

JESUS I TRUST IN YOU

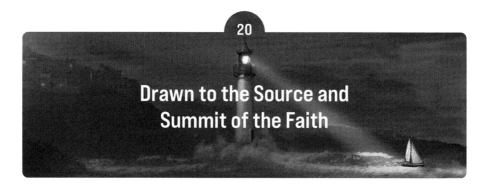

20

Drawn to the Source and Summit of the Faith

In the Eucharist we have Jesus, we have his redemptive sacrifice, we have his resurrection, we have the gift of the Holy Spirit, we have adoration, obedience and love of the Father. Were we to disregard the Eucharist, how could we overcome our own deficiency?

Saint John Paul II, The Church from the Eucharist, 60

Many years ago, I was with a long time Protestant friend who casually mentioned he had just met a priest from Africa studying at the Catholic University of America in Washington, D.C. He asked the priest what he was studying and the priest said he came to Washington to do his

Ph.D on the Eucharist. My friend was speechless and dumbfounded, and thoroughly confused how anyone could study the subject, because to him it was a symbol and celebration of unity. He shook his head in disbelief anyone could study the Eucharist, and actually devote time and effort to do a doctorate on the subject.

As we moved into the eighth full week of Covid lockdown in the State of Virginia, churches around me had different levels of activity and some without the Mass at all. One nearby parish didn't open its doors for any reason from day one of the lockdown. Other parishes had Eucharistic Adoration in the morning and night for a combined several hours a day all while abiding by the social distancing guidelines and limiting people in the church. Some had confession when Adoration was going on. There were hours of Adoration on Saturday and Sunday for a portion of the day in one parish, and another local parish broadcasted Mass on the internet daily with little else.

During the lockdown, I greatly enjoyed going to Adoration daily. It was not a new practice for me, but I had never been as regular or so consistent as this period of lockdown. It became a routine over the months of the pandemic where I enjoyed waking up and going the first thing in the morning. What was most satisfying was sitting in the quiet of a large church listening to Gregorian chant being played over the speaker system sung by a beautiful chorus of men. The serenity and contemplation were nothing I had ever experienced to this depth before. It is spiritually exhilarating to enjoy the stillness of the early morning in silence. I think one reason for my enjoyment was there was less havoc during that period of time, and it was a scheduled event for me with nowhere near the normal daily activity.

All during the lockdown a constant conversation took place about why government authorities had locked down churches preventing worship. Other businesses were allowed social distancing of 6 feet, but not churches.

I live in a heavily populated area in Northern Virginia. From my home are ten Catholic churches within one to ten miles. Some were outright closed; others offered limited services. What I noticed was that it was the same few people every day for Adoration. There was little variation in the number of people over a two-hour period in the mornings and a two-hour period in the evenings, when the church was open. It was the same few people sitting in their chosen spots each day. About thirteen to fifteen people total attended over a two-hour period on average. As one of the most densely populated areas in Northern Virginia with thousands of families per parish, only a few went to Adoration. All the while people were often complaining Mass had been suspended. It was an inconsistent view of Who is before them in the Tabernacle.

People like to complain, talk, and discuss philosophy, but few are willing to take the time, and do the work on their knees to change the culture. Saint Thomas Aquinas would spend two hours on his knees for every hour he spoke publicly. Archbishop Fulton J. Sheen often spoke of doing a Holy Hour every day of his life; a commitment he made as a young priest. He once joked he fell asleep on a park bench in Paris and counted it as a valid Holy Hour. He said since he fell asleep thinking about the Passion of Jesus, it counted as a Holy Hour. The Tabernacle is a treasure waiting to be visited. Our excuses dwindled for not attending Adoration during this period of lockdown.

Saints and scholars have had a lot to say about the important role of the Eucharist in the Church. The Catechism of the Catholic Church says, *"The Eucharist is **the source and summit of the Christian life.** The other sacraments, and indeed all the ecclesiastical ministries and works of the apostolate, are bound up with the Eucharist and are oriented toward it. For in the blessed Eucharist is contained the whole spiritual good of the Church, namely Christ himself, our Pasch"* (CCC 1324).

On June 14, 1979, to the Marian Movement of Priests, on the Feast of Corpus Christi in a message titled, Jesus in the Eucharist, the Blessed Mother spoke about the importance of the Eucharist. She said,

"Beloved sons, in these present times the darkness has alas obscured even the Tabernacle; around it there is so much emptiness, so much indifference, so much negligence. Each day, doubts, denials and sacrileges increase. The Eucharistic Heart of Jesus is wounded anew by his own, in his own House, in the very place where He has taken up His divine dwelling in your midst.

"Become again perfect adorers and fervent ministers of Jesus in the Eucharist who, through you, makes Himself again present, immolates Himself anew, and gives Himself to souls.

"Bring everyone to Jesus in the Eucharist; by adoration, by communion and by a greater love. Help everyone to approach the Eucharistic Jesus in a worthy manner, by cultivating in the faithful an awareness of sin, by inviting them to present themselves for the sacrament of Holy Communion in the state of grace, by educating them to the practice of frequent confession, which becomes necessary before receiving the Eucharist for those who are in mortal sin.

"Beloved sons, build a dam to hold back the flood of sacrileges; never before as in these present times have so many communions been made in such an unworthy manner.

"The Church is deeply wounded by the multiplications of sacrilegious Communions. **The time has come when your heavenly Mother says: enough!**

"I myself will fill up the great void about my Son Jesus, present in the Eucharist. I will form a barrier of love about His divine presence. I myself will do this through you, beloved sons, whom I wish to set up as a guard of love round about all the Tabernacles of the earth" (MMP #176).

Also on August 8, 1986, the Blessed Mother said to the Marian Movement of Priests, "And He becomes present in order to continue the work of the Incarnation and the redemption and in order to accomplish, in mystery the Sacrifice of Calvary, which He was able to offer to the Father because of his human nature....

"[T]oday Jesus in the tabernacle is surrounded by so much emptiness, much neglect, and much ingratitude" (MMP #330).

Saint Padre Pio of Italy would often say the Eucharist is more important to the world than the sun. We have Jesus waiting for us to adore Him in the tabernacles of the Catholic Churches all around us. Create a new normal. Go before Jesus in Adoration and make time to discern the days in which we are living and how we should act in these troubled times. Seek His thoughts. He waits for us. He thirsts for us.

Evil is being exposed now in every area — entertainment, media of all kinds, sports, political, the Church, finance, and commerce. The lockdown slowed us down and many positive spiritual things happened as a result of it. Do not abandon the lessons but continue to fight the battle. His ways are not our ways. We should be reminded good always wins. It may take awhile, but evil is always exposed to the light in the long run.

"For there is nothing hidden that will not be disclosed, and nothing concealed that will not be known and brought out into the open" (Luke 8:17).

JESUS I TRUST IN YOU

"'But what will become of men then?' I asked him, 'without God and immortal life? All things are lawful then, they can do what they like?'"

Fyodor Dostoevsky, The Brothers Karamazov

Wars Build Over Time, And Then a Spark Sets a Country Ablaze

The seeds of revolt are sown long before the actual spilling of blood. The conditions and circumstances that led us to the American Civil War (1860-1865) began well before 1860. Some 35 years prior to the onset of the war, there was a vocal anti-slavery movement that began in Massachusetts and New York and disseminated strong opinions in print. Even before that, the Founding Fathers said that the last act of the American Revolution would be the abolishment of slavery. Activity preceded the actual event of the Civil War that demonstrated neither side was willing to budge on ideology. The result was a bloodbath that changed the American landscape forever.

Fear that has not been seen since the U.S. Civil War has now gripped the nation. Similarly, the French Revolution was well on its way to civil disobedience 75 years before the events of 1789 and immediately beyond. The storming of the Bastille was just one single event that exploded after decades of governmental abuse of its citizens. A palace coup is the result of a repressive regime of some kind or another over an extended period of time. There is a point where the blood of citizens boils and one side feels it cannot be pushed any further. Exactly what that point is modestly varies, but the end result is the same. At some point someone starts shooting. As someone said, "*When I hear someone talk about changing the culture, it makes me want to grab my revolver.*"

What we are seeing fits the pattern of all insurrections. One party perceives an injustice, and the other reacts. Tempers and activities escalate, continue to fester, and brew over long periods of time. The rest is history. One could read modern history and see it widely commonplace: Germany under Hitler and the Third Reich; Italy under Mussolini; Poland and Eastern Europe under Soviet control until the Soviet Empire collapsed when the Berlin Wall came down; events prior to the Spanish Civil War; India under Imperialist Great Britain until Gandhi led the salt march in defiance — and the list goes on endlessly even until today. This is the history of civil conflict. If Christ is not at the center of man's rule, abuse will eventually set in where Godly authority does not have a check and balance on men's souls.

Founding Fathers Create a New Kind of Government

The hottest issue of our times is the precise role of the state or government in our lives. The conversation whether acknowledged or not is exactly what do we expect government to do for us. What is free, what is paid for, and who accepts the burden if nearly everything from education, health, and welfare of all kinds are all paid for by government? If government is made up by people, who pays and how much? Embedded inside that is the hot spot of the Second Amendment and gun rights. The Founding Fathers created the Second Amendment in case the First Amendment isn't working. Based on what we see in the cancel culture especially with tech, the First Amendment protections are struggling. The Founding Fathers had seen the abuses of the British Empire at home in Scotland, Ireland, and England. Many of the early immigrants came to U.S. shores from the British Isles. Those were the first, second, or third generation of Americans. Based on their experiences, they devised a Bill of Rights and a Constitution that would best assure them of a peaceful existence in their new country. They based their new system of government on thousands of years of what was considered acceptable and workable governance. They melded a blend of many civilizations and empires and took the very best from them. The U.S. system was designed on Greek logic, Roman law, the Magna Carta, and Christianity. This was no easy task for a fledgling nation and a new experiment of self-rule.

Then there is the story of what Alexis de Tocqueville saw when he came to America. Under the sponsorship of the French government, he came to find out what made America tick. As America's first social biographer he published a four-volume treatise in 1835 called Democracy in America, in which he wrote about what he saw. In short he wrote, *"I looked to find what made America great in her cities and did not find it. I looked in her countryside to find what made America great and did not find it. I looked in her factories to find what made America great and did not find it. I looked on her farms and did not find it. I looked in her homes to find what made America great, and did not find it, but when I looked in her churches I found what made America great."* As de Tocqueville roamed a young America and saw the vibrancy of her people, he recognized American exceptionalism was in America's faith.

Today we have lost those traditions in a thousand ways. As an ancient Greek philosopher said, *"A democracy ceases to exist when the public learns to raid the largesse of the treasury with impunity."* A democracy exists because the people obey the law voluntarily for the good of the individual, the family, and the public good. A democracy is not based on government mandates. It is principled self-governance based on individual virtue that desires to preserve freedom and liberty.

The root problem of what ails us as a nation is not the guns, mental health issues or psychotropic drugs. These are the surface problems manifesting themselves in the streets, classroom and in the community. It is the demise of the family, a structure that heaven ordained and which man has sought to dismantle, mocking God. The family has been devastated by sin, divorce, materialism, ungodly activity, addictions, alienation and isolation of youth. In our America today many find solace in a digital world communicating hour after hour with cyber beings that have no connection to community, with little adherence to family structures that have been the lifeblood of thousands of years, and generally with a lack of faith in the home. We have allowed ourselves to be overtaken by a relativism that allows a philosophy of "anything goes." As the 19th Century Russian writer Dostoevsky said, *"Without God anything is lawful."* By not allowing faith in the classroom, and not teaching virtue the result has been violence. When virtue or faith based education is not taught a void is created which is filled by all kinds of ungodly ideologies. In time, it becomes its own religion as we see today. These ultimately find their way into public policy whether a person is willing to admit it or not. Will it take more blood to allow God back in the classroom and our lives for order to be restored? A child will witness over 19,000 murders on television and video games by the time he or she is eighteen. We should not be surprised then if that desensitized child at some point resorts to violence.

Not allowing Christianity in the classroom has been a mistake that has festered for nearly sixty years now. We are well into our third generation of godless education that has been so humanistic and secular, the youth are lost. Secularism and humanism are religions. Shootings at Columbine, Colorado, Virginia Tech, Aurora, Colorado, and Newtown, Connecticut were events that happened due to the vacuum of God in our society. It should be noted that these, as many other similar mass shootings, did not occur in low-income and marginalized areas, but rather in middle class to affluent areas.

In a nation where it is illegal for a teacher to allow prayer or have a Bible in a classroom, yet allows a fifteen year old to have an abortion without parental knowledge, what would one expect the future to look like? What would one expect from a nation that has slaughtered over 60 million babies in the womb under government protection of the highest court in the land? Does this nation really deserve the Lord's blessing on the land? Until America recognizes our problems are spiritual, we are a hopeless nation that will be relegated to the ash heap of fallen nations. Legislation will not cure our ills. They will magnify them.

The Ten Commandments are about seventy-two words depending on what version you read. They seem pretty clear to most people and easy to understand. It is sin that clouds the mind and grace cannot enlighten unless there is confession. The longer we remain in sin, the less clarity we possess. The Federal Register contains regulations and laws that fill hundreds of thousands of pages and grows every day. Layer on top of layer is making it impossible to live. Until there is a recognition that the only solution is God and repentance, there will be no spiritual rebirth. America will continue to flounder and decline. It is just that simple. As the Babushka said, *"We forgot God."*

JESUS I TRUST IN YOU

Moses answered the people, "Fear not! Stand your ground,
and you will see what Yahweh will do to save you today: the Egyptians
you see today, you will never see again. Yahweh will do the fighting
for you: you have only to keep still."

Exodus 14:13-14

The above account is an act of Yahweh to make it clear to the Israelites during the Exodus from Egypt, that the yoke of Pharaoh had come to an end with the parting of the Red Sea. Their four-hundred year bondage was over as they walked on the dry ground of the Red Sea towards the Promised Land. If one looks at the geography of the Sinai Peninsula, there was another easier route that is seldom spoken of because Yahweh wanted to show His glory for the Israelites for all future generations. *"So shall I win myself glory at the expense of Pharaoh, of all his army, his chariots, his horsemen. And when I have won glory for myself, at the expense of Pharaoh and his chariots and his army, the Egyptians will learn that I am Yahweh"* (Ex. 14:17-18). The freedom from bondage of Egypt and the parting of the Red Sea was all show to establish the might and fidelity of Yahweh to His chosen people for all generations. What a show it was with a pillar of smoke by day in the form of a cloud and a fire by night in the form of a column guiding His people, establishing His physical presence among them.

The biblical account is well known about the grumbling, the complaining, and the whining from the people even while Yahweh was doing a great work answering their prayers of freedom.

"Here in the desert the whole assembly of the children of Israel grumbled against Moses and Aaron. The children of Israel said to them, 'Would that we had died at the Lord's hand in the land of Egypt, as we sat by our fleshpots and ate our fill of bread! But you had to lead us into the desert to make the whole community die of famine'" (Ex. 16:2-3).

The uncertainty of their future was the cause of the fear amongst the Israelites. In just days they had doubted what God had done with the ten plagues to free them. The people were still not operating in faith in spite of what had just happened: being miraculously freed from their four-hundred year bondage in Egypt.

Is it any different today with all the grumbling and the whining about the state of affairs around us? The confusion. The fear. The anxiety. The divisive conversations on so many issues. The command of Yahweh was resolute and strong. **Fear not. Stand your ground.** The response required from Moses is exactly as it is from the Psalmist: ***"Be still and know that I am God"*** (Ps. 46:10).

In times of outright fear, and the unknown of living in a desert ahead, Yahweh told the people, ***"Fear not, I will do the fighting for you; you have only to keep still."*** The Israelites had seen the miracles of Moses in Egypt yet still doubted. Is it any different for us today with our constant doubt the Lord is in control, and what lies ahead will be for His glory? For concerns about food, Yahweh sent quail and manna that was to be harvested daily to teach them He would provide daily for their needs. The Hebrew word for manna is, *"What is this?"* (Ex. 16:15) as food had never fallen from the sky. God provided in a way no man could have ever imagined, yet He did provide. To make provision for the Sabbath, Yahweh told the people to pick from the ground twice the amount of food on the sixth day to have enough for the seventh to honor Him as a day of worship with no manual work. Yahweh was about to etch in stone new laws, the Ten Commandments, to govern His people. All were satisfied from hunger while wandering in the desert by miraculous provision of the quail at evening and the manna in the morning.

Today, our concerns are many. No matter where we look there is uncertainty and fear. The anxiety is palpable with conversations among friends. The economy, vaccines, government intrusion, inflation, political concerns of every kind, health care, race, corrupt government, immigration, the direction of the church, and many more problems, are at the forefront that disturb us due to a widespread social and moral breakdown. What gives us peace of mind is certainty, and at the moment that is a hard commodity to come by. It was uncertainty to cause the grumbling and whining of the Israelites leaving for an unknown future. It is uncertainty with our social and religious structures crumbling that give us many questions, and thus anxiety, as it gave the Israelites at the time of the Exodus. The ease and comfort of the past generation(s) seems to have taken a hard turn towards the ensuing chaos that is in our midst.

Moses commanded twelve spies to go to Canaan for forty days to determine the general lay of the land and its agriculture before they proceeded to enter the Promised Land. Ten of the spies said there were giants in the land, and only Joshua and Caleb said the Lord could overcome the obstacles and win victory. They came back and gave their report to Moses and the people:

"At the end of forty days, they came back from the reconnaissance of the land. They sought out Moses, Aaron and the whole community of Israel, in the wilderness of Paran, at Kadesh…. They told them this story, 'We went into the land to which you sent us. It does indeed flow with milk and honey; this is its produce. At the same time, its inhabitants are a powerful people; the town are fortified and very big; yes, and we saw the descendants of Anak are there. The Amalekite holds the Negeb area, the Hittite, Amorite and Jebusite the highlands, and the Canaanite the sea coast and the banks of the Jordan.' Caleb harangued the people gathered about Moses: 'We must march in he said, and conquer this land; we are able to do it'" (Numbers 13:25-30). The ten other spies grumbled and said they could not defeat these giants. Caleb was speaking faith Yahweh was going to give them the land promised by Yahweh through Moses.

"At this, the whole community raised their voices and cried aloud, and the people wailed all that night. Then all the sons of Israel grumbled against Moses and Aaron, and the whole community said, 'Would that we had died in the land of Egypt, or at least we had died in the wilderness. Why did Yahweh bring us to this land, only to have us fall by the sword, and our wives and young children seized as booty? Should we not do better to go back to Egypt?' And they said to one another, 'Let us appoint a leader and go back to Egypt'" (Num. 14:1-4).

Then Caleb silenced the people of Israel before Moses and said, **"We should go up and take possession of the land, for we can certainly do it"** (Numbers 13:30). Only Joshua and Caleb after wandering for forty years from their generation entered the Promised Land. They spoke faith the Lord was going to do a mighty work even though they didn't know exactly how. **Fear not, and stand your ground.**

"Joshua son of Nun, and Caleb son of Jephunneh, two of those who had reconnoitred the country, tore their garments; and they said to the entire community and the sons of Israel, 'This land we went to reconnoitre is a good land. If Yahweh is pleased with us, He will lead us into this land and give it to us. It is a land where milk and honey flow. **Do not rebel against Yahweh. And do not be afraid of the people of this land; we shall gobble them up.... Do not be afraid of them'"** (Num.14: 6-9).

To take the Land of Canaan, Joshua had battles. At Gibeon against the Amorites (one of the tribes of Canaan) Joshua asked Yahweh that the sun and the moon would stand still so he could finish the battle in daylight (Joshua 10). It showed the Israelites again that Yahweh would fight for them and still they grumbled and doubted. It is interesting to note on the ancient Chinese calendar there is a day missing exactly as this event took place. Joshua lived in the time of the Bronze Age where a Chinese calendar did exist. Science validates this missing day on the calendar as authentic. In another battle while taking possession of the Promised Land, more Canaanites were killed by huge hailstones than the Israelites actually killed in battle. And still, they grumbled and doubted.

"I will be with you as I was with Moses; I will not leave you or desert you. **Be strong and stand firm,** *for you are the man to give this people possession of the land that I swore to their fathers I should give to them.* **Only be strong and**

stand firm and be careful to keep all the law which my servant Moses laid on you. Never swerve from this to right or left, and then you will be happy in all you do. Have the book of this law always on your lips; meditate on it day and night, so that carefully you may keep everything that is written in it. Then you will prosper in your dealings, then you will have success. Have I not told you: Be strong and stand firm? Be fearless then, be confident, for go where you will, Yahweh your God is with you" (Joshua 1:5-9). Notice how often the phrase **be strong and stand firm** is used above. That is Yahweh's demand in times of crisis. The same as Saint Faustina, Jesus I Trust in You. If God is with you, who can be against you? God plus one is a majority — all the time.

The greatest stories in the Bible are about the faith in action of heroic people in times of crisis. Hebrews 11 is the Jewish Hall of Fame, where St. Paul speaks about those who operated in faith and altered history due to their actions. *"And what shall I yet say? For the time would fail me to tell of Gideon, Barac, Samson, Jephthah, David, Samuel, and the prophets: who by faith conquered kingdoms, wrought justice, obtained promises, stopped the mouths of lions, quenched the violence of fire, escaped the edge of the sword, recovered strength from weakness, became valiant in battle, put to flight the armies of foreigners; and women received their dead raised to life again"* (Hebrews 11:32-35). The greatest traditions in the Church are acts of faith at a critical point in time where events can go one way or the other, then the Lord steps in. **We are at one of these times now to STAND FIRM** and not buckle to a godless state promoting such heinous practices as infanticide.

Our Response Today

The question must be asked, how do we respond? Do we raise the white flag of surrender? Do we roll over? Do we concede everything away? Do we draw a line of demarcation and say, this is where I will be pushed no longer? Do we stand firm? Resolute? **Fear Not, Hold your ground?** Do we lose our peace in the midst of the chaos? The instructions going forward for living in the Promised Land is obedience to what is asked of us. The Triumph of the Immaculate Heart is the next major mile marker for the believer. The Triumph of the Immaculate Heart is similar to what Moses and Joshua endured. Strong convictions were no different for Moses or Joshua than us today. Both were and are milestones of seismic change. The old has to be done away with for the new to be introduced. Unless there was a crucifixion, there would not have been redemption with the Resurrection. We have to trust, knowing what the Lord desires and go with His plan, not ours. *"My thoughts are not your thoughts, and My ways are not your ways"* (Isaiah 55:8).

We have to trust that Heaven has a plan as the culture collapses around us. But, we also need to be obedient to what is being asked of us. Jesus told Saint Faustina, **"Fear is useless, what is needed is TRUST."** FEAR is **False Evidence Appearing Real.** Before we can enter in the New Era of Peace promised for so long; the old must pass away. The pain we are witnessing at this very moment in the Church will continue as it was painful for the Israelites in the desert before there was a new beginning. We must endure until the end. *"If God is for us, who can be against us?"* (Romans 8:31)

We know the rubrics and fundamentals of the faith, and we must stick to them. The lack of faith, the distrust, and the discouragement need to be eliminated immediately if we are going to emotionally and spiritually prosper going forward. **Do we see the giants of big tech, big government, big pharma and the global elite as the giants** Joshua and Caleb saw? Do we see the Lord's work in the chaos around us?

Yahweh will do the fighting for us, we need to be obedient and remain still in spirit, knowing it is Heaven's hand to play now. This does not mean to sit around and do nothing. It is time to speak up, with the faith of Joshua. It is time to get down on our knees and storm Heaven in prayer like never before. A Red Sea moment awaits us.

Fear Not, and Stand Your Ground.

JESUS I TRUST IN YOU

23

The Prayer That Heaven Gave the World

*And when you pray, you must not be like the hypocrites; for they love
to stand and pray in the synagogues and at the street corners,
that they may be seen by men. Truly, I say to you, they have their reward.
But when you pray go into your room and shut the door and pray to your
Father who is in secret; and your Father who sees in secret will reward
you. And in praying do not heap up empty phrases as the Gentiles do;
for they think that they will be heard for their many words.
Do not be like them, for your Father knows what you need
before you ask Him. Pray then like this...."*

Matthew 6:5-9

In the gospel of Matthew Jesus told us how to pray. Then Jesus gave the Apostles the prayer which is known as the Lord's Prayer or the Our Father. Jesus must have thought it was important, because this is the only prayer during His earthly ministry that is recorded in Scripture that He gave the world.

In the Old Testament, it could be said that reading the Psalms is a continual prayer. They are often a comfort in times of stress as there is so much in the Psalms about praise. The Psalms are a consolation when we may need a lift of assurance that Heaven is by our side. Heaven has given us a specific prayer that saints and scholars alike agree is a divinely inspired prayer. Heaven has chosen to give us a prayer for the benefit of all humanity — and that is the Rosary. It is a prayer that many cherish, while others may look on it as a rote monotonous grouping of words not uttered directly from the heart. A form prayer so to speak for some. Depending on your outlook of what it is, and how it should be said, both may be correct.

Saint Dominic and the Rosary

Catholic tradition has its origins of the rosary with Saint Dominic (1170-1221) given in a vision from the Blessed Mother. Dominic was founder of the Dominicans; the Order of Preachers (OP). All is not clear when people began to recite it in its modern-day form. It has its origins in monasticism as early as the 3rd and 4th centuries where monks would pray on knotted ropes. After the First Council of Ephesus in 431, groups of Marian Prayers came about through the Middle Ages. Strings of beads would count the Hail Marys and Our Fathers then known in Latin as Paternosters.

Its set of mysteries were in time called the Life of Jesus Rosary. The rosary continued to evolve to its present form of meditation with sets of mysteries based on the life of Jesus. The rosary today depicts the highlights of the life of Jesus and Mary all the way to His resurrection. It was Heaven that gave mankind this prayer much in the same way Jesus gave His followers the Our Father. Heaven will dispense grace how it chooses for man's benefit. The tradition of the Church is that it was Saint Dominic that gave the rosary its fifty Hail Marys. Saint Dominic would use the rosary in his missionary work with the Albigensians (12th and 13th century), who professed the early heresy of denying the mystery of the divinity of Jesus Christ. What is irregular, is the early writers of Dominic do not attribute him to the rosary.

Whom do the Demons Fear the Most?

There are many stories about the power of the rosary with Dominic. One of the best is the time Saint Dominic put his rosary around an Albigensian heretic's neck and asked the devils to tell him of all the saints in Heaven, who was the one they feared the most, and who should be the most loved and revered by men. At this, they let out such unearthly screams that most of the people fell to the ground, faint from fear.

Then, using all their cunning so as not to answer, the devils wept and wailed in such a pitiful way that many of the people wept also, out of natural pity. The devils spoke through the mouth of the Albigensian, pleading in a heart-rending voice saying, *"Dominic, Dominic, have mercy on us — we promise that we will never hurt you. You have always had compassion for sinners and those in distress, have pity on us for we are in grievous straits.*

We are suffering very much already, so why do you delight in heightening our pains? Can't you be satisfied with our suffering without adding to it?"

Dominic was not one bit moved by the pathos of those wretched spirits, and told them that he would not let them alone until they answered the question. Then they said they would whisper the answer in such a way that only Saint Dominic would be able to hear. Then Dominic firmly insisted upon answering clearly and out loud.

Then the devils kept quiet and refused to say another word, completely disregarding Saint Dominic's orders. He knelt down and prayed to Our Lady. *"O powerful and wonderful Virgin Mary, I implore you by the power of the Most Holy Rosary, order these enemies of the human race to answer me."*

No sooner had he made the prayer than a glowing flame leaped out of the ears, nostrils, and mouth of the Albigensian. Everyone shook with fear, but remarkably, the fire did not hurt the man or anyone near him.

Let Us Leave

Then the devils cried: *"Dominic, we beseech you, by the passion of Jesus Christ and by the merits of His Holy Mother, and of all the saints, let us leave the body of this man without speaking further — for the angels will answer your question whenever you wish. After all, are we not liars? Why should you want to believe us? Please do not torture us anymore; have pity on us. Woe unto us wretched spirits, who do not deserve to be heard."* Saint Dominic kneeling down said to Our Lady:

"Oh Most worthy Mother of Wisdom, I am praying for the people assembled here who have already learned how to say the Angelic Salutation properly. Please. I beg of You, force Your enemies to proclaim the whole truth about this, and nothing but the truth, here and now, before the multitude."

Saint Dominic had hardly finished this prayer when he saw the Blessed Mother surrounded by a multitude of angels. She gently struck the man with a golden rod and said, *"Answer My servant Dominic at once."* The people didn't hear or see Our Lady, but only Dominic. Then the devils started screaming: *"O You who are our enemy, our downfall, and our destruction, why have You come from Heaven just to torture us so grievously? Oh, Advocate of sinners, You who snatch them from the very jaws of hell, You who are the surest path to Heaven, must we, in spite of ourselves, tell the whole truth and confess before everyone who it is who is the cause of our shame and our ruin? Oh, woe to us, princes of darkness."*

Listen Well

"*Then listen well, you Christians: the Mother of Jesus Christ is all powerful, and She can save Her servants from falling into hell. She is the sun which destroys the darkness of our wiles. **It is She who uncovers our hidden plots, breaks our snares, and makes our most intense temptations useless and ineffectual.***

"*We have to say, however reluctantly, that not a single soul who has really persevered in Her service has ever been damned with us, one single soul. What She offers to the Blessed Trinity is worth far more than all prayers, desires, and aspirations of all the other saints combined.*

"***We fear Her more than all the saints in Heaven together, and we have no success with Her faithful servants.** Many Christians who call upon Her, when they are at the hour of death, and who really ought to be damned according to our ordinary standards, are saved by Her intercession.*

"*Oh, if only that Mary (it is thus, in their intense fury that they call Her) had not pitted Her strength against ours, and had not upset our plans, we could have conquered the Church and destroyed it long before this … and we would have seen to it that all the Orders of the Church fell into error and disorder.*

"*Now that we are forced to speak, we must also tell you this: nobody who perseveres in saying the rosary will be damned, because She obtains for Her servants the grace of true contrition. By means of this, they obtain God's forgiveness and mercy."*

The Devils Leave

Then a wonderful thing happened. Saint Dominic had all the people say the rosary together slowly and with great devotion. At each Hail Mary that he and all the people said together, **a hundred devils issued forth from the wretched man's body under the guise of red-hot coals, which neither burned or harmed the man. This happened until all 15,000 devils left the man's body.**

Our Lady, who was still invisible to everyone other than Saint Dominic, gave her blessing to the crowd. They all felt joy, and a large number of heretics were converted and became devotees to the Blessed Mother.

If one were to study the lives of the saints, these stories are more common than people may think. The Church elevated men like Dominic to sainthood due to the extraordinary spiritual fortitude and phenomena around him. Few ever speak about it, but **Saint Dominic raised a young boy from the dead.**

A Time of Confusion and Chaos Precedes God's intervention— Why We Need Another Rosary Campaign Like the Past

Where previous generations and civilizations have had turmoil, we now have ours, and we are presently watching Western Civilization rapidly crumble in front of us. It is now happening at an accelerated pace manifest to all who have ears to hear and eyes to see. The Blessed Mother said to Father Gobbi in the Marian Movement of Priests, *"The Holy spirit will cause you to understand the times through which you are living"* (MMP #521f). The unbeliever will not be able to see this as his lens is of their own human nature and not attuned to the Lord's ways. Without the Holy Spirit, and with the darkness sin creates, the unbeliever is unable to see what the Lord is doing in the world.

The United States has run its course as empires that have preceded it. Previous empires rose the same way, and the steps of collapse are identical. The United States and other western countries forget that it is God who blesses a nation, and they seek answers independent of God and mock Him with their own arrogance. In their wealth and affluence, they believe they don't need God.

It would be hard for someone to choose any social index that is working as it was designed. The dollar is well on its way to not being accepted as the reserve currency of the world, which will greatly diminish its value in global markets overnight when that happens. Every day it seems there is another natural disaster on the morning news: uncontrolled fires in the West; hurricanes destroying the infrastructure in the East and South; and floods, great rivers and reservoirs drying up in the Midwest. Agriculture is in peril due to droughts. Uncontrolled inflation is around the corner due to trillions of dollars printed under Modern Monetary Theory (MMT-which is just printing money) to fund communist programs. Printing money is the solution to problems by politicians who largely never worked in the private sector and have lived off government largesse for their entire careers. Their elixir is taxing everyone else's hard work to collect taxes to fund their wild dreams of a godless utopian dream.

The goal of the globalists is to destroy the United States as a Constitutional Republic and Christianity in the world. The godless believe both are failed experiments and need to be eliminated for proper governance. It is a ferocious war waged by Satan and his followers against God and His followers. This war is manifesting now in a fascist power grab void of any just laws. The mistake many make using logic is things will work out politically. When a civilization reaches a point of depravity by using evil legislation and patronage, it makes the country a lawless state. America is under judgment and is now going to be tested in ways we never imagined. We are off our equilibrium, off balance, and getting it back will be an act of God. I think of the boxer Mike Tyson when he said, *"It's all theory until you get hit in the face and knocked down."* Our days of normalcy are over as so much collapses around us. It would be a tragic mistake to think we will return to normal.

The godless are well on their way to create destruction as we look at the laws passed in Congress. Meanwhile some Christians naively believed progressives were operating in good faith when they were not. They never had intentions to honor commitments they contracted. It was a one-way street while they made laws they never intended to obey. Believers were naïve and were played the fools for complying. They had no concept of the evil being planned because to them it was incomprehensible because there were so many participants in this evil agenda. There was a revolution with tactics of subversion done in plain sight using the legislative process. Their accomplice was a press controlled by progressive globalists spewing propaganda, covering for a liberal view, and refusing to print the truth of their agenda. Believers were lulled to sleep by injurious and false rhetoric. The onslaught of the culture war was relentless lacking any mercy or reason, yet believers were led to the slaughter in silence as Jews were in Germany prior to and during World War II. Jews asked all the while, *Could this really be happening? Can anyone really be doing this? Can anyone really be this evil?* The answer was yes — they did do it — and the people complied for financial security. Just like today.

To understand the globalists, one has to understand their nefarious agenda has been about depopulation for several generations. They simply believe the world has too many people to sustain a way of life which they deem appropriate, and they want it void of God. The negative propaganda news will continue to come at us like boxcars. Why the maniacal push to vaccinate against Covid when the empirical data shows there are inexpensive alternatives that work like Ivermectin and hydroxychloroquine? Their agenda makes no sense until one grasps the plan is to depopulate. The agenda is to radically transform the civilization at all levels, not just government. I highlighted this agenda in a book called **The Great Transformation** released in 2015. We are now here at full throttle, with radical implementation. Unless one understands the depopulation plan, they will not grasp where the elitists are hell bent to bring the world. The prize is communism (not socialism), and its implementation is called the Great Reset. This must be understood to grasp the murderous agenda of the enemy.

Countries and regions of the world have seen chaos before where they cry out to Heaven for relief and mercy. But, never at this level has the world seen this diabolical agenda. We will look at several instances in history where Heaven intervened in miraculous ways, and to those observing there was little doubt Heaven had a hand in the outcome. However, the holocaust that is in our midst now is global. The American Revolution and the Civil War were fought just in the United States. It was a local war. World War I was originally called The Great War until World War II came along. Wars were largely fought regionally over domestic or regional strife. What lies before us is a global conflagration that will require Divine intervention to solve our problems, because they are too complex to solve any other way. As the world is connected and joined at the hip in so many areas, what happens today in Beijing has a repercussion immediately in Washington, Moscow, Kabul, or Paris, and vice versa. With billions of dollars of U.S. armaments left behind in Afghanistan, we have armed millions of jihadists looking to harm not just the United States, but the entire Christian west. We have armed our enemies. It is as big a blunder of sheer incompetence as any in our history. Was it pre-planned to further destroy America from within? It is as great a sign of moral decline as one can imagine. Islamic experts are left speechless at what has happened and what will happen in the near future now that billions of dollars of military equipment is in enemy possession in the Middle East.

There is only one way out of this mess as the water is now well over the dam. Man needs Divine help at this moment like few other times in history. We are very far down river for the Great Reset to transform society for public-private partnership to control every transaction for transnational corporations, and to make people a ward of the state serving state interests. We are watching a digital coup d'etat using a propaganda scheme of the elitist-owned media outlets. We are watching humanity's last stand against authoritarian behemoth internet corporations creating and controlling the narrative of anti-god. One may think this is extreme, but could you have imagined just several years ago we would be where we are now? We are fast approaching **where we need to have a world-wide rosary campaign like those before us**. It will take such an act of repentance for mercy to save us.

If a child is lost, it looks for its mother. When all is lost man has always gone to the Mother. And the Mother who never disappoints is Our Lady. Civilization is now at the precipice, and the answer for man is to ask the Mother of Jesus for help as it has happened so many other pivotal times in history. The chosen prayer Heaven has given us is the rosary. It has worked when done with the multitudes in the past, and it will work again if there is compliance with the wishes of Heaven.

The Angel With the Key and the Chain: The Salvation for the World

On October 7, 1992, the Feast of Our Lady of the Rosary, Our Lady gave to Father Gobbi a message from the Marian Movement of Priests (MMP #479) that needs no interpretation on how important and efficacious Heaven says the prayer of the rosary is for all mankind. October 7 is the anniversary of the victory of Lepanto. Our Lady says,

"The rosary is my prayer, it is the prayer which I came down from Heaven to ask of you, because it is the weapon you must make use of, in times of the great battle, and it is the sign of my assured victory. My victory will be won

when Satan, with his powerful army made up of infernal spirits, will be shut up in his kingdom of darkness and death, from which he will no longer be able to escape in order to do harm to the world.

"For this reason, there is to come down from Heaven an angel to whom there is given a key to the abyss and a chain with which this angel will bind the great Dragon, the ancient serpent, Satan, with all his followers.

"An 'angel' is a spirit who is sent by God to carry out a particular mission. I am the Queen of the Angels because it is of the very nature of my role to be sent by the Lord to accomplish the very great and important mission of conquering Satan.

"In fact from the very beginning, I was announced as she who is the enemy of the serpent, she who does battle with him, she who in the end will crush his head: 'I will put enmity between you and the woman, between your offspring and hers. She will crush your head, as you attempt to bite at her heel' (Gen. 3:15). My offspring is Christ. In Him, who has carried out the work of redemption and set you free from the slavery of Satan, my complete victory is accomplished.

"And so, there has been entrusted to me the key with which it is possible to open and shut the door of the abyss. The key is the sign of the power which belongs to him who is the lord and the master of a place which belongs to him.

"In this sense, He who holds the key to the universe is the Incarnate Word alone, because all things have been made through Him, and therefore Jesus Christ is the Master and King of all the universe, namely, of heaven, of earth, and the abyss. My Son Jesus alone possesses the key of the abyss, because He Himself is the Key of David, who opens and no one can shut, who shuts and no one can open.

"Jesus consigns this key, which represents his divine power, into my hand because, **as his Mother, Mediatrix between you and my Son, there is entrusted to me the task of conquering Satan and all his powerful army of evil.** It is with this key that I am able to open and shut the door to the abyss.

"The **chain,** with which the great Dragon is to be bound, is made up of a prayer made with me and by means of me. **This prayer is that of the holy rosary.** A chain has in fact the function of first of all limiting action, then of imprisoning, and finally of making ineffective every activity of the one who is bound by it.

"*The chain of the holy rosary has first all the function of **limiting the action** of my Adversary. Every rosary which you recite with me has the effect of **restricting the action of the Evil One,** of drawing souls away from his pernicious influence, and of giving greater impetus to the expansion of goodness in the life of many of my children.*

"*The chain of the holy rosary has also the effect of **imprisoning Satan,** that is, of making his action impotent, and of diminishing and weakening more and more the force of his diabolical power. And so each rosary that is recited well deals a mighty blow to the power of evil, and it represents one part of his reign which is destroyed.*

"*The chain of the holy rosary brings about, in the end, **the result of making Satan completely harmless.** His great power is destroyed. All the evil spirits are cast into the pool of fire and sulfur; the door is shut by me with the key of the power of Christ, and thus they will no longer be able to go out into the world to do harm to souls.*

"*You understand now, my beloved children, why in these last times of the battle between me, the Woman Clothed with the Sun, and the great dragon, **I am asking you to multiply everywhere the cenacles of prayer, with the recitation of the holy rosary, meditation on my word, and your consecration to my Immaculate Heart.***

"*With these, you make it possible for your heavenly Mother to take action in binding Satan, so that I may carry out my mission of crushing his head, that is to say, of defeating him once and for all, shutting him up in his abyss of fire and sulfur.*

"***The humble and fragile cord of the holy rosary forms the strong chain with which I will take as my prisoner the dark ruler of the world, the enemy of God and of his faithful servants.*** *Thus, the pride of Satan will once again be defeated by the power of the little, the humble and the poor.*

"*As I announce to you today that this, my great victory, is near at hand, the victory which will bring you to your assured liberation, I give you the comfort of my motherly presence among you, and I bless you*" (MMP #479).

For those that may doubt how a well-intentioned rosary may be so powerful one may need to digest the above again. It is Heaven's prayer for our times. It has the power to render Satan useless against us. The rosary is an exorcism prayer that frees us to do God's will.

Decisive Battles That Altered History—
The Battle of Lepanto, October 7, 1571

The Bay of Lepanto lies beyond the Isthmus of Corinth connecting the Peloponnesus with mainland Greece. A great sea battle was fought there on October 7, 1571 where it would be decided whether Christianity or Islam would rule Europe and Asia Minor for coming centuries. The roots of the conflict started soon after Mohammed assumed power as the founder of a new religion, and said he was the prophet of Allah. Starting in the 7th Century, Islam spread rapidly among nomadic tribes as it could be explained so easily. In Christianity there was a virgin birth, a Mother of God, a Holy Spirit, a Trinity with three people in one God, miracles, the supernatural, and a resurrection. Islam was easier to grasp and understand for an illiterate and nomadic people. Islam then swept swiftly through North Africa and the Middle East. It was also a violent religion, if people did not submit to its rule. With significant numbers they marched across the Mediterranean region conquering with a quest of global domination. Turkey, Spain, and other regions fell to its horrors of violence, and Suleiman the Magnificent, who had never lost in battle vowed to stable his horses beneath the dome of Saint Peter and wrap the pope's head in a turban. Islam was defeated at a key battle on the island of Malta by a much smaller army, the Knights of Malta. Badly outnumbered, the Knights stood their ground and defeated the Turkish army. The Turks retreated and vowed to defeat the Christians.

A humble Dominican monk became Pope Pius V. As Christian Europe was caving in to Muslim pressure, St. Pius V saw Christian Europe was in trouble. Only Spain and the region of Venice Italy was ready to defend the faith as other nations had lost the will to defend their sovereign territory. As time progressed, it became more evident all of Christian Europe could be lost unless there was direct action. Pius V formed what became the Holy League to defend against the Turks, and then put the cause for victory in Our Lady's hands. Prayer became the weapon of choice to defeat the Turks, and the chosen prayer was the rosary.

St. Pius V called for a Europe-wide rosary campaign to save Christian Europe, even though they were outmanned, and out gunned in every capacity. However, the Holy League was ready for battle. They lost 8,000 lives and only 17 of their 100 ships were sunk, yet they freed 15,000 Christian galley slaves from the Turkish ships. The Sultan lost 260 ships out of his 300, and 30,000 men. The Holy League had won against great odds. **Admiral Doria, head of the Christian fleet, had the first missionary image of Our Lady of Guadalupe ever to leave Mexico in his stateroom during the battle.**

St. Pius V decreed that October 7 would be thereafter celebrated as Feast of Our Lady of Victories. Pope Gregory in 1573 instituted the victory as Feast of the Holy Rosary. In Venice a chapel was built with the inscription that read: **Neither Valor, Nor Arms, nor Leaders but Our Lady of the Rosary Gave Victory.** What is seldom spoken about is St. Pius V was shown in a vision the defeat of the Turks two weeks prior to the battle!

Austria, the Battle of Vienna 1683

Again, it was the Turks now looking to overtake Austria, a little over 100 years after Lepanto. Their strategy was not by sea, but by land. The Star and the Crescent of the Turkish empire ruled the Danube River, and flew over Budapest, and a short distance away was Vienna. On July 13, the Turks surrounded Vienna and the siege began. When news reached King John of Poland, he raised his heart to heaven and prayed, *"Blessed Virgin of Czestochowa allow me two miracles: that those in Vienna shall resist the siege until September and those of us outside reach there in time to save them."* Even though time was of the essence, the King of Poland and his advisors went to Jasna Gora to pray before the Black Madonna. After four days of prayer, as King John III Sobieski was preparing to leave the shrine, a priest handed him a picture of the Madonna suspended from a gold chain. The King gratefully accepted it and slipped it over his head and began the march with approximately 26,000 armed troops. The wall around Vienna was surrounded by a ring of Turks. The Turkish army had about 115,000 men. The Polish King received about 51,000 more men from Austria and Germany.

On September 12 (this is the Feast of **In the Name of Mary**), King John III arose, and put on the picture of Our Lady of Czestochowa, and attacked. The Polish soldiers had on their lips **Mary Help Us** marching into combat. The battle was a brief one and John Sobieski, King of Poland declared, **"I came, I saw, God Conquered."**

Austria, May 13, 1955, the Strategic Location of Austria — Heaven Intervenes Again

Located next to Eastern and Central Europe, Austria was now facing the mighty Soviet Union and advancing communism. Fearing Austria could fall under the hammer and the sickle as had its neighbors, Austria knew it was powerless and resorted to prayer. World War II had ended in 1945, and the fear was that the Soviet Union would look for further conquests to expand their borders as they took over country after country in Eastern and Central Europe, forming what became known as the Iron Curtain. Of Austria's 7 million people, about ten percent of the population, or 700,000 people, pledged to pray the rosary daily in compliance with Our Lady of Fatima's request. Prayer chains were set up for all hours of the day to have the rosary said over a period of seven years. On May 13, 1955 (the Feast of Our Lady of Fatma), the Soviets just picked up and left for home without a single life lost on either side. Historians were baffled why Russia would give up such a strategically located country without a fight. This was attributed to Our Lady of the Rosary by the Austrian people. The German stigmatist Therese Neumann said before her death on September 18, 1962, *"Definitely, definitely, it was the prayers and many rosaries of the Austrian people that purchased them their freedom from Russian domination."* **Neumann was resolute when she said any country that prayed the rosary could have similar results.**

This is similar to what happened to the fall of the Soviet Union with the end of the Berlin Wall in 1989/1990. The Soviet empire collapsed soon after as well. There was also no widespread blood shed (or extremely limited) during that period.

The Philippines, February 1986

The Philippines Under President Ferdinand Marcos was a corrupt government. **The Blue Army's Soul magazine** covered in great detail when Corazon (Corrie) Aquino ran for president against Marcos. Colman McCarthy of the Washington Post on March 9, 1986 wrote,

"As a weapon, prayer has mostly saints and martyrs to speak for its power: The language of faith says that no weapon is more effective. Now there are followers of Corazon Aquino. On the Sunday before the collapse of the Marcos regime, thousands of Filipinos knelt in a field before the tanks of the government's armed forces. **They recited the rosary....** *The military revving the engines of the tanks, ordered the people to clear a path. They refused to move.... The armored column, which had been on its way to attack a camp of dissident leaders, were turned around by the rosaries. It rolled back to the barracks instead of rolling over the citizens."*

It was not only the Washington Post that reported this, but the UPI, and Cardinal Jaime Sin, Primate of the Philippines, said the government troops held their fire and did not attack the crowd blocking the way to Camp Crame, because, as the soldiers told him, **"a very beautiful lady appeared. The soldiers told his eminence the lady in the vision said, 'Stop! Do not attack my people. I am the Queen of this land.'"**

Sister Lucy of Fatima of Fatima said, *"The Most Holy Virgin in these last times in which we live has given a new efficacy to the recitation of the rosary to such an extent that* **there is no problem, no matter how difficult, whether temporal or above all spiritual, in the personal life of each one of us, or of our families, that cannot be solved by the rosary."**

Pope Saint Pius X said, *"In our time more than ever before, the chief strength of the wicked, lies in the cowardice of good men. All the strength of Satan's reign is due to the easy-going weakness of Catholics."*

At Fatima, on June 13, 1917, the Blessed Mother said, *"I wish... that you pray the rosary every day."*

On July 13, 1917 she said again, *"Pray the rosary every day in honor of Our Lady of the Rosary, in order to obtain peace for the world and the end of the war for she alone can help."*

Again at Fatima on October 13, 1917, Our Lady said, *"I am the Lady of the Rosary. I have come to warn the faithful to amend their lives and ask for pardon for their sins. They must not offend the Lord anymore, for He is already grievously offended by the sins of men. People must pray the rosary. Let them continue saying it every day."*

What Some Have Said About the Rosary

The quotes below are found in *Champions of the Rosary, The History and Heros of a Spiritual Weapon*, 2016, by Father Donald Calloway, MIC. The following is a small number of the several hundred quotes about the power and value of the rosary from saints, and men and women of God.

The rosary is one of the greatest secrets to have come down from Heaven.

— St. Louis De Montfort

It would hardly be possible for me to put into words how much Our Lady thinks of the Holy Rosary and how vastly she prefers it to other devotions.

— Saint Louis de Montfort

I beg of you to beware of thinking of the rosary as something of little importance — as do ignorant people and even several great and proud scholars. Far from being insignificant, the rosary is a priceless treasure which is inspired by God.

— Saint Louis de Montfort

The rose is the queen of flowers, and so the rosary is the rose of all devotions, and it is therefore the most important one.

— Saint Louis de Montfort

The immense good that this noble devotion (the rosary) has done to the world is well known. How many, by its means, have been delivered from sin! How many led to a holy life! How many to a good death, and are now saved!

— St. Alphonsus Liguori, Doctor of the Church

A person who was leading an immoral life had not the courage to give it up: he began to say the rosary and was converted.

— St. Alphonsus Liguori, Doctor of the Church

It is well known that the devotion to the most holy rosary was revealed to St. Dominic by the Blessed Mother herself, at a time when the saint was in affliction, and bewailing, with his Sovereign Lady over the Albigensian heretics, who were at that time doing great mischief in the Church.

— St. Alphonsus Liguori

I could conquer the world if I had an army to say the rosary.

— Blessed Pope Pius IX

Among all the devotions approved by the Church, none has been so favored by so many miracles as the rosary devotion.   — Blessed Pope Pius IX

The single greatest treasury in the Vatican is the rosary.

— Blessed Pope Pius IX

Mother Mary, how good you have been to me and how ungrateful I have been to you! My mother, I wish to love you from now on with all my heart, and not only to love you myself, but to bring everyone else to know, love, serve, and praise you and to pray the holy rosary, a devotion that is pleasing to you.

— St. Anthony Mary Claret

The holy rosary is comprised of many holy elements; no one doubts that this devotion is very pleasing to God and His Holy Virgin. The devotion of the most holy rosary is powerful enough to transmit all the graces and, as we are aware from experience, it has proven to be a remedy during times of war, plagues, hunger and other calamities; in addition, those who have been troubled in body and soul, if they had recourse to the rosary always received consolation.

— St. Anthony Mary Claret

The rosary is a flower garden that contains all kinds of beautiful and aromatic virtues.   — St. Anthony Mary Claret

It is mainly to expand the kingdom of Christ that we look to the rosary for the most effective help.   — Pope Leo XIII

Experience has shown that to inculcate love for the Mother of God deeply in souls there is nothing more efficacious than the practice of the rosary.

— Pope Leo XIII

The rosary, if rightly considered, will be found to have in itself special virtues, whether for producing and continuing a state of recollection, or for touching the conscience for its healing, or for lifting up the soul.   — Pope Leo XIII

After the Holy Liturgy of the Eucharist, the prayer of the rosary is what better draws to our spirit the mysteries of Faith, Hope, and Charity. She (the rosary) is the spiritual bread of souls. — Servant of God Lucia Dos Santos

There are those who say that the rosary is an antiquated and monotonous prayer because of the constant repetition of the prayers that compose it. But, I put the question: Is there anything kept alive without the perseverance in the continual repetition of some actions? — Servant of God Lucia Dos Santos

The rosary is the prayer of the poor and the rich, of the wise and the ignorant. To uproot this devotion from souls is like depriving them of their daily spiritual bread. She (the rosary) is what supports that little flame of faith that has not yet been completely extinguished from many consciences. Even for those souls who pray without meditating, the simple act of taking the beads to pray is already a remembrance of God, the supernatural.

— Servant of God Lucia Dos Santos

The holy rosary, according to Lucia of Fatima, is so powerful that it can solve any problem, material or spiritual, national or international.

— Blessed Gabriele Allegra

One has to have great patience and trust in her. Moreover, one must pray much in times of trouble and suffering. One needs to invoke her most sweet name, "Mary," or say a "Hail Mary," and in the most difficult and crucial times it will not hurt to even recite a whole section of the rosary.

— St. Maximilian Kolbe

A prayer both simple and sublime that the Immaculata herself indicated when she appeared in Lourdes is the holy rosary. May it become the sword of each knight of the Immaculata, just as the Miraculous Medal is the bullet that strikes down evil. — St. Maximilian Kolbe

In her apparition at Lourdes, in 1858, the Mother of God held in her arms the rosary, and through (St) Bernadette, recommended to us the recital of the rosary. We can conclude, therefore, that the prayer of the rosary makes the Immaculata happy. Moreover, with this prayer we can easily obtain great graces and divine blessing. — St. Maximilian Kolbe

When very frequently we receive newly married couples in audience and address paternal words to them, we give them rosaries; we recommended these to them earnestly; and we exhort them, citing our own example, not to let even one day pass without saying the rosary, no matter how burdened they may be with many cares and labors. — Pope Pius XI

In climbing towards God for its salvation, the soul possesses the Key of Heaven in the rosary. — Servant of God Dolindo Ruotolo

The rosary is a weapon in our hands with which we can overcome the devil's attacks. — St. Pio of Pietrelcina

Our Lady has never refused me a grace through the recitation of the rosary. — St. Pio of Pietrelcina

The rosary is a great test of faith. What the Eucharist is in the order of sacraments, the rosary is in the order of the sacramental — the mystery and the test of faith, the touchstone by which the soul is judged in its humility. The mark of the Christian is the willingness to look for the Divine in the flesh of a babe in a crib, the continuing Christ under the appearance of bread on an altar, and a meditation and a prayer on a string of beads. — Venerable Fulton J. Sheen

Take care of them — they are mine. Bring them to Jesus — carry Jesus to them. Fear not. Teach them to say the rosary — the family rosary, and all will be well. — Our Lady's words to St. Teresa of Calcutta

The rosary is the prayer of the Christian who advances on pilgrimage of faith, in the following of Jesus, preceded by Mary. — Pope Benedict XVI

Our Lady's Promises to Those Who Pray the Rosary
15 Promises Given to Saint Dominic and Blessed Alan

Whoever shall faithfully pray my rosary:

1. Shall receive special graces.

2. Shall have my special protection and the greatest of graces.

3. Shall have a powerful armor against hell. It will destroy vice, decrease sin, defeat heresies.

4. Shall find it will cause virtue and good works to flourish. It will obtain for souls the abundant mercy of God. It will withdraw the hearts of men from the love of the world and its vanities, and will lift them from the desire of eternal things. Oh, that souls would sanctify themselves by this means.

5. Shall not perish.

6. Shall never be conquered by misfortune if he applies himself to the consideration of its sacred mysteries. God will not chastise him in His justice; he will not perish by an unprovided death; if he be just, he shall remain in the grace of God and become worthy of eternal life.

7. Shall not die without the Sacraments.

8. Shall have during their life and at their death the Light of God and the plenitude of His graces. At the moment of death they shall participate in the merits of the saints in paradise.

9. Shall be delivered from purgatory.

10. Shall merit a high degree of glory in Heaven.

11. Shall obtain all that you ask of me.

12. All who propagate the Holy Rosary shall be aided by Me in their necessities.

13. Shall have for intercessors the entire celestial court during their life and at the hour of death.

14. Are my sons, the brothers of my only Son, Jesus Christ.

15. Can consider it a great sign of predestination.

A Call to Prayer and Action — Now

In November 2017, 25 members of our group comprised of friends and the local Legion of Mary and the International Week of Prayer and Fasting (IWOPF.org) and **Signs and Wonders for Our Times Apostolate,** met to discuss what we could do to combat the evil that is accelerating. Rather than just do the 40 days of prayer and fasting that we have been doing for 29 years ending with the public event at the Shrine of the Immaculate Conception in Washington, D.C, we heard in prayer that we were to launch a program with subscribers of our magazine for a total of 365 days. We presently have over 300 people nationwide committed to finding groups of people and churches to participate. There are now several thousand people involved in a prayer campaign for a new Spiritual Revolution, and the seven steps for the restoration of America. This program is now in its 4th full year and growing as more people see the urgency of our times. We have called it: Pray and Fast for America.org.

The program is simple:

1. Attend the Holy Sacrifice of the Mass when possible — daily
2. Pray the Holy Rosary and Divine Mercy chaplet — daily
3. Spend one hour in adoration — weekly
4. Fast and do penance — weekly
5. Consecration to the Holy Family
6. Spiritual Purity Prayers — daily
7. Spiritual Warfare prayers — daily

If you would like to join the effort, go to **Pray and Fast for America.org** and join the prayer campaign or become a person to sign up other groups.

In the Garden of Gethsemane the night before His passion, *"Jesus came unto His disciples and found them asleep and said to Peter, 'What, could you not watch with me one hour?'"* (Matt. 26:40)

JESUS I TRUST IN YOU

24

Courage Is Contagious

Be strong and courageous. Do not be afraid or terrified
because of them, for the Lord your God goes with you.
He will never leave you nor forsake you.

Deut. 31:6-8

W hen Saint Paul wrote the book of Romans, he was at the end of his apostolic journey. It had begun after he was knocked off his donkey (he may have been on a horse as he was a Roman citizen) on the way to Damascus and blinded because of his zealous nature persecuting the new believers in Jesus Christ. Those looking to follow the teachings of Jesus as a way of life were fearful of what Saul was doing and didn't want anything to do with him.

Then after the Damascus road event, the Lord called on Ananias to minister healing to Saul. Annanias said to the Lord, *"Lord several people have told me about this man and all the harm he has been doing to your saints in Jerusalem. He has only come here because he holds a warrant from the chief priests to arrest everybody who invokes your name. The Lord replied, 'You must go all the same, because this man is my chosen instrument to bring my name before pagans and pagan kings and before the people of Israel. I myself will show him how much he himself must suffer for my name'"* (Acts 9:13-16).

Few know that Saul of Tarsus, now Paul went through a discipleship period for three years in the desert of Arabia after his radical conversion. On today's map that would be modern day Syria. Saint Paul had traveled throughout Asia Minor all the way to Rome to preach the gospel as it had been given to him directly by Jesus Christ.

Paul gives a brief biography in chapter 1 of Galatians of how while in Arabia he evolved into an apostle taught directly by the Holy Spirit and not the original apostles. Paul writes, *"I want you to realize this, the Good News I preach is not a human message, that I was given by men. It is something I learnt only through a revelation of Jesus Christ. Then God, who had specially chosen me while I was still in my mother's womb, called me through His grace to reveal His Son in me so that I might preach the Good News about Him to the pagans. I did not stop to discuss this with any human being, nor did I go to Jerusalem to see those who were already apostles before me, but I went to Arabia at once and later went straight back from there to Damascus. Even when after three years I went up to Jerusalem to visit Cephas and stayed with him fifteen days"* (Gal. 1: 11, 15-19).

Paul had a unique commission from God to preach the good news in the known world to pagan people not having any catechesis before he arrived. Therefore, he had to be very clear and direct on this new truth of Jesus that he was teaching. The writings of Saint Paul show a man who never compromised the truth.

There was no political correctness to a consensus to get along. Paul spoke pure unadulterated raw truth no matter the circumstance(s). It is why he had such a large and loyal following with those pure of heart. The human heart, soul, and mind seeks the truth, and Paul provided it everywhere he taught. People may not agree with him, but his teachings are clear. Paul understood the letter of the law from his ancestral traditions he learned as an observant zealous Jew. Once Saul, now Paul being taught directly by God, had been transformed to an understanding of a new law now written on men's hearts. Paul had a unique charism understanding what Jesus was trying to convey to the world in the Redemptive Plan as the Kingdom of God had come to men in the person of Jesus. Saint Paul was a principal agent in the early church as God's mouthpiece for a new emerging doctrine.

America over the last several generations has become a pagan land. Albeit, we have technology the world could never could have imagined years ago. In 1969 we sent three men to the moon and brought them home safely, we have broken the genetic code of man, and countless other technological feats. We are pagans in our beliefs and practices, with great technology in our hands. We have devolved into a moral wasteland filled with pagan people. If one were to look at what the U.S. government funds for our social policies, and what we practice and believe, we have become outright pagan, similar in practice and views to the people Paul visited on his mission journeys.

Saint Paul's writings are majestic truth in every sense of the word because of his uncompromising clarity. There is never any ambiguity where Paul stands on any moral issue. In an age where 2 + 2 = 5, and the truth is hard to find, it is going to take more of the directness of Paul to make Christian doctrine clear. The insanity of gender shows just how far we have drifted spiritually. When a woman can be called a man because someone wills it due to dysfunctional thinking, and the government endorses it, that is not just confusion, that is moral depravity. Moral relativism has taken us to another dimension when we can't make it clear there is a difference between something as simple as the differences between a man's and a woman's nature. The U.S. is a modern-day pagan Rome whether we care to admit it or not, and speaking directly, as Paul did to the Romans, is a partial remedy for the culture.

Saint Paul described the Roman's behavior and views in the first chapter in his letter to them. Paul is speaking as if he is on a street corner among friends. He is speaking in the vernacular and understandable. It is direct, clear, and brutally frank what he thinks these pagans in Rome really are, as he gives very emotive descriptions of their behavior. There is no confusion where he stands. It is not sugar coated like we see people talking about the state of American degeneracy and what we have become as a nation.

Paul writes to the Romans what he thinks of their behavior, *"Ever since God created the world His everlasting power and deity — however invisible — have been there for the mind to see in the things he has made. **That is why such people are without excuse: they knew God and yet refused to honor Him as God** or to thank Him; instead they made nonsense out of logic and their empty minds were darkened. The more they called themselves philosophers, **the more stupid they grew,** until they exchanged the glory of the immortal God for a worthless imitation of a mortal man, of birds, quadrupeds, and reptiles. That is why God left them to their filthy enjoyments, and the practices which they dishonor their own bodies since they have given up divine truth for a lie and have worshipped and served creatures instead of the creator, who is blessed forever. Amen!*

*"In other words, since they refused to see it was rational to acknowledge God, God has left them to their own irrational ideas and their monstrous behavior. And so they are steeped in all sorts of depravity, rottenness, greed and malice, slanderers, enemies of God, rude, arrogant, boastful, enterprising in sin, rebellious to parents, **without brains, honor, love, or pity.** They know what God's verdict is: that those who behave like this deserve to die — and yet they do it; and what is worse; **encourage others to do the same"** (Romans 1:20-25, 28-32).*

Paul is talking to people about the state of depravity in men's souls due to the ravages of illicit conduct. Sin clouds the mind from grace to have clear thoughts, thus you produce monstrous behavior and all the descriptions St. Paul uses to describe people who are lost. Ultimately, one's world view is based on a belief in God or not. Atheism brings out the beast in man and this is what is prevailing today.

History has shown man is capable of horrific crimes when the divine is removed from the affairs of man. Sin prevents grace and light from entering the soul of people, thus morally aberrant conduct that encourages others to do the same. Over the last generation in particular, as we have lost our moral standing, we are following the path of other great civilizations to the ash heap of history. Observing the insanity is hard to watch for people who grew up in 1940's to 1970's in the United States. *Sin is the ultimate enemy within.*

The Ignoring of Heaven's Remedy

Our state of depravity is so complex to fix today, most have given up trying to find a remedy. The national past time is talking about the problems and disseminating emails on the reprobate state of the country. Very few (yea verily) provide solutions. Believers have all the tools necessary to remedy the situation, but their silence is the problem. Jesus told Saint Faustina, *"Fear is useless. What is needed is trust."* Edmund Burke's famous quote is still appropriate, *"The only thing necessary for the triumph of evil is for good men to do nothing."* The left has a near monopoly on controlling the narrative, while most believers just respond to their nonsense. It is time to do as Heaven has asked with the spiritual tools it has given us. First and foremost is speaking the truth. The Word of God is an offensive weapon.

There are two thousand years of established doctrine and truth behind us. Philosophy, theology, natural law, and science backstop a believer yet they often cower when confronted for fear of appearing confrontational. II Timothy states, *"All Scripture is inspired by God for doctrine, reproof, correction, and instruction in righteousness, that we all may be made perfect"* (II Tim. 3:17).

One place to start in social settings is to be clear, as is Saint Paul, in what the culture has become when the subject comes up. Proverbs says *"A gentle answer turns away wrath, but a grievous word stirs up anger"* (Proverbs 15:1). A response to the left does not have to be rooted in sarcasm, anger or ending in a brawl. The truth if spoken by one meekly is still the truth. It can turn around a family, a parish, or even a community over time because it makes people think. **Speaking truth may also encourage another who shares your views to be more courageous in expressing the truth rather than getting beaten down by progressives.** *Courage is contagious.* But hiding the light is a mistake and has brought us to this place of insane behavior where we find ourselves today. We are in this spiritual malaise because good people ceased to speak up when lies were expressed. The day of being the turtle on a fence post must end if we are to save this generation.

JESUS I TRUST IN YOU

25

The Epic Battle We are in
and Heaven's Ultimate Protection

It has been discovered that with a dull urban population,
all formed under a mechanical system of state education,
a suggestion or a command, however senseless and unreasoned,
will be obeyed if it be sufficiently repeated.

Hilaire Belloc, An Essay on the Restoration of Property

The messages below are exclusively from the Marian Movement of Priests from the Blessed Mother to Father Stefano Gobbi over a twenty-five year period from the first public messages in 1973 to the very last message of December 31, 1997. In the final message Our Lady said, *"As of now, all that I had to say has been said, because all has been revealed to you"* (MMP #604). For those following her messages, what was first said back in 1973 has come to pass as it was stated. It has been similar to the messages of Fatima. What was said in 1917 at Fatima has come to pass concerning Russia and Church events. It happened as stated with historical accuracy. To a student of these messages, it is not a debatable point.

The Holy Spirit is dynamic (as opposed to static) and moves on with or without us. It is our choice. With coinciding events, Fatima and even MMP have moved on to the future where Medjugorje and Garabandal will soon take center stage. Events prophesied at Garbandal and Medjugorje will change the world forever, much like we speak in terms of Before Christ (BC) and After Christ (AD). The Marian Movement of Priests' messages laid out in great detail the direction of the Church decades in advance, when many people could not see the possibility of the events happening when the messages were first released. We have seen what was said at Fatima come to fruition in stunning accuracy. It is now the same for the MMP messages; we have seen in historical hindsight the prophesied events happen as foretold.

The messages of the Marian Movement of Priests are like modern day epistles for the faithful paying attention to our times. We are at the tail end of what the Blessed Mother told us decades ago. Those following the messages know that **"all has been revealed,"** taking much of the guess work out of interpreting the events of our day. The messages are a roadmap to know the times in which we live — and more importantly, how to respond as Heaven wishes. It is like having read today's newspaper years ago.

To win this battle, the believer must deeply contemplate Jesus's meaning when He said, *"For my thoughts are not your thoughts, neither are your ways, my ways, says the Lord. For as the heavens are higher than the earth so are my ways higher than your ways, and my thoughts than your thoughts"* (Isaiah 55:8-9). The believer has been given the necessary tools to fight evil, but often forgets to implement them even though they are at our constant disposal to win necessary battles.

Even nature has a profound understanding of how to sustain itself using its God-given abilities to its own advantage. The eagle will not fight the snake on the ground where it is the wisest and the strongest. It will change the battle to the sky where it is in control and the snake is vulnerable. So, it will snatch the snake off the ground and bring it into the sky where it is disoriented, weak, and helpless. We must utilize the weapons and tools God has given us to win this battle against evil. They are Consecration, prayer, fasting, and the full use of the arsenal of the Sacraments which we must realize are both offensive and defensive weapons; not merely talking all day about the problems we face. Change the nature of the battle to your advantage. Let God win your battles on His terms, with His methods.

The Blessed Mother as Prophetess of Our Times and God's Chosen Instrument for Our Times

Moses was tasked with leading the Jews out of bondage in Egypt where they had been slaves for four hundred years. If a generation is twenty-five years, that would mean sixteen generations of Hebrews had lived under the Egyptian yoke of oppression. To put this in an American historical perspective, four hundred years ago was 1621. It was December 18, 1620, that the Mayflower came to shore in Plymouth Harbor, Massachusetts, which became the Massachusetts Bay Colony under the leadership of William Bradford. Moses had an entrenched mindset to overcome where the people would believe it could be done after such a long time in bondage under generations of Pharaohs. It was Yahweh and the Most Holy Trinity who had given Moses the task to lead God's people to a new life. Surely many Hebrew slaves doubted it could be done, but God had chosen Moses to free His people. It was Heaven's will.

Just as Moses was chosen to lead God's people, it is now the Blessed Mother's role as the chosen instrument by the Most Holy Trinity to lead God's people as the prophetess of our age in these times. She is the daughter of the Father, mother of the Son, and the spouse of the Holy Spirit tasked to lead God's people to the New Era and the New Jerusalem which is spoken of many times throughout the ages. She has been given many titles as she is today the Mother of the New Advent, Mother of the Second Pentecost, Mother of the Eucharist, and the Mother of the New Evangelization to name just a few. She has said, *"These are My Times."* Yes, we are living a great mystery more profound than human words can possibly express. If Heaven wants it to be so, can we doubt Heaven's good intentions for us? We must live the mystery as only good can come from what she is asking us to do at this perilous moment in history. The globalists wish to reset the world without a Christocentric view, and the Blessed Mother will not allow it.

Many are near a point of despair as they look at the overwhelming negative societal issues in front of us. We will soon experience shortages of many things and will need to improvise. There will be further economic and moral collapse of every kind leaving us disoriented at the end of the day. Before the New Times are ushered in, the old must pass away — and it will be painful. We are watching evil being exposed in every genre of the culture. In essence, the puss is being pushed out as the infection is being lanced, and that is what is on the nightly news as Satan's cohort and Heaven's cohort battle. Now is the not the time to doubt as we near Heaven's prescribed victory.

We have to stand on the promises. The devil knows his time is short, thus the level of evil Satan is perpetrating upon the entire world is accelerating.

The Blessed Mother gave an encouraging message very early on (1973) to the Marian Movement of Priests titled The Triumph of My Immaculate Heart. Indicating there will be a huge battle in the future, she said, ***"In fact at the very moment when Satan will be enthroned as the lord of the world and will think himself now the sure victor, I myself will snatch the prey from his hands. In a trice he will find himself empty-handed, and in the end the victory will be exclusively my Son's and mine. This will be the triumph of my Immaculate Heart in the world"*** (MMP #29g).

The word trice means quickly or in an instant. This is how events will shift back to the believer. We will know the miracle is of God, and not man. Few really know what the Triumph of the Immaculate Heart really means. We are told it is the Triumph of Jesus as the Blessed Mother always points to her Son, never herself. His Triumph is His return in glory, and thus she triumphs. As Aaron spoke for Moses in the desert, she is speaking for the Trinity now. It will be a glorious day. **Here lies our great hope as Heaven is in control,** albeit it is hard for us to believe and understand the totality of our times because there is so much darkness at this moment.

Of the many necessary tools to fight evil, one which is misunderstood, and underutilized, is Consecration to the Immaculate Heart. Consecration means to be set aside, and when a person makes a Consecration, there are graces that come with that act. It is an anointing that Heaven gives that individual where there is an infusion of grace beyond human understanding. It is the single best thing a person can do for a truly spiritual response to understand our times, and as importantly, be spiritually and physically protected. The promises defy human reason in light of the spiritual malaise of our day. It is why MMP's entire message of Family Consecration has been included in its totality. In addition, considerable verbiage is provided making it clear the Blessed Mother has been appointed by the Most Holy Trinity as Heaven's messenger, as Moses was in the Old Testament to bring God's people out of bondage. Heaven tasks and entrusts people to execute their mission. It is the story of the Bible, and it is God's way.

The Families Consecrated to Me (MMP #358)

"How consoled I am by this day spent in prayer, in a simple and cordial fraternal gathering, with this family, consecrated to me and which belongs to

me! I want now to give you my word of consolation, that it may be a comfort for you in the midst of the daily difficulties of your life. I love you; I am present in your midst; I am speaking to you and leading you because you are the instruments of my motherly will.

"I look with love on the families consecrated to me. In these times, I am gathering the families and leading them into the depths of my Immaculate Heart, that they may be able to find refuge and security, comfort and defense. Just as I love to be invoked as Mother and Queen of my priests, so also, I love to be invoked as Mother and Queen of the families consecrated to me.

"I am the Mother and the Queen of families. I watch over their life; I take their problems to heart; I interest myself not only in their spiritual good but also in the material good of all their members. When you consecrate a family to my Immaculate Heart, it is as though you open the door of your house to your heavenly Mother, invite her to come in, and give her the opportunity to exercise her motherly function in an ever stronger way. This is why I desire that all Christian families consecrate themselves to my Immaculate Heart. I ask that they open the doors of all their homes to me so that I may come in and take up my motherly dwelling among you. I then come in as your Mother, I dwell with you, and I take a part in all your life.

"Above all I see to the care of your spiritual life. I seek to bring the souls of those who compose the family to live always in the grace of God. There where I enter in, sin goes out; there where I stay, grace and divine light are always present; there where I dwell, purity and holiness dwell with me. That is why my first motherly task is that of making the members of the family live in the state of grace and of making them grow in the life of holiness, through the exercise of all the Christian virtues.

"And because the sacrament of Matrimony confers on you a particular grace to make you grow together, my task is that of cementing deeply the unity of the family, to bring the husband and wife to an ever deeper and more spiritual communion, to perfect their human love, to make it more perfect, to bring it into the Heart of Jesus, so that it may assume the new form of a greater perfection, which expresses itself in a pure and super-natural charity. I strengthen more and more unity within families. I bring them to a greater and reciprocal understanding; I make them feel the new exigencies of a more delicate and profound communion.

"*I lead their members along the road of sanctity and of joy, which must be built up and traveled through together, that they may be able to attain the perfection of love and thus enjoy the precious gift of peace. Thus, I form the souls of my children, and through the way of the family, I lead them to the summit of holiness.*

"*I want to enter families to make you saints, to bring you to the perfection of love, to stay with you, to make your family unity more fruitful and strong. And then I see also to the material good of the families consecrated to me.*

"*The most precious good of a family is its children. The children are a sign of a particular predilection on the part of Jesus and of me. The children must be wanted, welcomed and cultivated like the most precious gems of a family estate.* **When I enter into a family, I immediately look after the children; they become also mine.** *I take them by the hand; I lead them to walk along the road of the realization of a plan of God, which has from all eternity already been clearly traced out for each one of them. I love them.* **I never abandon them. They become a precious part of my maternal estate.**

"*I see to your work in a special way. I never allow you to be lacking in the assistance of divine providence. I take your hands, and I open them upon the plan which the Lord is carrying out each day, by means of your human collaboration.*

"*As my humble, faithful and daily motherly action in the little and poor house of Nazareth made possible the fulfillment of the Father's plan, which was realized in the human growth of the Son, called to carry out the work of redemption for your salvation, so too I am calling you to second the plan of the Father, which is being realized through your human collaboration and by means of your daily work.*

"*You must do your part, as the Heavenly Father does His. Your action must be espoused to that of divine providence, that the work may produce its fruit in those goods which are useful for the sustaining of your life, for the enrichment of the family itself, in such a way that its members can always enjoy spiritual and material well-being.*

"*And then I will help you to carry out the plan of the Will of God. Thus, I make the work more fruitful spiritually, because I make of it a source of merit for you and an occasion of salvation for many of my poor lost children. Then, in your person, action is united to love, work to prayer, fatigue to the burning thirst of an ever-greater charity. In this way, by your collaboration with the Will of the Father, you form the masterpiece of a providence which, by means of you, becomes a day-to-day reality.*

"Do not be afraid; there where I enter in, security enters in with me. **Nothing will ever be lacking to you.** *I make your activity more perfect; I purify your very work.*

"I share also in all your preoccupations. I know that the preoccupations of a family today are many. They are yours, and they become mine. I share with you your sufferings. That is why, in such difficult times as those of the present purification, I am present in the families consecrated to me, as a concerned and suffering Mother, who really takes part in all your suffering. Be therefore consoled.

"These are my times. 'These,' that is to say the days in which you are living, are 'mine,' because they are times marked by my great and strong presence. These times will become even more mine, the more my victory will broaden out and become stronger, surpassing the victory which at present is that of my Adversary. This presence of mine will become very strong and extraordinary, above all in the families consecrated to my Immaculate Heart. It will become apparent to all and will become for you a source of a special consolation.

"So then go forward in confidence, in hope, in silence, in your daily work, in prayer and in humility. Go forward more and more in purity and with an upright intention; advance with me along the difficult road of peace of heart and of peace in your families.

"If you all walk along the road which I have traced out for you, if you listen to and put into practice what I have said to you today, your families will be the first buds of my triumph: small, hidden, quiet buds, which are already sprouting in every part of the earth, as though to anticipate the new era and the new times which are even now at your doors."

I Am the Beginning of the New Times (MMP #302)

"My dearly beloved children, never lose confidence and hope. Beneath the great and vast clamor which evil is managing to spread everywhere, many sprouts of goodness and holiness are budding forth in silence and hiddenness. These precious sprouts of new life are being daily cultivated in the secret garden of my Immaculate Heart....

"Entrust yourselves, all of you, to your heavenly Mother that you may be consoled. In the great battle which you are fighting, find strength and comfort there, and never lose your courage in the face of the difficulties which you meet.

"During the new year, the trials and sufferings which await you will become even greater, because you have already entered into the final phase of what I have foretold to you. **A great and bloody trial is about to shake the whole earth, to prepare it for its complete renewal in the triumph of my Immaculate Heart.**

"But the more severe the trial will become, the greater will be my presence at the side of each one of you, that you may be comforted and encouraged by me. If you live in my Immaculate Heart, nothing that can happen will be able to disturb you; within this motherly refuge of mine, you are always safe, wrapped in the light and the presence of the Most Holy Trinity, who loves you and surrounds you with its divine protection....

"You must be my powerful help, which I wish to offer today to all humanity in order to lead it to return along the road of goodness and of love. I am the way of this, its return. I am the doorway of divine mercy. I desire that, through you, all my lost children may be able to come back to the Lord, who awaits them with the anxiety and the joy of a Father who loves them and wants to save them. Thus, you become also instruments of divine mercy, in these times in which the greatest triumph of the merciful love of my Son Jesus is in preparation."

All Has Been Revealed to You (MMP #604)

"Truly Satan, with the cup of lust, has succeeded in seducing all the nations of the earth. He has replaced love with hatred; communion with division; justice with many injustices; peace with continuous war. In fact, this entire century has been spent under the sign of cruel and bloody wars, which have claimed millions of innocent victims.

"So then, the Most Holy Trinity has decreed that your century be placed under the sign of my powerful, maternal and extraordinary presence. Thus, at Fatima I pointed out the way along which humanity must journey for its return to the Lord: that of conversion, prayer and penance. And as a safe refuge, I offered you my Immaculate Heart.

"All has been revealed to you: my plan has been pointed out to you even in its painful realization. Humanity has fallen under the domination of Satan and of his great power, exercised with the satanic and masonic forces; my Church has become obscured by his smoke which has penetrated into it. Errors are being taught and propagated, causing many to lose true faith in Christ and in his Gospel; the holy Law of God is openly violated; sin is committed and often even justified, and thus the light of grace and of the divine presence is lost; unity is deeply split apart by a strong contestation directed against the Magisterium, and especially against the Pope; and the wound caused by painful lacerations becomes ever wider. (Author's note: this message was given during the papacy of St. John Paul II).

"In order to give the suffering and crucified Church of your time my motherly help and a safe refuge, I have brought the Marian Movement of Priests into being and have spread it through every part of the world by means of my book, which traces out for you the road along which you must journey in order to spread my light. With this book, I teach you to live the consecration to my Immaculate Heart with the simplicity of children, in a spirit of humility, of poverty, of trust and of filial abandonment....

"Then the words which I have caused to come down from my Immaculate Heart, as drops of heavenly dew upon the desert of your life, so threatened by snares, will produce fruits of grace and holiness....

"All has been revealed to you: my plan has been foretold to you especially in its wonderful and victorious fulfillment."

I have announced to you the triumph of my Immaculate Heart in the world. In the end my Immaculate Heart will triumph.

"This will come about in the greatest triumph of Jesus, who will bring into the world His glorious reign of love, of justice and of peace, and will make all things new.

"Open your hearts to hope. Throw open the doors to Christ who comes to you in glory. Live the trembling hour of this Second Advent.

"Become thus the courageous heralds of this, His triumph, because you—little babes consecrated to me who live from my very own spirit—are the apostles of these last times.

"Live as faithful disciples of Jesus, in contempt for the world and for yourselves, in poverty, in humility, in silence, in prayer, in mortification,

in charity and in union with God, while you are unknown and despised by the world....

"Fight, children of the light, because the hour of my battle has now arrived. In the harshest of winters, you are the buds which are opening up from my Immaculate Heart and which I am placing on the branches of the Church to tell you that her most beautiful springtime is about to arrive."

Do Battle, Beloved Sons! (MMP #296)

"For this I need much prayer. More is obtained through one day of intense prayer than through years of continuous discussions.... [L]et Holy Mass be the center of your apostolic day."

If there is any doubt about what Heaven thinks of how powerful prayer is, nothing can be more important to turn a negative situation around than a day of intense prayer versus talking about it for years. In addition, Our Lady says Mass should be at the center of our apostolic life.

I Am the Queen of Peace (MMP #298)

"Never before as today has the human race been so threatened by the danger of war and of an immense destruction. Look to me as to her who has the task from God of bringing peace to the world."

Mother of the Second Advent (MMP #417)

"Beloved children, begin this new year in the immaculate light of my divine maternity. I am your Mother as well, by the Will of my Son Jesus....

"During these years I am preparing you, by my motherly action, to receive the Lord who is coming. This is why I have asked you for the consecration to my Immaculate Heart: to form all of you, in that interior docility which is necessary for me in order that I may be able to work in each one of you, bringing you to a profound transformation which should prepare you to receive the Lord worthily.

"I am the Mother of the Second Advent."

Only in the Hearts of the Little Ones (MMP #418)

"Look at all these children of mine: they are simple; they are little; they are so tried by suffering and by poverty. And yet, see how they have responded with generosity to my request for consecration and for prayer."

Promises of Consecration

The Heart of My Priests (MMP #9)

"One who has consecrated himself to me belongs totally to me. He cannot, at any moment of the day, decide freely what he is to do with himself."

This Month of May (MMP #264)

*"At this time above all, I am asking you to pray with fervor and joy by means of the Holy Rosary. It is the weapon which is to be used by you today in fighting and winning this bloody battle; it is the golden chain that binds you to my heart; **it is the lightening rod that will keep far from you, and those who are dear to you, the fire of the chastisement; it is the sure means of having me always close to you.**

*"Finally, I ask you to renew often and to live fully the consecration to my Immaculate and Sorrowful Heart. **Enter at once into this refuge to be protected by me.** My protection should become ever more manifest to all because the days in which you are living are marked by great sufferings, and for so many of my poor children, who are so menaced today, the danger of being lost is increasing."*

There is today, in many sincere circles in the Catholic community and beyond, an over emphasis on places of physical refuge. The Blessed Mother is clear: the refuge is in the Immaculate Heart. There are so many potential contingencies where places of physical refuge will not suffice for all the issues in the future which we may encounter. The Deep State has a long reach into our lives for methods of compliance and their dictates for control. However, living and being squarely in the refuge of the Immaculate Heart, which Heaven is asking, will cover all the necessary elements for our physical and spiritual welfare.

The Blessed Mother Entrusted to Provide the Messages for Humanity

The Bloody Years of the Battle (MMP #495)

"The powers which are directing and arranging human events, according to their perverse plans are the dark and diabolical powers of evil. They have succeeded in bringing all humanity to live without God. They have spread

everywhere the error of theoretical and practical atheism. They have built the new idols before which humanity is bowing down in adoration: pleasure, money, pride, impurity, mastery over others, and impiety....

"The forces of Masonry have entered into the Church, in a subtle and hidden way, and have set up their stronghold in the very place where the Vicar of my Son Jesus lives and works.

In My Immaculate Heart (MMP #177)

"Here you will be formed by me according to the plan which the Heart of My Son Jesus has entrusted to me. Thus, each one of you will be helped by me to carry out in a perfect manner the divine Will alone....

"Thus, your life is becoming daily more conformable to my motherly plan, and the Most Holy Trinity can reflect its light in you and receive greater glory....

"And so it must be apparent to the Church what that refuge is which I, the Mother, have prepared for all: my Immaculate Heart.

My Plan (MMP #558)

"I have been conceived without original sin, and thus I have been able to realize in my life, in a perfect way, the plan of the Most Holy Trinity and to respond to the task which It entrusted to me on my becoming the Mother of the Incarnate Word.

"My plan is that of leading in battle the cohort of the sons of God to fight and overcome the snares of those who have put themselves at the service of Satan and who are battling to spread in the world the reign of evil, error, sin, hatred, and impurity.

"My plan is to lead all creation back to its primal splendor, in such a way that the Heavenly Father may again be pleased to be reflected in it and to receive His greatest glory from all creation.

"My plan is to lead all my children along the road of perfect imitation of Jesus, in such a way that He may live again in them and contemplate with joy the copious fruits which are born from His great gift of redemption.

"My plan is to prepare hearts and souls to receive the Holy Spirit, who will pour Himself out in fullness to bring upon the world the second Pentecost of fire and love.

"My plan is to point out to all my children the way of faith and of hope, of love and of purity, of goodness and of holiness. Thus, in the garden of my Immaculate Heart, I am preparing the little remnant who, in the midst of the tempestuous waves of the apostasy and the perversion, will remain faithful to Christ, to the Gospel and to the Church.

"And it will be with this little flock, guarded in the Immaculate Heart of your heavenly Mother, that Jesus will bring about his glorious reign in the world."

The Great Sign of Divine Mercy (MMP #560)

"For this, I am manifesting myself, in so powerful and extraordinary a way, through my apparitions, my numerous weepings, and the messages which I give to the heart of the little son of mine, whom I myself am leading along the roads of the world, in search of sinners, of the sick, of those who have fallen, of the straying, of the despairing, of those who are succumbing to the seduction of sin and of evil.

*"For this, I invite all to consecrate themselves to my Immaculate Heart, and I am extending this, my request, to the most extreme limits of the earth through my Marian Movement of Priests. In this way, **I am offering you a safe refuge, which the Most Holy Trinity has prepared for you, for those stormy times of the great tribulation and of the painful trial that has come for the Church and for all humanity....***

"This is why I am calling you each day to follow me. I am the Mother of Fair Love and Holy Hope. I am the Queen of Peace and the dawn which announces the new time which awaits you and which is drawing ever closer!"

At this point in time, we are living a profound mystery. Some bishops and cardinals, such as Cardinal Raymond Burke and others, have stated numerous times over the last several years that we are living in the end times. Heaven is responding in kind with an abundance of messages because of the strong presence of evil today. *"Where sin abounds, grace abounds all the more"* (Romans 5:20).

My Heart is Bleeding (MMP #332h)

The Blessed Mother speaks of infiltration in the Church by men with evil intent.

"There has also entered into the Church disunity, division, strife and antagonism. The forces of atheism and Masonry, having infiltrated within it, are on the point of breaking up its interior unity and of darkening the splendor of its sanctity. These are the times, foretold by me, when cardinals will be set against cardinals, bishops against bishops, and priests against priests, and the flock of Christ will be torn to pieces by rapacious wolves, who have found their way in under the clothing of defenseless and meek lambs. Among them there are some who occupy posts of great responsibility, and by means of them, Satan has succeeded in entering and operating at the very summit of the Church…. Repent; seek pardon; make amends; and above all, be once again faithful to the task which has been entrusted to you."

The Beast Like a Lamb (MMP #406g)

"The black beast like a leopard indicates Freemasonry; the beast with the two horns like a lamb indicates Freemasonry infiltrated into the interior of the Church, that is to say, ecclesiastical masonry, which has spread especially among members of the hierarchy. This masonic infiltration, in the interior of the church, was already foretold to you by me at Fatima, when I announced to you that Satan would enter even to the summit of the Church. If the task of Masonry is to lead souls to perdition, bringing them to the worship of false divinities, the task of ecclesiastical Masonry on the other hand is that of destroying Christ and His Church, building a new idol, namely a false christ and false church."

The enemy of the Church at the deepest level is Freemasonry. They are the puppet masters operating behind the curtain. Few will confront this reality because they do not understand it. People hack at the branches of evil rather than the root. Social activist and leader for many years in the American Communist Party, Bella Dodd, wrote in her autobiography, *School of Darkness* (her conversion story to the Catholic faith with the help of Archbishop Fulton Sheen), how the communists successfully infiltrated Catholic seminaries and the hierarchy. She wrote how the communist party had been effective in placing several influential cardinals, bishops, and many priests in key positions of the hierarchy to promote their views from within the Church. This started as early as the 1930's and continued long after. To properly comprehend the intentional auto-demolition of the Church from within, Masonry with all of its tentacles must be understood. The enemy of the Church and state is not a liberal or progressive, but highly organized Masonry which is now called **"The Deep Church"** at the ecclesiastical level.

I Have Intervened Forcefully (MMP #386c)

"I have intervened forcefully as well in the life of the Church. At the present time, the tenebrous forces of evil are laying snares for her on all sides. The dark conspiracies woven by Masonry, by means of its many followers who have insinuated themselves at the summit of the Church, have succeeded in paralyzing her activity and in extinguishing her apostolic ardor."

The words above are very emotionally charged. The Blessed Mother is saying she is intervening with the tenebrous forces of evil. Tenebrous means dark, gloomy and obscure. Snares are by design hidden traps meant to injure and thus kill. She is saying there are many followers of Masonry that have penetrated to the summit. The summit of a mountain is the very peak. **Most importantly, she said they have succeeded** in paralyzing fervent behavior of people, most notably good priests, who are precluded from speaking the truth for fear of their bishop's wrath, and being marked for the rest of their priestly life. As a result, apostolic ardor is snuffed out and the people die a slow death in the pew and the classroom. The reality in front of us is why that Consecration is so critical to maintain peace of heart, mind, and soul in such tumultuous times. Consecration keeps the believer going forward in spite of all the obstacles in our path.

In the Name of Mary (MMP #456)

"In the name of your heavenly Mother, yes, in the name of Mary, the Turks were defeated, when they laid siege to the city of Vienna and threatened to invade and destroy the whole Christian world. They were far superior in strength, in numbers and in weapons, and they felt that their victory was assured. But I was publicly invoked and called upon; my name was inscribed upon their banners and shouted out by the soldiers, and thus through my intercession, there took place the miracle of this victory which saved the Christian world from its destruction. It is for this reason that the Pope instituted, on this day, the feast of the Name of Mary.

"In the name of Mary, Marxist communism, which for decades had been exercising its rule and holding so many of my poor children, in oppressive and bloody slavery has been defeated in these countries. Not because of political movements or persons, but through my personal intervention, has your liberation finally come about.

"It will again be in the name of Mary that I will bring to my completion my work with the defeat of Masonry, of every diabolical force, of materialism, and of practical atheism, so that all humanity will be able to attain its encounter with the Lord and be thus purified and completely renewed, with the triumph of my Immaculate Heart in the world."

Of everything that could be a target of Heaven and the promotion of evil, Our Lady has said it is Masonry. If you were to talk to someone about it, they would generally glaze over and say something like, my father, my uncle, or grandfather was a member while thinking it is a boy's night out having dinner on a regular basis at the Lodge. It is no such thing. It is Satan's army on earth. It needs to be studied to understand their anti-Christian agenda, masquerading as a compliment to Christianity, funding hospitals and burn centers for their social activism. Against such evil institutional forces is why Consecration is so necessary for our families. With the defeat of Freemasonry, we will witness a new Lepanto.

Come, Holy Spirit (MMP #521)

"Come, Holy Spirit.

"Come by means of the powerful intercession of my Immaculate heart. My hour is the hour of the Holy Spirit. The triumph of my Immaculate Heart will coincide with the great prodigy of the second Pentecost.

"A new fire will come down from heaven and will purify all humanity which has again become pagan. It will be like a judgment in miniature, and each one will see himself in the light of the very truth of God.

"Thus sinners will come back to grace and holiness; the straying to the road of righteousness; those far away, to the house of the Father; the sick, to complete healing; and the proud, the impure, the wicked collaborators with Satan will be defeated and condemned forever.

"Then my motherly Heart will have its triumph over all humanity, which will return to a new marriage of love and of life with its Heavenly Father."

We will witness pain before there is a New Era, because there is no way around it. Old structures that have stood for generations must pass, and the transition phase will be hard to watch as things crumble. However, with Consecration and the promises we can stand on, we will endure, and actually even prosper. Senator Robert F. Kennedy's favorite poet in times of personal tragedy was the ancient Greek Aeschylus, considered the father of Greek tragedy. The quote below is on Bobby Kennedy's grave stone at Arlington National Cemetery. Aeschylus wrote:

"And even in our sleep, pain which cannot forget, falls drop by drop upon the heart, until in our own despair, against our own will, comes wisdom through the awful grace of God."

JESUS I TRUST IN YOU

26

Gen E — A Generation Soft and Entitled

Go your way; behold, I send you out as lambs in the midst of wolves.

Luke 10:3

There was a chemistry professor in a large college that had some exchange students in the class. One day while the class was in the lab, the professor noticed one young man, an exchange student, who kept rubbing his back as if his back hurt. The professor asked the young man what was the matter. The student told him he had a bullet lodged in his back.

He said he had been shot while fighting the communists in his native country who were looking to overthrow his country's government, and install a new communist regime. In the midst of his story he asked the professor a strange question. "Do you know how to catch a herd of wild pigs?" The professor thought it was a joke, and asked the punch line. The young man said it was no joke.

"You catch wild pigs by finding a suitable place in the woods, and then put corn on the ground. The pigs find it and begin to come everyday to eat the free corn. When they are used to coming everyday, you put a fence on one side of the place where they are used to coming. When they are used to the fence, they begin to eat the corn again and you then put up another side of the fence. They get used to that and they start to eat again. You continue until you have all four sides of the fence up with a gate on the last side.

The pigs now used to free corn, start to come through the gate to eat that free corn again. You then slam the gate on them and catch the whole herd. Suddenly the wild pigs have lost their freedom. They run around and around inside the fence, but they are caught. Soon they go back to eating the free corn. They are so used to it that they have forgotten how to forage in the woods for themselves, so they accept the captivity."

The young man said to the professor that is exactly what he sees happening in America. The government keeps pushing its citizens towards socialism and communism by spreading the free corn out in the form of social welfare programs. Supplemental income, tax credits for unearned income, tax exemptions, tobacco subsidies, dairy subsidies, welfare and pharmaceutical exemptions, drug exemptions, and dozens of more large programs are just a few as we continually lose our freedom, just a little at a time.

One should always remember three things:

1. *There is no such thing as a free lunch; someone is paying for it.*
2. *When you begin to think that government will provide for you and make your decisions, realize that you have also given up the freedom that goes with making your own choices.*
3. *God help you when the gate slams shut.*

(The above is from an e-mail that was floating around the internet.)

Several years ago, I had a conversation with a man I have known for many years. He was 90 years old and still engaged in a variety of activities. Intellectually he did remarkably well and was still a constant reader. Only after a mild stroke did he stop driving, but was still a daily communicant with friends picking him up for church. We were talking about World War II, and he made a casual comment that America won World War II so quickly because the men and women of America were tough. He explained they had been the sons and daughters of depression era parents who worked hard with often two and three jobs to provide for their families. Nothing came easy with these men and women, and they learned from their parents that hard work overcame many obstacles. This group didn't have a welfare state as a safety net so they put their nose to the grindstone to make a better life for their families. If they wanted to get ahead, they worked more. Social programs were non-existent for these people where precious little was ever for free. Self-discipline and self-reliance were necessary. There was no utopian view of the world with someone else paying their way. If they wanted something, they saved up to buy it. The best they could do then was a lay away program at a department store. Deficit spending by the government was more limited and nowhere near as reckless. There was also much more common sense thinking among the general population on the role of the government dole giving free passes to do nothing. As Proverbs says, *"The borrower is servant to the lender"* (Proverbs 22:7).

A partial, but substantive, answer of how we ended up where we are today is due to the government providing so many *"free things."* It has lulled us to sleep like the herd of pigs. If you walk into many homes today, you will walk over *"things."* Most are trinkets of some sort of something and time sapping, because we think they will make us happy. All the while much of this is on a credit card and financed by the majority of Americans accumulating debt, and then often renting a storage unit to store *"things."*

We ended up in this situation because the baby boomers watched their immigrant parents, and often immigrant grandparents suffer and go without. They vowed as Scarlet O'Hara outside Tara in Gone with the Wind, *"As God is my witness, I'll never be hungry again."* Hardship was a fact of life for most people during the depression and beyond, but there was a great deal more safety in civic society where people in neighborhoods watched out for each other. America really wasn't free from the effects of the depression until after World War II. It was faith that brought them to America's shores for a better life, but by the baby boomer generation, they forgot it was faith and God's providence that brought them blessings. Their parents worked hard to make a better life for their kids. SAT scores and the finer things in life then began to matter far more than the confessional and the Sacraments. The baby boomers incrementally abandoned their faith, as did their sons and daughters. The drift to what we have become today can be traced directly to that mentality of forgetting that God is most important in lives. Jewelers get used to fine stones.

Both sides of the political aisle are at fault, and have blame in this regard by buying off the voters by giving them *"free things."* Today's insane lunacy thinking everything can be free is most dominant coming from the democratic socialists as a group. Their thinking is not socialist, but Marxist Communism. It defies human nature, logic, rational thought, natural law, economics, and Scripture. People who think everything can be free are looking for a utopia that will and has never existed on this earth. That thinking leads to anarchy, which in turn leads to bloodshed. Only a revolution will quell it if it continues, and based upon the softness of so many of the public getting *"free stuff,"* they won't go down without a fight if anyone tries to take *"free things"* away.

This is why the battle in the political realm is so ferocious. If someone pledges a political platform of free everything, people will demand it if they once get it. If they get it once, they will demand it in the next election cycle. The phrase of *"if you keep giving, they'll keep taking"* is real. The scandal (Varsity Blues) of parents paying to get their kids into elite schools is just one symptom of this behavior of getting something for doing nothing. Entitled people act that way. Personal liberty has to be rooted in moral responsibility to have enduring and positive results.

Politicians and others, who think and act this way, have largely been recipients of government largesse themselves without working and paying for what they were given in the past. Often they are still on government programs for their living. Governments never voluntarily reduce their budgets. They continue to grow and expand through taxing, when they pledged to serve. *They have largely seen a system of government providing for them, so they want it to continue — by any means.* In reality, others footing the bill for them is how they have lived since youth. They want it to continue, and they expect it to continue, so they will just print money to mandate it to continue — at any cost as long as it's *"free stuff."*

Few who think this way have ever run a business or been responsible for a Profit and Loss Statement, and many had parents giving them most everything without needing to work for it. They expect everything to be free, because they largely lived a good life getting everything for free, and this is how they vote today.

Since the baby boomers that came after World War II (1946-1964), we have had Generation, X, Y (Millennials), and Z. Each of these have somewhat different characteristics and traits, and cross over into each other in years without a clear line of demarcation. However, social science has designated each of them with a different view of life and habits than the previous one. Over the last several generations they have grown so soft on the realities of life, all of the above X, Y, Z, and whatever you wish to call it for a generation, could cumulatively be called **Generation Entitled.** That such a large section of the population has become entitled is why socialism is gaining such momentum.

The government has captured us with free goods and services, all the while people are numb to the reality of what it will bring just a few years up the road. Free everything, fast food while sitting in your car, talking and observing social media — all contribute to a mentality of *"I want it, and I want it now."* If I don't get it I will demand it, and if I don't get it, I'll sue to get it. Better yet, I'll sue on discrimination and label my enemy a racist bigot to get it. But, the under lying issue, is they want *"free things."* A lot is spoken about people's rights, but little is spoken about personal responsibility.

The era of connectivity to social media has led to higher suicide rates, prescriptions for anti-depressants by the bushel barrel, and increased loneliness due to isolation. What we have reaped from *"free everything"* is miserable, anxious and despondent people, and a life of despair with broken marriages and families. Self-indulgence has led to a lack of purpose. A recent poll found that 80% of Generation Z born in the mid 1990's and after say they feel lonely due to *"a lack of social support and infrequent meaningful social interaction,"* according to a national study of 10,000 adults by insurance provider Cigna. Instead of church, youth adopted Facebook and social media as their community of salvation, and it has failed them.

It is only faith in God that leads to fulfillment and joy in this life. As the Blessed Mother told a young Bernadette Soubirous at Lourdes, *"I cannot give you happiness in this life, but I can in the next."* If people think the government will solve their problems, they are ignorant of history.

JESUS I TRUST IN YOU

27

The Mind of an Unbeliever

The whole modern world has divided itself into Conservatives and Progressives. The business of Progressives is to go on making mistakes. The business of Conservatives is to prevent mistakes from being corrected.

G.K. Chesterton

I, as everyone else in life, encounter people with views other than my own. It is life. In youth I never gave conservative versus liberal much thought, probably due to wise parents who arranged activities to keep their kids out of trouble instead of talking politics. However, as I grew older, I became fascinated with how people develop intellectually, politically, socially, and spiritually, with world-views that shape who we are, and what we do as a person, a family, and as a nation. What is it exactly that molds us into who we become? Is there a common denominator? What defines our actions? What is the thought process that develops so acutely it defines what we do on a daily basis?

There are many forms of thought that indicate where we are on the political spectrum. We are what we think. There are progressives, democrats, leftists, socialists, Marxists, communists, liberals, fascists, Stalinists, Maoists, Leninists, and other indicators of our views based on the way we think and what we support. Likewise, there are words for what could generally be in the category or genre of conservative: traditional, republican, main street, right-wing. In political philosophy, the above words mean profoundly different things as they relate to our ideology.

Where is the intersection of disordered affections due to sin and a political philosophy that is acceptable and civil, or one that flies in the face of what is contrary to Scripture and ungodly? Jesus said, *"My sheep hear my voice and obey"* (John 10:27). Obedience to His word is paramount for an ordered life. Jesus said, *"I come to give you life and give it more abundantly,"* and Satan is out to *"kill, destroy, and steal"* (John 10:10). Satan said, I will not serve and the rebellion of mankind began. There is sin — and it has consequences.

We are living in times Sister Lucia of Fatima labeled *"diabolical disorientation."* Our present times are of great confusion and division. As a nation we are on the cusp of violence due to such radically differing views of the populace. No matter the subject there is great discord that has grown to hatred. What will be the spark to send people over the edge into societal chaos is unknown, but as the anger and animosity builds it may not take much for some form of eruption.

Spiritually, over a lifetime I have learned that every aberrant human behavior is due to a wound or a hurt. We act out our hurts or virtues in the marketplace whether we are aware of them or not. Behavior has an origin spoken or unspoken, acknowledged or not acknowledged, aware or not aware, confronted or ignored.

G. K. Chesterton called the mind of a progressive, *"The modern and morbid habit of always sacrificing the normal to the abnormal."* As Isaiah said, *"It has been your sin that has separated you from God."* The rebellion in the streets and the hearts and souls of man are an alienation from God. If one is alienated from God, they are alienated from self, and thus others — everyone and everything. The result is a life of chaos for individuals, families, cities, and countries. The angry man is not even able to articulate why he is angry. Anarchy is his utopia.

Together as they march and vent their anger with the heel of their shoes, their pen, or their voice, they are rejecting tradition, virtue, the normal for the abnormal, something that works for something that doesn't work, order for chaos, and supplanting new forms of *"social justice"* in all of its ill formed thinking. All the while the unbeliever is rejecting the tradition of the Gospel and the very words of Jesus, and striving to build a new world with no foundations other than living by their glands. The liberal is looking to replace any traditional thinking for the chaos of the unknown. In short, the liberal wants a world without God because they think they have a better way to order society. The liberal also wants to end any connection to the traditional normal and desires to have the state supreme. The state cannot reform man's soul, but only the Lord can. It is for this reason Jesus did not come as a political ruler. He came to change hearts — and no matter the politics, a person becomes better if a heart is changed towards God.

When man believes in nothing, he will believe in anything. Likewise, if he believes in no one, he will believe in anyone. Or the old adage, *"If a man doesn't stand for something, he will fall for anything."* The fruit of unbelief is tyranny. Reject God, and blood runs in the streets. It will take more blood in the streets to bring the Lord back into the classrooms of America. The only blueprint for peace of soul comes from God — nowhere else. That is the history of civilization.

As Archbishop Fulton J. Sheen often said, *"Marry the age and you become a widow in the next."* Man's whimsy is fleeting because the grass withers and the flower fades, but the Word of God endures forever. (Isaiah 40:8) Truth is timeless and not wrapped up into the ideology or the fancy of the culture of the day. Truth will always win. Sometimes it takes longer than we may desire, but truth always prevails.

I have no doubt there are many well-intentioned people with liberal views. But, at the very foundation of their thinking is an individual rejecting the plan and order of God, and His ordained plan for civility and order in a fallen world. In their actions they say, I will do it my way. I will not serve — I have a better way. Jesus was clear when he said, *"My ways are not your ways, and unless a seed falls into the ground and dies, it cannot bear fruit"* (John 12:24). Man's rebellion is rooted in pride. Sin alienates us from everyone and everything, and the result is a life of chaos.

JESUS I TRUST IN YOU

28

The Afterlife—Heaven, Hell & Purgatory, What Some Saints and Others Have Said Who Have Visited Them

My sheep hear my voice, and I know them, and they follow Me:
and I give unto them eternal life; and they shall never perish,
neither shall any man pluck them out of My hand.

John 10: 27-28

If one were to search the internet for "Purgatory," "what is Heaven like," "Hell," "near death experiences," (NDEs) "life after death," and similar subjects, he will find those categories get millions of hits. Subjects like NDEs have been a topic of fascination for over thirty years. Yet we rarely hear about **Heaven, Hell, Purgatory or the Four Last Things — Death, Judgment, Heaven, or Hell — being taught in the Church.** Is there a connection between not hearing the most fundamental of truths that were taught for nearly 2,000 years and the sugar water we often hear today from some ecclesiastical and political leaders as we watch in real time the destruction of our culture?

The data is clear that people are very interested in this genre of spirituality given that they research and read about these subjects. Many books on these subjects are best sellers. Jesus addressed Heaven and Hell in the Gospels, and He was not ambiguous as to their reality. A person could possibly go to Church for a life-time and never hear a sermon on Purgatory or Hell. A priest might be considered too extreme or negative by many as the talk may offend someone. To deny the devil is to deny sin, and as a result of not being taught about these most basic truths, people have become desensitized to sin, and therefore, deny sin as a reality along with its repercussions. Sin has virtually drenched our culture and become normalized.

In the same vein, people today know something is very wrong in our culture. Society is talking and operating on the extremes, with a festering civil disturbance on the horizon. Based on many conversations, we can tell immediately if someone we meet is on the same political and spiritual wavelength as us. It is obvious to everyone now as the divide is so great. Bring up names like Pope Francis, Hillary Clinton or President Trump, and the waters part as if Moses waved his walking stick over the Red Sea. It doesn't take long to find out if one has a starkly contrary view from yours.

It has only been in the last generation with the ubiquitous and viral forms of social media, that people have recognized the events around NDEs are very similar worldwide. There is speculation in the NDE community that their experiences are the norm, and not the exception for hundreds of thousands who do not tell their story in public. Information is traded much more openly and freely without censorship or detractors on the internet, thus there are so many similar stories. What is most interesting is that many who experience a life review see their lives in slow motion: for major events in their lives; areas of their life that hurt people; the long-term impact of sin; sins of omission and commission; not forgiving someone; harming themselves and others; and sins against the commandments. If there is a profound lesson to be learned, it is that sin has consequences, much in the same way as an act of love has consequences. As a stone is thrown on a still pond, sin ripples for great distances. It is God's justice that determines one's fate. The Lord said, *"My thoughts are not your thoughts, and My ways are not your ways"* (Isaiah 55:8). If the justice of God is odd to you, remeber the Lord views our lives through a different prism.

It would be a safe bet that most readers have not heard the words **"Mortal Sin"**, **"Hell"** or **"Purgatory"** from the pulpit for a long time — if at all. Generations of the past were more spiritually and Scripturally literate, and had a more sober view of life after death for millennia based upon teachings of the Catholic Church. Now, if one attends a funeral, it is often mentioned that the deceased is *"now lovingly looking down upon us from on high."* However, the Church has taught that upon death few go directly into the presence of God.

The Church has deemed **Heaven, Hell,** and **Purgatory** real, and there are considerable Scriptural passages where all of these places are addressed. I will rely primarily on what the saints said about them as the Church has laid hands on these people as authentic. The Church heavily scrutinizes an individual before sainthood is granted, and this is prudent and wise. Testing them over time to assure their validity for the benefit of the mystical body of Christ now and in the future, is the approach of the Church. It is not abnormal for people in previous times as well as today to be taken to **Heaven, Hell,** and **Purgatory**, and come back to tell their story. For those operating in the spiritual realm, it is normal to know and speak of such things. To someone not versed in spirituality, it is considered an abnormality, or something not real.

The Apocalypse means the *"Unveiling."* As evil is being exposed in every sphere of the human condition, and being brought to light, we just might be watching the seeds of the Triumph of the Immaculate Heart that was promised at Fatima, taking on a new acceleration or quickening. The Triumph is when we enter a new dimension, a New Era. Sin is being exposed that has operated in stealth for generations, and the *"Unveiling"* is taking place. The body can't heal until a disease is exposed and excised. Removing the cancerous growth and puss is unpleasant, but necessary if the body is to heal. This is the painful time we are witnessing for the ecclesiastical profession, and it is necessary to clean the rot.

Some of the stories were written several hundred years ago in the vernacular of the day, and not in the conversation of the modern era. The words have not been altered to maintain as they were either dictated or written.

Saint Faustina on Heaven (1905-1938)

After Holy Communion, I was carried in spirit before the throne of God. There I saw the Heavenly Powers which incessantly praise God. Beyond the throne I saw a brightness inaccessible to creatures, and there only the Incarnate Word enters as Mediator (Diary 85).

I learned in the Heart of Jesus that in Heaven itself there is a Heaven to which not all, but only chosen souls, have access. Incomprehensible is the happiness in which the soul will be immersed. O my God, oh, that I could describe this, even in some little degree. Souls are penetrated by His divinity and pass from brightness to brightness, an unchanging light but never monotonous, always new though never changing. O Holy Trinity, make Yourself known to souls! (Diary 592).

Today I was in Heaven, in spirit, and I saw its inconceivable beauties and the happiness that awaits us after death. I saw how all creatures give ceaseless praise and glory to God. I saw how great is happiness in God, which spreads to all creatures, making them happy: and then all the glory and praise which springs from this happiness returns to its source: and they enter into the depths of God, contemplating the inner life of God, the Father, the Son, and the Holy Spirit, whom they will never comprehend or fathom.

This source of happiness is unchanging in its essence, but it is always new, gushing forth happiness for all creatures. Now I understand St. Paul, who said, **eye has not seen, nor has ear heard, nor has it entered into the heart of man what God has prepared for those who love Him** (Diary 777).

The sight of this great majesty of God, which I came to understand more profoundly and which is worshipped by the heavenly spirit, according to their degree of grace and the hierarchies to which they are divided, did not cause my soul to be stricken with terror or fear; no, no, not at all! My soul was filled with peace and love, and the more I come to know the greatness of God, the more joyful I become that He is as He is. And I **rejoice immensely in His greatness and am delighted that I am so little because, since I am little, He carries me in His arms and holds me close to His Heart** (Diary 779).

O my God, how I pity those people who do not believe in eternal life: how I pray for them that a ray of mercy would envelop them too, and that God would clasp them to His fatherly bosom (Diary 780).

A vivid presence of God suddenly swept over me, and I was caught up in spirit before the majesty of God. I saw how the angels and the saints of the Lord gave glory to God. The glory of God is so great that I dare not try to describe it, because I would not be able to do so, and souls might think that all I have written is all there is.... And all that has come forth from God returns to Him in the same way and gives Him perfect glory (Diary 1604).

Saint Faustina on Purgatory

[The next night] I saw my Guardian Angel, who ordered me to follow him. In a moment I was in a misty place full of fire in which there was a great crowd of suffering souls. They were praying fervently, but to no avail, for

*themselves; only we can come to their aid. The flames which were burning them did not touch me at all. My Guardian Angel did not leave me for an instant. I asked these souls what their greatest suffering was. They answered me in one voice that their greatest torment was longing for God. I saw Our Lady visiting the souls in Purgatory. The souls call her "**The Star of the Sea.**" She brings them refreshment. I wanted to talk with them some more, but my Guardian Angel beckoned me to leave. We went out of that prison of suffering. [I heard an interior voice] which said, **My mercy does not want this, but justice demands it.** Since that time, I am in closer communion with the suffering souls* (Diary 20).

*Once I was summoned to the judgment [seat] of God. I stood alone before the Lord. Jesus appeared just as we know Him during His Passion. After a moment, His wounds disappeared except for the five, those in His hands, His feet, and His side. **Suddenly I saw the complete condition of my soul as God sees it. I could clearly see all that is displeasing to God. I did not know that even the smallest transgressions will have to be accounted for.** What a moment! Who can describe it? To stand before the Thrice-Holy God! Jesus asked me, Who are you? I answered, "I am your servant, Lord." **You are guilty of one day of fire in purgatory.** I wanted to throw myself immediately into the flames of purgatory, but Jesus stopped me and said, which do you prefer, suffering now for one day in purgatory or for a short while on earth? I replied, "Jesus I want to suffer in purgatory, and I want to suffer also the greatest pains on earth even if it were to the end of the world." Jesus said, **One [of the two] is enough; you will go back to earth, and there you will suffer much, but not for long; you will accomplish My will and My desires, and a faithful servant of Mine will help you to do this. Now, rest your head on My bosom, on My Heart, and draw from it strength and power for these sufferings because you will find neither relief nor help nor comfort anywhere else. Know that you will have much, much to suffer, but don't let this frighten you, I am with you"* (Diary 36).

One evening, one of the deceased sisters, who had already visited me a few times, appeared to me. The first time I had seen her, she had been in great suffering, and then gradually these sufferings had diminished; this time she was radiant with happiness, and she told me she was already in heaven.... And further, as a sign that she only now was in Heaven, God would bless our house. *Then she came closer to me, embraced me sincerely, and said, "I must go now." I understand how closely the three stages of a soul's life are bound together; that is to say, life on earth, in purgatory, and in Heaven* [the Communion of Saints] (Diary 594).

After Vespers today, there was a procession to the cemetery. I could not go, because I was on duty at the gate. But that did not stop me at all from praying for the souls. As the procession was returning from the cemetery to the chapel, my soul felt the presence of many other souls. I understood the great justice of God, how much each one had to pay off the debt to the last cent (Diary 1375).

Saint Faustina on Hell

"*Most of the souls there are those who disbelieved that there is a Hell.*"
Today I was led by an Angel to the chasms of Hell. It is a place of great torture; how awesomely large and extensive it is! The kinds of torture I saw: the first torture that constitutes Hell is the loss of God; the second is perpetual remorse of conscience; the third is that one's condition will never change; the fourth is the fire that will penetrate the soul without destroying it — a terrible suffering, since it is purely a spiritual fire, lit by God's anger; the fifth torture is continual darkness and a terrible suffocating smell, and, despite the darkness the devils and the souls of the damned see each other and all the evil, both others and their own; the sixth torture is the constant company of Satan; the seventh torture is horrible despair, hatred of God, vile words, curses and blasphemies. These are the tortures suffered by all the damned together, but that is not the end of the sufferings.

There are special tortures destined for particular souls. These are the torments of the senses. Each soul undergoes terrible and indescribable sufferings, related to the manner in which it has sinned. *There are caverns and pits of torture where one form of agony differs from another. I would have died at the very sight of these tortures if the omnipotence of God had not supported me. Let the sinner know that he will be tortured throughout all eternity, in those senses which he made use of to sin. I am writing this at the command of God, so that no soul may find an excuse by saying there is no Hell, or that nobody has ever been there, and so no one can say what it is like.*

I, Sister Faustina, by the order of God, have visited the abyss of Hell so that I might tell souls about it and testify to its existence. I cannot speak about it now; but I have received a command from God to leave it in writing. The devils were full of hatred for me, but they had to obey me at the command of God. What I have written is but a pale shadow of the things I saw. **But I noticed one thing: that most of the souls there are those who disbelieved that there is a Hell.** *When I came to, I could hardly recover from the fright. How terribly souls suffer there! Consequently, I pray even more fervently for the conversion of sinners. I incessantly plead God's mercy upon them. O my Jesus, I would rather be in agony until the end of the world, amidst the greatest sufferings, than offend You by the least sin* (Diary 741).

The Repercussions of the Choices We Make

Saint Faustina recorded an image of what she saw as one road to Heaven, and the other to Hell. **Few people in the history of the Church can match her writings since it was Jesus Himself who gave her instruction on the splendor of Heaven, and the torments of Hell.**

One day, I saw two roads. One was broad, covered with sand and flowers, full of joy, music and all sorts of pleasures. People walked along it, dancing and enjoying themselves. They reached the end without realizing it. And at the end of the road there was a horrible precipice; that is, the abyss of Hell. The souls fell blindly into it; as they walked, so they fell. And their number was so great that it was impossible to count them. And I saw the other road, or rather, a path, for it was narrow and strewn with thorns and rocks; and the people who walked along it had tears in their eyes, and all kinds of sufferings befell them. Some fell down upon the rocks, but stood up immediately and went on. At the end of the road there was a magnificent garden filled with all sorts of happiness, and all these souls entered there. At the very first instant they forgot all their sufferings (Diary 153).

The Location of Purgatory — St. Frances of Rome (1385-1440)

The Jesuit priest Father F. X. Schouppe wrote *Purgatory Explained by the Lives and Legends of the Saints.* His purpose, he stated, was to make purgatory "better known to the pious faithful who believe with a divine faith this dogma revealed of God." The following accounts are excerpted from his work.

It has pleased God to show in spirit the gloomy abodes of Purgatory to some privileged souls, who were to reveal the sorrowful mysteries thereof for the edification of the faithful. Of this number was the illustrious **St. Frances,** *foundress of the Oblates, who died in Rome in 1440. God favored her with great lights concerning the state of souls in the other life. She saw Hell and its horrible torments: she saw also the interior of Purgatory, and the mysterious order — I had almost said hierarchy of expiations — which reigns in this portion of the Church of Jesus Christ.*

In obedience to her supporters, who thought themselves bound to impose this obligation upon her, she made known all that God had manifested to her; and her visions, written at the request of the venerable Canon Matteotti, her spiritual director, have all the authenticity that can be desired in such matters. Now, the servant of God declared that, after having endured with unspeakable horror that vision of **Hell,** *she came out of the abyss and was conducted by her celestial guide into the regions of* **Purgatory.** *There reigned horror nor disorder, nor despair nor eternal darkness; there divine hope diffused its light, and she was told that this place of purification was called also* **sojourn of hope.** *She saw there souls which suffer cruelly, but angels visited and assisted them in their sufferings.*

Purgatory, she said, is divided into three distinct parts, which are as the three large provinces of that kingdom of suffering. They are situated the one beneath the other, and occupied by souls, of different orders. These souls are buried more deeply in proportion as they are more defiled and farther removed from the time of their deliverance.

The lowest region is filled with a fierce fire, but which is not dark like that of Hell; it is a vast burning sea, throwing forth immense flames. Innumerable souls are plunged into its depths: **they are those who have rendered themselves guilty of mortal sin, which they have duly confessed, but not sufficiently expiated during life....** *Although the souls are enveloped in the same flames,* **their sufferings are not the same; they differ according to the number and nature of their former sins.**

In this lower Purgatory the saint beheld laics (one of the laity) and persons consecrated to God. The laics were those who, after a life of sin, had had the happiness of being sincerely converted; the persons consecrated to God were those who had not lived according to the sanctity of their state. At that same moment she saw descend the soul of a priest whom she knew, but whose name she does not reveal. She remarked that he had his face covered with a veil which concealed a stain. Although he had lead an edifying life, this priest had not always observed strict temperance, and had sought too eagerly the satisfaction of the table.

The saint was then conducted into the intermediate Purgatory, destined for souls which had deserved less rigorous chastisements. It had three distinct compartments; one resembled an immense dungeon of ice, the cold of which is indescribably intense; the second, on the contrary, was like a huge caldron of boiling oil and pitch; the third had the appearance of a pond of liquid metal resembling molten gold or silver.

The upper Purgatory, which the saint does not describe, is the temporary abode of souls which suffer little, except the pain of loss, and approach the happy moment of their deliverance. Such, in substance, is the vision of St. Frances relative to Purgatory.

St. Magdalen de Pazzi, Her Vision of Purgatory

The following is an account of St. Magdalen de Pazzi, a Florentine Carmelite, as related in her life by Father Cepari. It gives more of a picture of Purgatory, while the preceding vision traces its outlines.

Some time before her death, which took place in 1607, the servant of God, Magdalen de Pazzi, being one evening with several other Religious in the garden of the convent, was ravished in ecstasy, and saw Purgatory open before her. At the same time, as she made known later, a voice invited her to visit all the persons of Divine Justice, and to see how truly worthy of compassion are the souls detained there.

At this moment she was heard to say, "Yes, I will go." She consented to undertake this painful journey. In fact, she walked for two hours round the garden, which was very large, pausing from time to time. Each time she interrupted her walk, she contemplated the sufferings which were shown to her. She was then seen to wring her hands in compassion, her face became pale, her body bent under the weight of suffering, in presence of the terrible spectacle with which she was confronted.

She began to cry aloud in lamentation, "Mercy my God, mercy!"

"Descend, O Precious Blood, and deliver these souls from their prison. Poor souls! you suffer so cruelly, and yet you are content and cheerful. The dungeons of the martyrs in comparison with these were gardens of light. Nevertheless, there are others still deeper. How happy should I esteem myself were I not obliged to go down into them."

She did descend, however, for she was forced to continue her way. But when she had taken a few steps, she stopped terror-stricken, and sighing deeply she cried, "What! Religious also in this dismal abode! Good God! How they are tormented! Ah, Lord!" She does not explain the nature of their sufferings; but the horror which she manifested in contemplating them caused her to sigh at each step. She passed from thence into less gloomy places. These were the dungeons of simple souls, and of children in whom ignorance and lack of reason extenuated many faults. Their torments appeared to her much more endurable than those of the others. Nothing but ice and fire were there. She noticed that these souls had their angel guardians with them, who fortified them greatly by their presence; but she saw also demons whose dreadful forms increased their sufferings.

Souls of Hypocrisy

Advancing a few places, she saw souls still more unfortunate, and she was heard to cry out, "Oh! how horrible is this place; it is full of hideous demons and incredible torments! **Who, O my God, are the victims of these cruel tortures? Alas! They are being pierced with sharp swords, they are being cut into pieces." She was answered that they were the souls whose conduct had been tainted with hypocrisy.**

Advancing a little, she saw a great multitude of souls who were bruised, as it were, and crushed under a press; and **she understood that they were those souls who had been addicted to impatience and disobedience during their life.** *Whilst contemplating them, her looks, her sighs, her whole attitude betokened compassion and terror.*

A moment later her agitation increased, and she uttered a dreadful cry. It was the dungeon of lies that now lay open before her. After having attentively considered it, she cried aloud, "Liars are confined in a place in the vicinity of

Hell, and their sufferings are exceedingly great. Molten lead is poured into their mouths; I see them burn, and at the same time tremble with cold."

She then went to the prison of those souls who had sinned through weakness, and she was heard to exclaim, "Alas! I had thought to find you among those who have sinned through ignorance, but I am mistaken; you burn with an intenser fire."

Further on, she perceived souls who had been too much attached to the goods of this world, and had sinned by avarice.

"What blindness" said she, "thus eagerly to seek a perishable fortune!" Those whom riches could not easily satiate, are here gorged with torments. They are smelted like metal in a furnace.

From thence she passed into the place whose souls which were imprisoned which had formerly been stained with impurity. She saw them in so filthy and pestilential a dungeon that the sight produced nausea. She turned away quickly from that loathsome spectacle. Seeing the ambitious and the proud, she said, "Behold those who wished to shine before men; now they are condemned to live in this frightful obscurity."

She was then shown those souls which had been guilty of ingratitude towards God. They were a prey to unutterable torments, and, as it were, drowned in a lake of molten lead, for having by their ingratitude dried up the source of piety.

Finally, in the last dungeon, she was shown souls that had not been given to any particular vice, but which, through lack of proper vigilance over themselves, had committed all kinds of trivial faults. She remarked that these souls had a share in the chastisements of all vices, in a moderate degree, because those faults committed only from time to time rendered them less guilty than those committed through habit.

After this last station the saint left the garden, begging God never again to make her witness of so heartrending a spectacle; she felt that she had not strength to endure it. Her ecstasy still continued, and, conversing with Jesus, she said to Him, "Tell me Lord, what was Your design in discovering to me those terrible prisons, of which I knew so little, and comprehended still less? Ah! I now see; You wished to give me the knowledge of Your infinite sanctity, and to make me detest more and more the least stain of sin, which is so abominable in Your eyes."

Dr. Gloria Polo, Bogota, Columbia, Sees the Afterlife

On May 5, 1995, Gloria Polo a dentist from Bogota, Columbia was struck by lightning and had either a near death, or life after death experience. She was judged and came back to life. She was taken to Heaven, Hell, and Purgatory. Her book **Struck by Lightning** has been a best seller. Dr. Polo has been an inspiration to hundreds of thousands of people at speaking events around the world on the necessity of repentance and confession and the reality of an afterlife. The following account is based on her book, a speech she gave at the Shrine of the Immaculate Conception in Washington, D.C for the International Week of Prayer and Fasting, and a three hour personal interview in 2011. The story is told in her words as a native Spanish speaker. I watched an audience sit in rapt attention not moving a muscle when she spoke.

Gloria was walking with her husband, and her twenty-three-year-old nephew, who was also a dentist, when she and her nephew were both struck by lightning. Her nephew immediately died (giving off smoke for some time after being struck), and Gloria lived to tell the story. Her husband was unharmed. The lightning bolt struck her nephew from behind on the shoulder and came out his feet and carbonized his body.

She says, *"As for me, the lightning bolt entered my shoulder, burning terribly the whole body, inside and out; in short my flesh disappeared including my breasts, especially the left one, leaving a hole. It caused to disappear the flesh of my abdomen, of my legs, of the ribs; it carbonized the liver, it greatly burned the kidneys, the lungs, the ovaries... and came out through the right foot.*

"For my contraceptive, I was using a spiral (an intrauterine device in the form of a T), and because of the material with which it is made (copper) it is a good conductor of electricity, the lightning bolt carbonized and pulverized also the ovaries which became like two raisins. I remained in cardiac arrest, just about without life, with the body that was jumping due to the electricity that was still present in that place.

"But this is only the physical part.... The good part is that, while my body lay there carbonized, in that same moment I found myself inside a beautiful white tunnel of light, a wonderful light, which made me feel a joy, a peace, a happiness, that I do not have words to describe the greatness of that moment.

It was a true ecstasy. I looked, and in the end of that tunnel I saw a white light, like a sun, a beautiful light.... I say white to tell you a color, but we are talking about colors that cannot be compared to those that exist on the earth. It was a splendid light; I felt from it a source of peace, of love, of light....

"When I went up in this tunnel toward the light, I said to myself: 'Caramba, I'm dead!' So I thought about my children and I sighed: 'Woe is me my God, my little children! What will my children say? This mother so occupied, that she never had time for them....' In fact, I left early every morning, and I did not return before eleven at night.

"And so, I saw the reality of my life, and I felt much sadness. I had left my home determined to conquer the world, but at what price? Putting in second place my home and my children! In that moment of emptiness, due to the absence of my children, without feeling any more of my body, nor of the dimension of time or of space, **I looked, and I saw something very beautiful: I saw all of the people of my life.... In one single moment in the same moment, all of the people, those living and those dead. I was able to embrace my great grandparents, grandparents, parents (who were dead)... everyone!**

"In an instant I heard the voice of my husband. He laments and cries with a profound sentiment, and cries, 'Gloria!!! Gloria! Please, do no leave me! Look at your children, your children need you. Gloria, go back! Do not be a coward, return!'

"I heard everything, and I saw him cry with such pain. **Alas, in that moment our Lord granted me to leave. But I did not want to return! That peace, that peace in which I was wrapped, fascinated me! But, slowly, I began again to descend toward my body, which I found without life. I saw it lifeless on a stretcher at the National Nursing University. I saw the doctors who were giving me electric shocks to my body, to pull me out of cardiac arrest. I and my nephew remained more than two hours laid on the ground, because our bodies were giving off electric discharges, and they could not be touched. Only when the electric charge was completely discharged, could they help us. And then they began the attempts to revive me."**

Gloria goes on to speak at length about the physical manifestations of dying by a lightning strike. Gloria is very honest that she was a worldly woman seeking financial success with adulation from an admiring world. As a physical fitness fanatic she focused primarily on accentuating the beauty of her legs and breasts. In the moment of the lightning strike, her breasts were torn off, and her legs were left severely deformed. In a flash, vanity had been stripped from her, and all that she most cherished was taken from her. Up until that point in her life, she had no interest in spirituality other than the cultural events that were fun activities. She explains,

"It was a terrible suffering, I felt the intense pain of my burned flesh, the body totally burned caused an indescribable pain; it was blazing terribly and gave off smoke and vapor. I heard the doctors cry out; 'She is coming back! She is coming back!'

"They were very happy, but my suffering was indescribable! My legs were frightfully black, there was live flesh on the body, and on the arms! The problem of the legs was complicated when they considered the possibility of amputating them."

I Was a Slave to My Body, Beauty, and Fashion

"But, there was another terrible pain; the vanity of a worldly woman, intellectual, the student... slave to the body, to beauty, to fashion. I dedicated four hours every day to aerobics; enslaved to having a beautiful body. I underwent massages, diets, and injections. Basically, everything you can imagine. This was my life, a routine of slavery in order to have a beautiful body. I used to say: If I have two beautiful breasts, they are there to show them, so why hide them? I said the same thing about my legs. Because I knew I had spectacular legs, nice abdominal muscles....

"But in an instant, I saw the horror—how my whole life had been only a continual and useless care of the body. Because this was the center of my life: love for my body. And now, I no longer had a body! I had startling holes where my breasts were, especially the left one, which was practically gone. The legs were a sight to be seen, like fragments, but without flesh, and black as coal. The parts of the body that I held in highest esteem were the most completely burned and literally without flesh.

Gloria Describes Her Life as a Catholic

In a nut shell, she really could have cared less about spiritual matters. She considered herself an atheist, but went to Mass to cover the bases and to ease the sense of guilt. She specifically found a Mass where she could get in and out in twenty-five minutes or less. Adultery never bothered her, as she knew her father had been an adulterer by the time she was fourteen years of age.

Once hearing a sermon that Hell does not exist, she decided anything goes. So she reasoned, "If everyone goes to Heaven, what is there to fear?" She says, *"What makes me most sad now, and I confess to you with great shame, is that the only tie that held me in the Church, was the fear of the devil. When I heard that Hell does not exist, I immediately said: 'Very good, if we all go to Heaven it is not important what we are or what we do.'*

*"**I no longer had any fear of sin, and I began to ruin my relationship with God.** I began to say to everyone that demons do not exist, that they are the inventions of the priests, that they are the manipulations on the part of the Church, and finally… I arrive to the point of saying to my colleagues at the University that God does not exist, that we were products of evolution, etc., succeeding in influencing many people."*

No one can blame anyone for the bad decisions they make but themselves. But there are influences in our lives that do have profound effects on our ideological perspective, which shapes our outlook on life. **For a priest to say, "There is no Hell," shows the dramatic impact in a negative way for bad catechesis. Here is a perfect example of someone being taught incorrectly and manifesting her lifestyle in an unfavorable and immoral life.**

Gloria Descends to Hell

Gloria, while being worked on by surgeons after being struck by lightning, had been taken to Hell and Purgatory. She speaks of her descent into darkness, and how she was shown the impact of her sins of commission and omission.

She says, *"And, I ever more terrified, continued to descend, seeking to get out of there, while the light was going away diminishing.… I carried on roaming in those tunnels in a frightening darkness, until I arrived to an obscurity that cannot be compared to anything else.… I can only say that, in comparison, the darkest obscurity on earth is not even comparable to the full sunlight at midday. Down there, that same obscurity generates pain, horror, shame, and stinks terribly. It is a living obscurity, yes, it is alive: there the mind is dead or inert.*

"Even though I was an atheist, but there I began to cry out: 'Souls of Purgatory! Please, pull me out of here! I beg you, help me!' **While I was crying out, I began to hear the crying of thousands and thousands of persons, youth... yes, above all youth, with so much suffering! I perceived that there, in that horrible place, in that quagmire of hate and suffering, they were gnashing their teeth, with screams and laments that filled me with compassion and that I will never be able to forget. Already ten years have passed, but I still cry and suffer, when I remember the suffering of all those persons.**

"Do you know what is the greatest torment? It is to see how one's own parents, or relatives who are [still] alive [after their earthly death], are crying and suffering with a tremendous sense of guilt: if I would have punished, or if I would not have punished, if I had said to him, or not have said to him, If I had done this or that.... In the end, these regrets so terrible — a true Hell for those who love them and remain in this life — they are what makes them suffer the most. It is the greatest torment for them, and it is here that the demons rage."

Gloria Sees the Evil She Has Done

"Jesus showed me how I was in no way grateful in regard to Him, and in the laziness I had in going to Mass. When I still lived with my parents, and my mother obliged me to go, I said to her, 'But mom, if God is everywhere, what need do I have to go to Mass?'

"Clearly for me it was very convenient for me to talk like this. And Jesus showed this to me. I had the Lord twenty-four hours a day for me, all my life God took care of me, and I was too lazy to dedicate to Him a little time on Sunday, to show him my gratitude, my love for Him. But the worst thing was to know that, to frequent the church meant to nourish my soul. Instead, dedicated myself totally to the care of my body. I became a slave to my flesh, and forgot that I had a soul. And never did I take care of it.

"*Regarding the Word of God, I even said, imprudently, that the one who read the Bible a lot became crazy. I arrived at the point not to be a blasphemer, and the incoherence of my life brought me to say, 'But what Most Holy? And God would be present there? In the ciborium and in the chalice? The priest should add brandy to give it flavor.'*

"*At what point did I arrive to degrading my relationship with God? I left my soul without nourishment, and if that were not enough, the only thing I did was to criticize the priests. If you knew brothers, how bad I felt about this before Jesus. The Lord showed me how my soul was reduced due to all of these criticisms. Beyond everything else, consider the fact I declared a priest to be a homosexual, and the whole community came to know this. You cannot imagine the evil I did to that priest. No, you cannot imagine it. I tell you that one word has the power to kill or destroy souls. Now I saw all the evil I had done.*

"*And then, who says that adultery does not kill? Moreover, how many abortions are done due to adultery? For example, how many women who had been unfaithful became pregnant, have had recourse to abortion so their husband may not discover it? They kill an innocent one that is not able to speak, nor defend himself! And this is only some examples. Adultery kills in so many ways and diverse forms. Then, we still have the courage to protest against God when things do not go well, when we have problems, when sicknesses arrive; while it is we who procured these things with our sins, drawing evil on our life.*"

She was taken to Heaven by Jesus, and when she looked down she saw the map of the world in darkness with many white lights. She saw that North America had the most twinkling lights. Our Lord told her this was the place that had the most Eucharistic Souls feeding on Him.

She Saw Her Parents in Purgatory

She was in a deep coma and in agony while in Purgatory. She saw her father who had died five years before she was struck by lightning, and he was at the entrance of the abyss due to his continued adultery. He had a little bit of light, near the lowest level of Purgatory. She saw her mother who was in a higher level of Purgatory closer to Heaven. She was shown how her father's unfaithfulness was a grievous sin that afflicted his relationship with God, his wife, and his children. He used to brag about his other women and Gloria's mother would cry. Gloria also admits she had a hyper critical spirit of everything and everyone, and its root was envy. Our Lord showed her the greatest sin is abortion. Gloria said, *"Every time that the blood of a baby is shed, it is a holocaust to Satan, who acquires still more power."* She was also shown how resentment limits our growth in God by taking us away from God, and others.

Maria Simma is Visited by the Souls in Purgatory

The book *Get Us Out of Here, Maria Simma Responds to This Call From the Poor Souls in Purgatory,* by Nicky Eltz, and approved by Maria (1915-2004), explains how the souls in Purgatory come and visit, and tell her what Purgatory is like. She was a very simple and humble woman who was born and died in the same village in Austria. Many souls would come and tell her their stories of the sins they committed and how they ended up in Purgatory. Maria's book was released in 2002, and had gone through ten printings as of March of 2013, and had sold half a million copies by that date. Since my copy is a 2013 edition, it is unknown how many more have been printed, but an estimate would be well over a million as it has gained traction worldwide with each printing. The total page count in the book is 340 pages, and I am only presenting here a tiny vignette on an important subject. I have chosen Divorce because it has been so devastating to families. The total chapter on **Marriage, Family, and Children** is fifteen pages and I have only presented a little over two pages of that chapter. There is a heavy emphasis in the chapter on the devastation of divorce to families. She is asked questions and answers them.

"In a marriage where the wife must suffer a lot at the hands of the husband or vice versa, is it all right for one to leave the other?

"They may, but it is certainly better that they do not. They should offer it all up. But the line one ought to draw is if physical suffering occurs."

What have the Poor Souls said about divorce?

"*They have said that it is one of the greatest of all sins against God Himself. It hurts everyone tremendously and, of course, the innocent ones the most. It is NOTHING LESS than spiritual, mental, and emotional murder committed upon God's greatest gift to us, that being our ability to participate in the creation of life and its fruit — our children. No child of divorce will ever grow to the fullness God had planned for it. In this century, millions of times more than ever before, Satan is ripping into the families and wombs of women, poisoning and cutting to pieces the Holy threads that keep families in His plan, poisoning and cutting to pieces the babies God has given to them. It is reparation for these two sins that the souls say is coming soon and will be earth shattering. And in the countries like the USA where more than 50% of marriages now break up, God will soon arrange for these matters to change quickly. He will step in for the humble, the innocent, prayerful and loving people and will punish the others for the never-ending insults against love. The industries, the organizations, the attorneys, the cults, the physicians, and psychologists who lie, confuse, collude, make profits, and thereby distort the truth to keep this most horrid of wars going will soon experience God's wrath as it has NEVER been experienced before! God have mercy on the ones who know what they are doing! And we have the duty to inform the unknowing ones of what they are doing.*"

Have the Poor Souls ever told you anything about annulments in the Church?

"*Yes, they have told me that the Church grants far too many annulments today. Such matters must be examined far more thoroughly today. I am afraid it is true to some degree that the well-connected and well-endowed have easier access to annulments and that is hardly God's wish. Of course, there are cases where coercion or emotional limitations of other situations in place at the time did invalidate the marriage to begin with, but these are serious matters that must be handled very lovingly but thoroughly as well.*"

What else can you think of that the Poor Souls communicate to their families?

"They can ask a family member to make something good that the soul itself had done badly or unfairly while here. And by following the instruction the living ones will be assisting the soul to go on its way. They can warn them to avoid this or that. They protect them, guide them, and convey love and security in various ways."

Have the Poor Souls said anything about the women's movement?

"No, not in those terms, except that no women should be around the altar. In the secular world it is quite all right that they compete with men on an equal basis. Having their own careers is fine but ONLY as long as the family is not in any way ignored. Here too, both women and men commit many great sins today. If either the children or the spouse are in any way neglected, the other one will have to suffer a lot for it later. This is most definitely a serious and most divisive sin."

What in the spiritual realm might happen more between a couple married in the Church and a couple not married in the Church, or a couple not married at all?

"God's Blessing, the marriage vows, which are after all vows before God, the Marriage Mass and the support of all family members are all such powerful protective graces that the lack of any one or several of these will seriously weaken its needed strength and unity. In calling on God and His Church's Blessing, things certainly unfold far stronger and thus happier than without them."

"Things do happen that are similar to what I see when the Poor Souls come to visit me, and among the living we would call it bilocation. Or it also happens that an angel takes on the appearance of the one spouse to bring the other a message. He or she would then hear, or both see and hear the other, and thereby receive protective or guiding words. This happens often and must be seen as a wonderful gift from God for a holy couple. It certainly will not happen when people live together in sin. In those cases, there is far less

protection from outside of this world. I would caution them very urgently to step away from that and to come back to God's protection."

"It is also common that a deceased spouse would come close to accompany the still living one through the death process. What a tremendous joy this must be for both to experience! True, giving a holy love never, never dies. Yet it is only this when God has blessed the marriage and is always near to them in prayer and in their acts of selfless love."

What should parents do to form the consciences of their children?

"A good example is the most important thing. Then by praying a lot for them and also with them. Also, by blessing them often; that too is worth a lot. And then a good education and the most important one is before they go off to regular school. Jesus told us to bring His children to Him and not to block them."

JESUS I TRUST IN YOU

The above information on the stories were taken directly from:

Saint Faustina's Diary, Divine Mercy in My Soul, based upon the contents of her diary from 1934 until her death in 1938.

Purgatory: Explained by the Lives and Legends of the Saints, by Fr. F.X. Schouppe, S.J., Imprimatur, 1893, translated from the French.

Struck by Lightning, Death, Judgment, & Conversion by Dr. Gloria Polo, 2009.

Get Us Out of Here, Maria Simma Responds to This Call from the Poor Souls in Purgatory, Maria Simma Speaks with Nicky Eltz, 2002.

All of the above books, and more on this and other spiritual subjects, are sold by:
Signs and Wonders for Our Time
sign.org • 703. 707. 0799

Index

Other Works by Ted Flynn

Garabandal and Its Secrets
The Warning and the Miracle of Garabandal, Like Nothing Before in all History — Two Supernatural Events That Will Change the World, The Global Reset — Heaven Resets on their Terms, 2022.
An explanation of the events and circumstances of the Illumination of Conscience or Life Review, and how the Great Miracle will follow The Warning as prophesied at Garabandal, Spain. How the Warning and the Miracle Will be Heaven's version of the Global Reset on their terms. These events will be the ultimate game changer for civilization.

Diabolical Disorientation, The Roots of the Crisis in the Church, the Family, the Nation, and the Culture, 2020.
Essays on the direction of the church, and the family in turbulent times with a unique orthodox Marian theme and how to thrive in times of crisis.

The Great Transformation, Finding Peace of Soul in Troubled Times, 2015.
A description of how the world was being transformed before our very eyes based on many data points.

The Thunder of Justice, The Warning, The Miracle, The Chastisement, And The Era of Peace, 2010, revised and updated from the original 1993 best seller. Translated in 6 languages. Ted & Maureen Flynn.
An overview of the major and most impactful Marian apparition sites in history and their primary messages.

Idols in the House, 2002.
Shows the destiny of a family, and thus the nation that abandons the first commandment of honoring God first. Examples from Scripture and prior civilizations. Proven to be prophetic to America and the world today.

The Hope of the Wicked, The Master Plan to Rule the World, 2000.
The political philosophy and ideology of rulers in the world in their own words (over 1,200 footnotes), and how they want to govern the world. We are now living what they proposed generations ago. Provides a description of the Deep State before the term was ever used. A book 20 years ahead of its time.

Key to the Triumph, The Final Marian Dogma of Co-redemptrix, Mediatrix, Advocate, 1997, DVD.
Filmed in Italy with the words of leading individuals and clergy on the importance of the Dogma being proclaimed.

Prophecy and the New Times, 1995, DVD.
Providing information from leading authorities and mystics from the apparitions in the Thunder of Justice, it is as informative as when it was first made.

See **Sign.org** (Signs and Wonders for Our Time) for a greater selection of books and other spiritual products. (703) 707-0799

About the Author

Ted Flynn is an author and Executive Producer of several films. He is the founder and president of MaxKol Communications, Inc. (1994). He attended the University of Massachusetts/Amherst, American University, the University of Fribourg, Switzerland, and the London School of Economics (England).

He was Chief Economist of a government agency, worked in consulting. been active in not for profits, real estate development, energy development, President and founder of a publishing company, worked in Poland on retrofitting power plants after the fall of the Berlin Wall, and then to Belarus after the fall of USSR during glasnost, distributing food aid with funds from USAID and the Department of Agriculture. He has spoken in over 700 venues in the world on the types of subjects addressed in this book and previous works, as well as giving over 300 radio and television interviews. He has traveled to over 50 countries in his career. He can be reached at: tflynn333@icloud.com.